KB087085

적중100

영어 기출 문제집

중3

금성 | 최인철

Best Collection

구성과 특징

교과서의 주요 학습 내용을 중심으로 학습 영역별 특성에 맞춰 단계별로 다양한 학습 기회를 제공하여 단원별 학습능력 평가는 물론 중간 및 기말고사 시험 등에 완벽하게 대비할 수 있도록 내용을 구성

Words & Expressions

Step1　Key Words 단원별 핵심 단어 설명 및 풀이
　　　　Key Expression 단원별 핵심 숙어 및 관용어 설명
　　　　Word Power 반대 또는 비슷한 뜻 단어 배우기
　　　　English Dictionary 영어로 배우는 영어 단어

Step2　실력평가 단원별 수시평가 대비 주관식, 객관식 문제풀이

Step3　서술형 대비 학업성취도 및 수행능력평가 대비 서술형 문제풀이

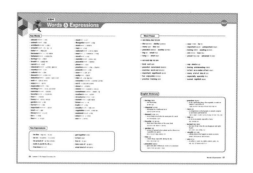

Conversation

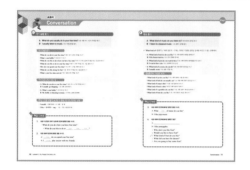

Step1　핵심 의사소통 소통에 필요한 주요 표현 방법 요약
　　　　핵심 Check 기본적인 표현 방법 및 활용능력 확인

Step2　대화문 익히기 교과서 대화문 심층 분석 및 확인

Step3　교과서 확인학습 빈칸 채우기를 통한 문장 완성 능력 확인

Step4　기본평가 시험대비 기초 학습 능력 평가

Step5　실력평가 단원별 수시평가 대비 주관식, 객관식 문제풀이

Step6　서술형 대비 학업성취도 및 수행능력평가 대비 서술형 문제풀이

Grammar

Step1　주요 문법 단원별 주요 문법 사항과 예문을 알기 쉽게 설명
　　　　핵심 Check 기본 문법사항에 대한 이해 여부 확인

Step2　기본평가 시험대비 기초 학습 능력 평가

Step3　실력평가 단원별 수시평가 대비 주관식, 객관식 문제풀이

Step4　서술형 대비 학업성취도 및 수행능력평가 대비 서술형 문제풀이

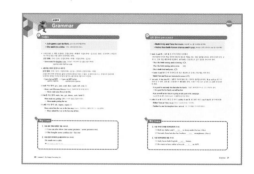

Reading

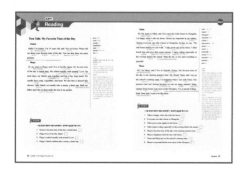

Step1　구문 분석 단원별로 제시된 문장에 대한 구문별 분석과 내용 설명
　　　　확인문제 문장에 대한 기본적인 이해와 인지능력 확인

Step2　확인학습A 빈칸 채우기를 통한 문장 완성 능력 확인

Step3　확인학습B 제시된 우리말을 영어로 완성하여 작문 능력 키우기

Step4　실력평가 단원별 수시평가 대비 주관식, 객관식 문제풀이

Step5　서술형 대비 학업성취도 및 수행능력평가 대비 서술형 문제풀이
　　　　교과서 구석구석 교과서에 나오는 기타 문장까지 완벽 학습

Composition

|영역별 핵심문제|
단어 및 어휘, 대화문, 문법, 독해 등 각 영역별 기출문제의 출제 유형을 분석하여 실전에 대비하고 연습할 수 있도록 문제를 배열

|단원별 예상문제|
기출문제를 분석한 후 새로운 시험 출제 경향을 더하여 새롭게 출제될 수 있는 문제를 포함하여 시험에 완벽하게 대비할 수 있도록 준비

|서술형 실전 및 창의사고력 문제|
학교 시험에서 점차 늘어나는 서술형 시험에 집중 대비하고 고득점을 취득하는데 만전을 기하기 위한 학습 코너

|단원별 모의고사|
영역별, 단계별 학습을 모두 마친 후 실전 연습을 위한 모의고사

교과서 파헤치기

- **단어Test1~3** 영어 단어 우리말 쓰기, 우리말을 영어 단어로 쓰기, 영영풀이에 해당하는 단어와 우리말 쓰기
- **대화문Test1~2** 대화문 빈칸 완성 및 전체 대화문 쓰기
- **본문Test1~5** 빈칸 완성, 우리말 쓰기, 문장 배열연습, 영어 작문하기 복습 등 단계별 반복 학습을 통해 교과서 지문에 대한 완벽한 습득
- **구석구석지문Test1~2** 지문 빈칸 완성 및 전문 영어로 쓰기

이책의 차례
Contents

Lesson 7

Careers Day

🎤 의사소통 기능

- 선호 표현하기
  I prefer science to literature.
- 의견 묻기
  How do you feel about becoming a writer?

🎤 언어 형식

- 난이 형용사+to부정사
  Jobs are hard **to come** by.
- 도치
  Are you excited about meeting them? **So am I.**

Words & Expressions

Key Words

- **alternative** [ɔ:ltə́:rnətiv] 형 대체 가능한, 대체의
- **architect** [á:rkətèkt] 명 건축가
- **architecture** [á:rkitèktʃər] 명 건축학, 건축 양식
- **avoid** [əvɔ́id] 동 피하다, 방지하다
- **bloomer** [blú:mər] 명 재능을 발휘하는 사람
- **boring** [bɔ́:riŋ] 형 지루한
- **calm** [kɑ:m] 형 침착한
- **career** [kəríər] 명 경력, 직업
- **climate** [kláimit] 명 기후
- **control** [kəntróul] 동 통제하다
- **cost** [kɔ:st] 동 비용이 들다
- **counselor** [káunsələr] 명 상담 전문가
- **classical** [klǽsikəl] 형 고전적인, 클래식의
- **disaster** [dizǽstər] 명 재난, 재해
- **end-of-life** 형 인생 말기의
- **energy-saving** 형 에너지를 절약하는
- **environment** [inváiərənmənt] 명 (주변의) 환경
- **exercise** [éksərsàiz] 동 운동하다
- **experience** [ikspíriəns] 동 경험하다
- **feed** [fi:d] 동 먹이를 주다
- **fellow** [félou] 형 동료의
- **graduate** [grǽdʒuət] 동 졸업, 졸업생 동 졸업하다
- **global warming** 지구 온난화
- **handle** [hǽndl] 동 다루다, 처리하다
- **helpful** [hélpfəl] 형 도움이 되는, 유용한
- **however** [hauévər] 부 그러나, 하지만
- **impossible** [impásəbl] 형 불가능한
- **increase** [inkrí:s] 동 증가하다, 증가시키다
- **invest** [invést] 동 투자하다
- **invite** [inváit] 동 초대하다
- **job** [dʒab] 명 직업
- **literature** [lítərətʃər] 명 문학
- **minute** [mínit] 명 (시간 단위의) 분, 잠깐
- **modern** [mádərn] 형 현대의, 근대의
- **moment** [móumənt] 명 잠시, 순간, 때
- **operate** [ápərèit] 동 작동하다, 가동시키다
- **perfectly** [pə́:rfiktl] 부 완벽하게
- **personality** [pə̀:rsənǽləti] 명 성격, 인격
- **prefer** [prifə́:r] 동 선호하다
- **prevent** [privént] 동 방지하다, 막다
- **purpose** [pə́:pəs] 명 목적
- **reduce** [ridjú:s] 동 줄이다, 낮추다
- **regularly** [régjulərli] 부 정기적으로, 규칙적으로
- **retirement** [ritáiərmənt] 명 은퇴, 퇴직
- **season** [sí:zn] 명 계절
- **seeding** [sí:diŋ] 명 씨 뿌리기
- **side effect** 부작용
- **source** [sɔ:rs] 명 원천, 근원
- **storm** [stɔ:rm] 명 폭풍
- **system** [sístəm] 명 체제, 시스템
- **taste** [teist] 동 맛이 ~하다, 맛보다
- **wash** [waʃ] 동 씻다
- **wealthy** [wélθi] 형 부유한, 재산이 많은
- **weather** [wéðər] 명 날씨
- **while** [hwail] 접 ~하는 동안에, 반면에
- **will** [wil] 명 유언장
- **wind power** 풍력

Key Expressions

- **as well** 또한
- **believe in** ~를 믿다
- **come by** (힘쓴 끝에) ~를 얻다
- **feel proud** 긍지를 느끼다
- **for example** 예를 들어
- **get along well with** ~와 잘 지내다
- **give a big hand** 크게 박수 치다
- **have a hard time ~ing** ~하는 데 힘든 시간을 보내다
- **instead of** ~ 대신에
- **keep on ~ing** 계속해서 ~하다
- **make a will** 유서를 작성하다
- **not only A but also B** A뿐만 아니라 B도
- **since then** 그 이후로
- **succeed in** ~에 성공하다
- **thanks to** ~ ~ 덕분에
- **these days** 요즘에
- **think about** ~에 대해 생각하다
- **try one's best** 최선을 다하다
- **turn off** ~를 끄다
- **welcome to** ~에 온 것을 환영하다

Word Power

※ 서로 비슷한 뜻을 가진 어휘

- □ **calm** 침착한 – **composed** 침착한, 차분한
- □ **career** 경력, 직업 – **occupation** 직업, 업무
- □ **disaster** 재난, 재해 – **catastrophe** 재앙, 참사
- □ **handle** 다루다, 처리하다 – **deal with** 다루다, 상대하다
- □ **helpful** 도움이 되는, 유용한 – **useful** 도움이 되는

- □ **personality** 성격, 인격 – **character** 성격, 성질
- □ **purpose** 목적 – **goal** 목적, 목표
- □ **source** 원천, 근원 – **origin** 유래, 기원
- □ **while** ~하는 동안에, 반면에 – **whereas** 반면에

※ 서로 반대의 뜻을 가진 어휘

- □ **boring** 지루한, 재미 없는 ↔ **exciting** 흥미진진한
- □ **impossible** 불가능한 ↔ **possible** 가능한
- □ **perfectly** 완벽하게 ↔ **imperfectly** 완벽하지 않게
- □ **regularly** 정기적으로, 규칙적으로 ↔ **irregularly** 비정기적으로

- □ **calm** 침착한 ↔ **nervous** 초조한
- □ **increase** 증가하다, 증가시키다 ↔ **decrease** 줄이다, 감소시키다
- □ **reduce** 줄이다, 낮추다 ↔ **increase** 증가하다, 커지다
- □ **wealthy** 부유한, 재산이 많은 ↔ **poor** 가난한

※ 형용사 + 접미사 -ly → 부사

- □ **actual** + **ly** → **actually** 사실은
- □ **easy** + **ly** → **easily** 쉽게
- □ **happy** + **ly** → **happily** 행복하게
- □ **loose** + **ly** → **loosely** 느슨하게
- □ **sudden** + **ly** → **suddenly** 갑자기

- □ **cheap** + **ly** → **cheaply** 저렴하게
- □ **exact** + **ly** → **exactly** 정확히
- □ **late** + **ly** → **lately** 최근에
- □ **lucky** + **ly** → **luckily** 다행스럽게
- □ **tight** + **ly** → **tightly** 단단히, 꽉

English Dictionary

- □ **alternative** 대체 가능한, 대체의
  - → offering a choice between two or more things
    두 개 혹은 더 많은 것 사이에서 선택을 제공하는

- □ **career** 경력, 직업
  - → the job or series of jobs that you do during your working life, especially if you continue to get better jobs and earn more money
    직업 또는 더 많은 돈을 벌고 더 좋은 일을 계속한다면 일하는 생활 동안에 하는 일련의 직업

- □ **climate** 기후
  - → the general weather conditions usually found in a particular place
    보통 특정한 장소에서 발견되는 일반적인 날씨 조건들

- □ **control** 통제하다
  - → to order, limit, or rule something, or someone's actions or behavior
    어떤 것이나 어떤 사람의 행동과 움직임을 지배하거나 명령, 제한하다

- □ **environment** (주변의) 환경
  - → the air, water, and land in or on which people, animals, and plants live
    사람과 동식물이 사는 곳의 공기, 물, 땅

- □ **exercise** 운동하다
  - → to do physical activities to make your body strong and healthy
    몸을 강하고 건강하게 만들기 위해 신체적인 활동을 하다

- □ **experience** 경험하다
  - → to have something happen to you, or to do or feel something
    당신에게 일어나는 일을 가지거나 혹은 어떤 일을 느끼거나 하다

- □ **personality** 성격, 인격
  - → the type of person you are, shown by the way you behave, feel, and think
    행동하고 느끼고 생각하는 것에 의해 보여지는 사람의 유형

- □ **prefer** 선호하다
  - → to like, choose, or want one thing rather than another
    어떤 것을 다른 것보다 좋아하거나 선택하거나 원하다

- □ **retirement** 은퇴, 퇴직
  - → the act of leaving your job and stopping working, usually because you are old
    보통 늙어서 일을 그만 두고 떠나는 행위

- □ **side effect** 부작용
  - → an unexpected result of a situation
    어떤 상황의 예상치 못한 결과

- □ **source** 원천, 근원
  - → the place something comes from or starts at, or the cause of something
    어떤 일이 시작된 장소 혹은 어떤 일의 원인

- □ **will** 유언장
  - → an official statement of what a person has decided should be done with their money and property after their death
    사람이 사망한 뒤 그들의 돈이나 재산으로 어떤 일이 행해져야 한다고 적은 공식 문서

01 다음 짝지어진 단어의 관계가 같도록 빈칸에 알맞은 말을 쓰시오.

> helpful : useful = career : _____

02 다음 중 밑줄 친 부분의 뜻풀이가 바르지 않은 것은?

① A new team was appointed to handle the crisis. (다루다, 처리하다)

② A key to protect environment is to keep energy-saving lifestyle. (에너지를 절약하는)

③ It was a good opportunity to develop her career. (경력, 직업)

④ He got poisoned by minute amounts of chemicals in the water. ((시간 단위의) 분, 잠깐)

⑤ Nicole is studying to be an architect. (건축가)

03 다음 우리말을 주어진 어휘를 이용하여 영작하시오.

(1) 태양광 판은 오직 햇빛 속에서만 작동한다. (operate, solar panel)

➡ _____

(2) 비가 그들이 밖에서 식사하는 것을 못하게 했다. (prevent, outdoors)

➡ _____

(3) 그는 정기적으로 우리를 위해 아이들을 봐준다. (regularly, babysit)

➡ _____

04 다음 영영풀이가 가리키는 것을 고르시오.

> an unexpected result of a situation

① side effect ② environment
③ prevention ④ system
⑤ personality

05 다음 문장의 빈칸에 들어갈 말을 〈보기〉에서 골라 쓰시오.

> ┤ 보기 ├
> for example / instead of / since then / as well / welcome to

(1) You are _____ use my car.

(2) The woman has been avoiding me _____.

(3) Now I can walk to work _____ going by car.

06 다음 문장의 (A)와 (B)에 각각 공통으로 들어갈 말이 바르게 짝지어진 것은?

> • All power was turned ___(A)___ in the room.
> • We have to put ___(A)___ our wedding until April.
> • The ancient Greeks believed ___(B)___ many different gods.
> • Three colorful flowers are put ___(B)___ the vase.

① off – on ② off – in
③ on – on ④ on — in
⑤ away – in

01 다음 짝지어진 단어의 관계가 같도록 빈칸에 알맞은 말을 쓰시오.

> boring : exciting = increase : _____

02 다음 우리말에 맞게 빈칸에 알맞은 말을 쓰시오.

> 그들은 수업에 주의를 집중하는 데 어려움을 겪었다.

➡ They _____ _____ _____ _____
　 paying attention to class.

03 다음 문장의 빈칸에 들어갈 말을 〈보기〉에서 골라 쓰시오.

> ┤ 보기 ├
> counselor / purpose / source / will /
> moment

(1) This is the important _____ of my
　 life.
(2) The boy wanted to ask some advice of
　 the _____.
(3) The _____ of industry is to create
　 wealth.

04 우리말과 일치하도록 주어진 어구를 배열하여 영작하시오.

(1) 그 돈은 특정 기간 동안 투자해 놓았다.
　 (for / has been / the money / a certain
　 period / invested)
　 ➡ _____
　 _____

(2) 그 평론가는 내 작업에 대해 도움이 되는 논평
　 을 해 주었다.
　 (comments / made / on / the critic / my
　 work / helpful)
　 ➡ _____

(3) 우리는 밖에서 기다리는 한 무리의 기자들을 피
　 해 갔다.
　 (avoided / outside / we / waiting /
　 journalists / a pack of)
　 ➡ _____

05 다음 우리말에 맞게 주어진 단어를 사용하여 영작하시오.

(1) 인터뷰에서 가장 중요한 것은 침착성을 유지하
　 는 것이다. (calm)
　 ➡ _____

(2) 대기만성형인 그녀는 52살 때 훌륭한 소설을
　 썼다. (bloomer, late)
　 ➡ _____

(3) 그는 모든 일이 아주 지루했다. (whole, boring,
　 find)
　 ➡ _____

1 선호 표현하기

A: Which fruit do you prefer, apples or strawberries? 사과랑 딸기 중에 어느 과일을 더 좋아하니?
B: I prefer apples to strawberries. 난 딸기보다 사과를 더 좋아해.

■ 상대방의 선호를 묻는 표현으로는 'Which one do you prefer, A or B?'라는 표현을 쓸 수 있다. 같은 표현으로 'Which (one) do you like better, A or B?', 'Which (one) do you like more, A or B?', 'Which one do you want to ~ more?' 등을 쓸 수 있다.

■ 대답할 때는 'I prefer ~.' 또는 'I like 목적어 better.', 'I like 목적어 more.'라고 말한다. 'B보다 A를 더 선호한다'라고 대답할 때는 'I prefer A to B.' 또는 'I like A better than B.', 'I like A more than B.', 'I prefer A over B.'라고 말한다.

선호에 대해 묻기

• Which (one) do you prefer, A or B?
• Which (one) do you like better, A or B?
• Which (one) do you like more, A or B?
• Which (one) do you want to ~ more?

선호 표현하기

• I prefer ~. / I prefer A to B.
• I like 목적어 better. / I like A better than B.
• I like 목적어 more. / I like A more than B.
• I would like 목적어 better.
• I would like 목적어 more.

핵심 Check

1. 다음 대화의 밑줄 친 우리말을 바르게 영작하시오. (8 words)

> W: What do you like doing better than making shoes?
> B: <u>전 신발 만드는 것보다 음악을 연주하는 게 더 좋아요!</u> I want to be a musician.

➡ _____

② 의견 묻기

> **A:** How do you feel about this book? 이 책에 대해서 어떻게 생각하니?
>
> **B:** I think it's very fun. 난 그 책이 참 재미있는 것 같아.

■ 상대방의 의견을 묻는 표현으로는 'How do you feel about ~?'과 'What do you think about ~?', 'What do you think of ~?'와 같은 표현이 있다. 이 표현들 모두 '~에 대해서 어떻게 생각하니/느끼니?' 라고 해석한다. 이와 같은 표현으로는 'How about ~?' 또는 'What about ~?' 등이 있다.

■ 상대방의 의견을 되물을 때에는 'What about you?', 'How about you?' 등이 있다.

■ 의견을 나타내는 표현으로는 대표적으로 'I think ~.'가 있다. 이외에도 다음과 같은 표현을 쓸 수 있다.

의견 표현하기

- I think (that) 주어 + 동사 ~.
- I believe (that) 주어 + 동사 ~.
- I feel (that) 주어 + 동사 ~.
- It seems to me that 주어 + 동사 ~.
- I want / would like to ~ more.
- In my opinion, 주어 + 동사 ~.
- From my perspective, 주어 + 동사 ~.

핵심 Check

2. 다음 대화의 빈칸에 들어갈 말로 적절하지 <u>않은</u> 것은?

> **A:** How do you feel about this book?
> **B:** _____ it's very fun.

① I think   ② I feel

③ I want   ④ In my opinion,

⑤ I believe

Everyday English 1 B Listening Activity

W: Are you ❶looking for a job? And are you an animal lover? ❷If you are, ❸here is the best job for you. We need someone ❹to take care of some pets ❺while their family is on vacation. You will need to wash the pets, feed them regularly, and play with ❻them. By the way, we ❼prefer people who can work with us for a long time to those who can only work for a short time. You will work ❽ from 9 to 5, Monday to Friday. If you are interested in taking care of pets, please call 567-1234.

W: 일을 찾고 계시나요? 그리고 동물을 사랑하시는 분이신가요? 그렇다면, 여기 당신을 위한 최적의 일이 있습니다. 저희는 애완동물 키우는 가족들이 휴가를 갔을 때 애완 동물을 돌봐줄 사람을 찾고 있습니다. 애완동물들을 씻기고 정기적으로 밥을 주고 놀아 주시면 됩니다. 그건 그렇고, 우리는 단기간만 일할 사람보다는 우리와 장기간 일할 수 있는 사람을 선호합니다. 월요일부터 금요일까지, 9시부터 오후 5시까지 일하게 될 겁니다. 애완동물을 돌보는 데 관심이 있으면, 567-1234로 연락 주세요.

❶ look for ~를 찾다 ❷ 'If you are looking for a job and an animal lover'의 줄임말이다. ❸ 도치 구문으로, 주어가 긴 경우 동사의 뒤에 위치한다. ❹ to부정사의 형용사적 용법으로 someone을 수식한다. ❺ while ~하는 동안에 ❻ 대명사 them은 pets를 가리킨다. ❼ prefer 더 좋아하다, 선호하다 ❽ from 9 to 5 9시부터 5시까지

Check(√) True or False

(1) The speaker is looking for a job. T ☐ F ☐

(2) Those who apply for the job should take care of pets. T ☐ F ☐

Everyday English 2 B Listening Activity

(*Phone rings.*)

B: Hello?

G: Hello, Minwoo. ❶This is Yena.

B: Hi, Yena. ❷What's up?

G: I received your present for my birthday today. Thank you so much.

B: Do you like ❸it? How do you feel about its bright color?

G: I really like it. ❹It can help drivers see me well in the rain.

B: I'm glad to hear that.

G: Thank you again. I hope ❺it rains soon so that I can use it.

B: Haha. ❻I hope so. See you soon!

(전화벨이 울린다.)
B: 여보세요?
G: 안녕, 민우야. 나 예나야.
B: 안녕, 예나야. 요즘 잘 지내니?
G: 오늘 네가 준 생일 선물 받았어. 너무 고마워.
B: 마음에 드니? 그 선물의 밝은 색은 어떠니?
G: 그거 정말 마음에 들어. 빗속에서도 운전자들이 나를 잘 볼 수 있도록 도와줄 수 있잖아.
B: 그 말을 들으니 기쁘다.
G: 다시 한번 고마워. 내가 이걸 사용해 볼 수 있게 어서 비가 내렸으면 좋겠다.
B: 하하하. 나도 그래. 또 보자!

❶ 'This is ~.'는 전화에서 자신을 나타내는 표현이다. ❷ 'What's up?'은 상대방에게 안부를 묻는 표현이다.
❸ 대명사 it은 앞서 언급된 B가 G에게 준 생일 선물을 의미한다. ❹ 대명사 It은 앞서 언급된 B가 G에게 준 생일 선물을 의미한다. ❺ 이때의 it은 날씨, 시간, 날짜, 거리 등을 언급할 때 주어로 사용하는 it이다. ❻ 'I hope it rains.'라는 의미이다.

Check(√) True or False

(3) Minwoo has given Yena a gift for her birthday. T ☐ F ☐

(4) Yena wants to use what she was given as soon as possible. T ☐ F ☐

Think Back

W: Miguel! ❶Let's make some shoes together.

B: Grandma, I don't want to make shoes.

W: You don't like ❷it? Then, what do you like doing better than making shoes?

B: ❸I like playing music better than making shoes! I want to be a musician.

B: ❹What do you think about music?

W: Music is bad! My grandfather left the family ❺because of music.

❶ 'Let us ∼'의 줄임말로, '∼하자'라는 의미이다. ❷ 대명사 it은 making shoes 를 의미한다. ❸ 'I prefer playing music to making shoes.'라고 바꿔 쓸 수 있 다. ❹ 'How do you feel about music?'이라고 바꿔 쓸 수 있다. ❺ because of + 명사 ∼ 때문에

Everyday English 1 A Listen and Check (1)

G: Do you like basketball?

B: Yes, I do. But ❶I prefer soccer to basketball.

G: Oh, really? Can you teach me ❷how to play soccer.

B: Sure.

❶ 'I prefer ∼.'는 '나는 ∼를 더 좋아한다.'는 의미로 선호를 나타내는 표현이다.
❷ how to∼ ∼하는 방법

Everyday English 1 A Listen and Check (2)

B: I'm ❶looking forward to the music festival.

G: Me too. Which do you prefer, singing or dancing?

B: ❷I prefer dancing to singing.

G: I like singing. It would be very fun if we can sing and dance together.

❶ look forward to + 명사 ∼를 학수고대하다
❷ 'I like dancing better[more] than singing.'이라고 바꿔 쓸 수 있다.

Everyday English 2 A Listen and Check (1)

B: ❶How do you feel about going on a picnic this weekend?

G: ❷I don't think it's a good idea. It's going to rain this weekend.

B: Then, ❸how about going to a concert?

G: Sounds great.

❶ 'How do you feel about ∼?'은 대화 상대방의 의견을 묻는 표현으로, 'What do you think about ∼?'이라는 표현으로 대체 가능하다. ❷ '나는 그것이 좋은 의견이라고 생각하지 않아.'라고 말할 때, 'I think it's not a good idea.'라고 쓰지 않도록 주의한다. ❸ 'How about ∼?'는 상대방의 의견을 묻는 표현으로, 'What about ∼?'와 바꿔 쓸 수 있다.

Everyday English 2 A Listen and Check (2)

M: ❶How can I help you?

G: I'd like to buy a hat for my mother.

M: How do you feel about this red ❷one? It's very popular.

G: ❸It looks good. I'll take it.

❶ '무엇을 도와 드릴까요?'라는 표현으로, 'May I help you?' 또는 'What can I do for you?'라고 바꿔 쓸 수 있다. ❷ 대명사 one은 앞서 언급된 hat을 가리킨다. ❸ 대명사 It은 앞서 언급된 the red one[hat]을 가리킨다.

Everyday English 2 A Listen and Check (3)

G: What are you doing?

B: I'm making a new soup. ❶Would you like to taste it?

G: Sure. Um... (*Tasting the soup*)

B: Do you like ❷it? ❸How do you feel about this new recipe?

G: Well, I think you need to put some salt in ❹ it.

B: You're right. Thank you.

❶ 'Do you want to taste it?'이라고 바꿔 쓸 수 있다. ❷ 대명사 it은 the soup을 가리킨다. ❸ 'What do you think about this new recipe?'라고 바꿔 쓸 수 있다. ❹ 대명사 it은 앞서 언급된 the soup을 가리킨다.

In Real Life

Jisu: Hello, Mr. Brown. Are you busy now?

Mr. Brown: ❶Not really.

Jisu: Then, can I talk to you ❷for a minute?

Mr. Brown: Of course. Jisu, what's wrong? You look ❸worried.

Jisu: I'm worried about my future. I don't know ❹what I want to be in the future.

Mr. Brown: How do you feel about becoming a writer? You like literature, ❺don't you?

Jisu: Well, no. ❻I prefer science to literature. But I don't know what kinds of jobs I could do.

Mr. Brown: Why don't you come to the student hall tomorrow? Our ❼graduates will talk about their jobs.

Jisu: That will be very ❽helpful. Thank you.

Mr. Brown: No problem.

❶ Not really. 별로 그렇지 않다 ❷ for a minute 잠깐만, 잠시만 ❸ worried 걱정하는 ❹ 의문사 what이 쓰인 간접의문문으로 동사 know의 목적어로 사용되었다. ❺ 부가의문문이다. ❻ 'I like science better[more] than literature.'라고 바꿔 쓸 수 있다. ❼ graduate 졸업생; 졸업하다 ❽ helpful 도움이 되는, 유용한

Check Your Progress 1

B: Mom, can you come to my room?

W: Yes. What are you doing?

B: I'm ❶getting ready for a date. It's Jina's birthday.

W: Aha! So, you're ❷trying your clothes on several times.

B: Yes. Mom, how do I look in this blue shirt?

W: It ❸looks good on you, but are you going to wear those blue jeans, too?

B: I think so. I prefer jeans to my other pants.

W: ❹How do you feel about wearing a white shirt instead?

B: I think the white one and the jeans ❺match better. Thanks for your advice.

W: ❻No problem.

❶ get ready for ~에 준비하다 ❷ try on ~를 입어 보다 ❸ look good on ~ ~에 잘 어울리다 ❹ 'How do you feel about ~?'이라는 표현은 상대방의 의견을 묻는 표현으로, 'What do you think about ~?'이라는 표현으로 대체 가능하다. ❺ match 어울리다, 맞다 ❻ 'No problem.'은 고맙다는 표현에 대한 대답으로 사용할 수 있다.

Check Your Progress 2

B: I got a ticket for the Coolboys concert.

G: You're so lucky! When is ❶it?

B: It's next Saturday. I'm ❷thinking of going there with my friends.

G: ❸By the way, how do you feel about their new album?

B: I like it. All the songs are so ❹exciting, aren't they?

G: Yes, but I ❺prefer their last album to the new one.

B: Why?

G: ❻It has more songs of different genres.

❶ 대명사 it은 앞서 언급된 the Coolboys concert를 가리킨다.
❷ think of ~ ~를 생각하다
❸ By the way 그건 그렇고, 그런데
❹ exciting 흥분되게 하는, 신나게 하는
❺ prefer ~를 선호하다, 더 좋아하다
❻ 대명사 It은 앞서 언급된 their last album을 가리킨다.

Check Your Progress 3

M: ❶Have you heard about the new STARS camera? It is a smart camera ❷which will catch your best moments. It is very small, but very strong. ❸It's very easy to take good pictures with this camera. ❹All you have to do is just talk to the camera ❺without having to use your fingers. Oh, and this is the last chance to get ❻one at a good price. It's 30 percent off ❼at the moment. How do you feel about visiting our store to see one?

❶ 현재완료의 경험 용법이 사용된 문장으로, '~해 본 적 있니?'라는 뜻으로 사용되었다.
❷ 관계대명사 which가 이끄는 절은 앞서 언급된 a smart camera를 수식해 준다.
❸ 가주어 It은 뒤에 나오는 to부정사절을 대신하는 가주어이다.
❹ 'All you have to do'가 문장의 주어로 사용되었다. talk은 to부정사의 to가 생략된 것으로 is의 보어이다.
❺ without ~ing ~하지 않고
❻ 대명사 one은 앞서 언급된 'a smart camera'를 가리킨다.
❼ at the moment 현재에, 지금

다음 우리말과 일치하도록 빈칸에 알맞은 말을 쓰시오.

Think Back A

W: Miguel! Let's make some shoes _____.

B: Grandma, I don't want to make shoes.

W: You _____ like it? Then, what do you like _____ better _____ making shoes?

B: I like playing music _____ than making shoes! I want to be a _____.

B: What do you think _____ music?

W: Music is bad! My grandfather left the family _____ of music.

Everyday English 1 Listen and Check

(1) G: Do you like _____?

B: Yes, I do. But I prefer soccer to basketball.

G: Oh, really? Can you _____ me how to_____ soccer?

B: Sure.

(2) B: I'm looking _____ to the music festival.

G: Me too. Which do you _____, singing or dancing?

B: I prefer dancing _____ singing.

G: I like singing. It _____ be very fun _____ we can sing and dance together.

Everyday English 1 B Listening Activity

W: Are you _____ for a job? And are you an animal lover? If you are, _____ is the best job for you. We need _____ to take _____ of some pets _____ their family is on _____. You will need to wash the pets, feed them _____, and play with them. _____ _____, we prefer people who can work with us for a _____ _____ to those who can only work for a short time. You will work from 9 to 5, Monday to Friday. If you are interested in _____ care of pets, please call 567-1234.

Everyday English 2 A Listen and Check

(1) B: How do you _____ about going on a picnic this _____?

G: I _____ think it's a good idea. It's _____ to rain this weekend.

B: _____, how about going to a concert?

G: _____ great.

(2) M: _____ can I help you?

G: I'd like to buy a hat for my mother.

M: How do you feel _____ this red one? It's very _____.

G: It _____ good. I'll take it.

(3) G: What are you _____?

B: I'm making a new soup. Would you like to _____ it?

G: Sure. Um... (Tasting the soup)

B: Do you _____ it? How do you _____ about this new recipe?

G: Well, I think you need to _____ some salt in it.

B: You're _____. Thank you.

Everyday English 2 B Listening Activity

(*Phone rings.*)

B: Hello?

G: Hello, Minwoo. This is Yena.

B: Hi, Yena. What's _____?

G: I _____ your present for my birthday today. Thank you so much.

B: Do you _____ it? How do you _____ about its bright color?

G: I really like it. It can _____ drivers see me _____ in the rain.

B: I'm glad to _____ that.

G: Thank you again. I hope it _____ soon so that I can _____ it.

B: Haha. I _____ so. See you soon!

In Real Life

Jisu: Hello, Mr. Brown. Are you _____ now?

Mr. Brown: Not really.

Jisu: Then, can I talk to you for a _____?

Mr. Brown: Of course. Jisu, what's wrong? You look _____.

해석

(1) B: 이번 주말에 소풍 가는 것에 대해 어떻게 생각하니?
G: 난 좋은 생각은 아닌 것 같아. 이번 주말에 비가 올 거야.
B: 그럼, 콘서트에 가는 건 어때?
G: 좋아.

(2) M: 어떻게 도와드릴까요?
G: 제 어머니를 위한 모자를 사고 싶은데요.
M: 이 빨간색은 어떻게 생각하세요? 매우 인기가 많아요.
G: 괜찮아 보이네요. 그걸로 살게요.

(3) G: 뭐 하는 중이니?
B: 새로운 수프를 만들고 있어. 맛볼래?
G: 좋아. 음… (수프를 맛본다)
B: 마음에 드니? 이 새 요리법에 대해 어떻게 생각해?
G: 글쎄, 내 생각엔 소금을 좀 더 넣어야 할 것 같다.
B: 그러네. 감사해.

(전화벨이 울린다.)
B: 여보세요?
G: 안녕, 민우야. 나 예나야.
B: 안녕, 예나야. 요즘 잘 지내니?
G: 오늘 네가 준 생일 선물 받았어. 너무 고마워.
B: 마음에 드니? 그 선물의 밝은 색은 어떠니?
G: 그거 정말 마음에 들어. 빗속에서도 운전자들이 나를 잘 볼 수 있도록 도와줄 수 있잖아.
B: 그 말을 들으니 기뻐.
G: 다시 한번 고마워. 내가 이걸 사용해 볼 수 있게 어서 비가 내렸으면 좋겠다.
B: 하하하. 나도 그래. 또 보자!

Jisu: Brown 선생님. 안녕하세요. 지금 바쁘신가요?
Mr. Brown: 아니 별로.
Jisu: 그럼, 잠깐 이야기할 수 있을까요?
Mr. Brown: 물론이지. 지수야, 무슨 일이니? 걱정되어 보이는구나.

Jisu: I'm worried about my _____. I don't know what I _____ to be in the future.

Mr. Brown: How do you feel about _____ a writer? You like _____, don't you?

Jisu: Well, no. I prefer _____ to literature. But I don't know what kinds of jobs I could do.

Mr. Brown: Why don't you come to the _____ _____ tomorrow? Our _____ will talk about their jobs.

Jisu: That will be very _____. Thank you.

Mr. Brown: No problem.

Check Your Progress 1

B: Mom, can you _____ to my room?

W: Yes. What are you doing?

B: I'm getting _____ for a date. It's Jina's _____.

W: Aha! So, you're trying your clothes on _____ times.

B: Yes. Mom, _____ do I _____ in this blue shirt?

W: It looks _____ on you, but are you going to _____ those blue jeans, too?

B: I think so. I _____ jeans to my other pants.

W: _____ do you feel _____ wearing a white shirt instead?

B: I think the white one and the jeans _____ better. _____ for your advice.

W: No problem.

Check Your Progress 2

B: I got a _____ for the Coolboys concert.

G: You're so _____! When is it?

B: It's next Saturday. I'm _____ of going there with my friends.

G: By the way, _____ do you feel about their new album?

B: I like it. All the songs are so _____, aren't they?

G: Yes, but I prefer their last _____ to the new one.

B: Why?

G: It has more songs of _____ genres.

[01~02] 다음 대화를 읽고 물음에 답하시오.

G: Do you like basketball?
B: Yes, I do. (A)하지만 나는 농구보다 축구를 선호해.
G: Oh, really? Can you teach me how to play soccer?
B: Sure.

01 위 대화의 밑줄 친 (A)의 우리말을 바르게 영작하시오. (6 words)

➡ _____

02 What does G want to learn from B? (10 words)

➡ _____

[03~04] 다음 대화를 읽고 물음에 답하시오.

B: How do you feel about going on a picnic this weekend?
(A) Sounds great.
(B) I don't think it's a good idea. It's going to rain this weekend.
(C) Then, how about going to a concert?

03 위 대화가 자연스럽게 이어지도록 순서대로 배열한 것은?

① (A) – (B) – (C)　　② (B) – (A) – (C)
③ (B) – (C) – (A)　　④ (C) – (A) – (B)
⑤ (C) – (B) – (A)

04 What are the two speakers going to do this weekend? (8 words)

➡ _____

[01~03] 다음 글을 읽고 물음에 답하시오.

W: Are you looking for a job? And are you an animal lover? If you ⓐare, here is the best job for you. We need someone ⓑto take care of some pets while their family is on vacation. You will need to wash the pets, feed them regularly, and play with them. _____(A)_____, we prefer people ⓒwho can work with us for a long time ⓓto those who can only work for a short time. You will work from 9 to 5, Monday to Friday. If you are interested in ⓔtake care of pets, please call 567-1234.

01 위 글의 밑줄 친 ⓐ~ⓔ 중 어법상 어색한 것은?

① ⓐ ② ⓑ ③ ⓒ ④ ⓓ ⑤ ⓔ

02 다음 중 위 글의 빈칸 (A)에 가장 알맞은 것은?

① Nevertheless ② By the way
③ In spite of ④ In addition
⑤ Therefore

03 다음 중 위 글의 목적으로 가장 적절한 것은?

① to recruit a pet sitter
② to promote a pet shop
③ to go on a vacation
④ to replace a pet sitter
⑤ to advertise a pet care program

[04~06] 다음 대화를 읽고 물음에 답하시오.

G: Hello, Minwoo. This is Yena.
B: Hi, Yena. What's up?
G: I (A)[receive / received] your present for my birthday today. Thank you so much.
B: Do you like it? How do you feel about its bright color?
G: I really like it. It can help drivers (B)[see / saw] me well in the rain.
B: I'm glad to hear that.
G: Thank you again. I hope it (C)[rains / rained] soon so that I can use (a)it.
B: Haha. I hope so. See you soon!

04 위 대화의 괄호 (A)~(C)에서 알맞은 것을 바르게 짝지은 것을 고르시오.

(A) (B) (C)
① receive – see – rained
② receive – saw – rains
③ received – see – rains
④ received – saw – rained
⑤ received – see – rained

05 위 대화의 밑줄 친 (a)it이 가리키는 것을 두 단어로 쓰시오.

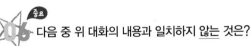

06 다음 중 위 대화의 내용과 일치하지 않는 것은?

① Minwoo gave Yena a birthday present.
② Minwoo asks Yena if she likes the present.
③ Yena thinks the present helps drivers see her well.
④ Yena is not very fond of what she was given.
⑤ Yena hopes it rains because she wants to use the present.

[07~08] 다음 글을 읽고 물음에 답하시오.

> A: (A)저는 수학보다 역사를 더 좋아합니다, but my favorite subject is music. I want to be a singer in the future. Next, I prefer pizza to chicken. I like pizza very much. Lastly, I prefer comedy movies to action movies. Watching comedy movies makes me feel better when I'm sad.

서답형

07 위 글의 밑줄 친 (a)의 우리말을 바르게 영작하시오. (5 words)

➡ _____

08 다음 중 위 글의 내용과 일치하지 <u>않는</u> 것은?

① A's favorite subject is music.

② A wants to be a singer in the future.

③ A likes pizza more than chicken.

④ A likes action movies better than comedy movies.

⑤ A feels better when watching comedy movies.

중요

09 다음 중 짝지어진 대화가 어법상 <u>어색한</u> 것을 고르시오.

① A: Which fruit do you like better, apples or strawberries?

B: I like apples better than strawberries.

② A: Which do you prefer, singing or dancing?

B: I prefer dancing to singing.

③ A: How do you feel about this book?

B: In my opinion, it's very fun.

④ A: How do you feel about this red shirt?

B: It really looks good. I'll take it.

⑤ A: Which fruit do you prefer, pears or strawberries?

B: I prefer pears than strawberries.

[10~11] 다음 대화를 읽고 물음에 답하시오.

> A: (A)클래식 음악에 대해서 어떻게 생각하니?
> B: I don't like it, because it's too boring. How about you?
> A: I think it's very good. I feel calm when I listen to classical music.
> B: Then why don't you become a musician in the future?
> A: That's a good idea.

중요

10 위 대화의 밑줄 친 (A)의 우리말을 바르게 영작한 것을 고르시오.

① What do you think classical music?

② How do you think of classical music?

③ How do you feel to classical music?

④ How did you feel about classical music?

⑤ How do you feel about classical music?

서답형

11 How does A feel when he/she listens to classical music?

➡ _____

_____

[01~03] 다음 대화를 읽고 물음에 답하시오.

Jisu: Hello, Mr. Brown. Are you busy now?

Mr. Brown: Not really.

Jisu: Then, can I talk to you for a minute?

Mr. Brown: Of course. Jisu, what's wrong? You look worried.

Jisu: I'm worried about my future. I don't know what I want to be in the future.

Mr. Brown: (A)How do you feel about becoming a writer? You like literature, don't you?

Jisu: Well, no. (B)저는 문학보다는 과학을 선호해요. But I don't know what kinds of jobs I could do.

Mr. Brown: Why don't you come to the student hall tomorrow? Our graduates will talk about their jobs.

Jisu: That will be very helpful. Thank you.

Mr. Brown: No problem.

01 위 대화의 밑줄 친 (A)를 What으로 시작하는 문장으로 바꿔 쓰시오. (8 words)

➡ _____

02 위 대화의 밑줄 친 (B)의 우리말을 바르게 영작하시오. (5 words)

➡ _____

03 위 대화에서 주어진 영영풀이가 가리키는 것을 찾아 쓰시오.

written artistic works, especially those with a high and lasting artistic value

➡ _____

04 다음 대화의 밑줄 친 우리말에 맞게 주어진 어구를 바르게 나열하시오.

A: 패스트푸드를 먹는 것에 대해서 어떻게 생각하니?(about / fast food / do / eating / you / how / feel)

B: I think eating fast food is bad for health.

➡ _____

[05~07] 다음 대화를 읽고 물음에 답하시오.

B: Mom, can you come to my room?

W: Yes. What are you doing?

B: I'm getting ready for a date. It's Jina's birthday.

W: Aha! So, (A)네가 여러 번 옷을 입어보고 있는 거구나.

B: Yes. Mom, how do I look in this blue shirt?

W: It looks good on you, but are you going to wear those blue jeans, too?

B: I think so. I prefer jeans to my other pants.

W: How do you feel about wearing a white shirt instead?

B: I think the white one and the jeans match better. Thanks for your advice.

W: No problem.

05 위 대화의 밑줄 친 (A)의 우리말을 바르게 영작하시오. (7 words)

➡ _____

06 What kind of pants does B prefer? (8 words)

➡ _____

07 What is B going to wear in the end? (12 words)

➡ _____

교과서
Grammar

① 난이 형용사+to부정사

> • Jobs are hard **to come** by. 직업을 얻기가 어렵다.
> • The weather was impossible **to control**. 날씨를 조절하는 것은 불가능했다.

■ 난이 형용사란 일반적으로 어려움과 쉬움을 나타내는 형용사를 말한다.
  • 어려운 / 쉬운: difficult, hard, easy
  • 위험한 / 안전한: dangerous, safe
  • 불편한 / 편리한: inconvenient / convenient, comfortable
  • 고통스러운 / 즐거운: painful, pleasant
  • 이외의 난이 형용사: fun(재미있는), impossible(불가능한), tough(힘든) 등
  • The accident was impossible **to avoid**. (그 사고는 피하기가 불가능했다.)
  • Bicycles are fun **to ride**. (자전거는 타기에 재미있다.)

■ 'It(가주어)+동사+난이 형용사+to부정사(진주어)' 구문에서 to부정사의 목적어를 문장의 주어로 써서 나타낼 수 있다. to부정사의 의미상의 주어는 for+목적격을 쓴다.
  • It is easy **to please** John. (John을 기쁘게 하는 것은 쉽다.)
    → John is easy **to please**. (John은 쉽게 즐거워한다.)
  • It is fun **to study** English. (영어를 공부하는 것은 즐겁다.)
    → English is fun **to study**. (영어는 공부하기에 즐겁다.)
  • It is easy for him **to ride** horses. (그가 말을 타는 것은 쉽다.)
  • Horses are easy for him to ride. (○)
  • He is easy to ride horses.　　　(×)
  • It is impossible for me **to win** him. (내가 그를 이기는 것은 불가능하다.)
  • I am impossible to win him. (×)
    → 그를 이기는 것이 불가능한 것이지 '내가' 불가능한 것이 아니므로 비문에 해당한다.
※ impossible은 위의 형용사에 해당하지만 'possible'은 위의 형용사에 해당하지 않는다.

핵심 Check

1. 다음 괄호 안에서 알맞은 말을 고르시오.
  (1) The situation is difficult (understanding / to understand).
  (2) It is dangerous (for / to) her to feed the tigers.
  (3) The machine is convenient to (use it / use).

② 도치

> • Are you excited about meeting them? **So am I.** 그들을 만나는 게 신나나요? 저도 그렇습니다.
>
> • People thought the weather was impossible to control. **So did I.** 사람들은 날씨를 조절하는 것이 불가능하다고 생각했습니다. 저도 그랬습니다.

■ 앞 문장의 동의를 나타낼 때, 'So'를 이용하여 표현할 수 있다. 이때 주어와 동사의 위치는 도치가 된다. 'So+동사+주어'로 쓰고 '~도 그렇다'라고 해석한다.
  • **A:** I'm so tired. (아주 피곤해.)
    B: So am I. Let's take some rest. (나도 그래. 우리 좀 쉬자.)

■ 앞 문장에 조동사가 쓰인 경우: 조동사를 활용하여 시제를 일치시켜 사용한다.
  • **A:** I can play the piano. (나 피아노 칠 수 있어.)
    B: So can I. (나도 칠 수 있어.)

■ 앞 문장의 동사가 be동사인 경우: be동사를 활용하여 주어의 수와 시제를 일치시켜 사용한다.
  • **A:** I am happy to meet you. (너를 만나서 기뻐.)
    B: So am I. (나도 그래.)

■ 앞 문장의 동사가 일반동사인 경우: 대동사 'do'를 활용하여 주어의 수와 시제를 일치시켜 사용한다.
  • **A:** I played tennis yesterday. (나 어제 테니스를 쳤어.)
    B: So did my brother. (우리 오빠도 쳤어.)

■ 부정문의 문장을 동의할 때는 'So' 대신에 'Neither'를 이용하여 표현하고 역시 주어와 동사의 위치는 도치된다.
  • **A:** She isn't busy.
    B: Neither am I. (혹은 I am not, either. / Me, neither.)
  • **A:** She didn't play the piano then.
    B: Neither did I. (혹은 I didn't, either. / Me, neither.)
  • **A:** I haven't seen Sarah for a long time.
    B: Neither have I. (혹은 I haven't, either.)

핵심 Check

2. 다음 문장에서 <u>어색한</u> 곳을 찾아 바르게 고쳐 다시 쓰시오.

  (1) The students in my school are exercising hard for their health. So I am.

  ➡ _____

  (2) My younger sister got sick while studying math. So her classmates did.

  ➡ _____

 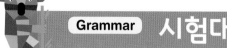

01 다음 문장에서 어법상 <u>어색한</u> 부분을 바르게 고쳐 쓰시오.

(1) It is pleasant to taking a trip around the world.

_____ ➡ _____

(2) My father was a soldier, and so did I.

_____ ➡ _____

(3) It is easy for him climbing this wall.

_____ ➡ _____

(4) It is difficult of her to do her work.

_____ ➡ _____

(5) My sister doesn't like to eat out. So do I.

_____ ➡ _____

02 다음 A와 B를 알맞게 연결하시오.

(A)	(B)
(1) I hate rainy days. •	• (a) So was I.
(2) I was glad to talk to her. •	• (b) Neither have I.
(3) I haven't heard that breaking news. •	• (c) So do I.

03 다음 밑줄 친 우리말에 맞게 3 단어로 영작하시오.

A: I think eating fast food is not good for the health.
B: <u>나도 그렇게 생각해.</u>

➡ _____

04 빈칸에 들어갈 적절한 한 단어를 쓰시오.

A: I preferred comedy movies to action movies.
B: So _____ I.

01 다음 대화에서 어법상 틀린 부분을 찾아 바르게 고쳐 쓰시오.

> **A:** My grandmother always treats me well. How about your grandmother?
>
> **B:** So is she. And she tells me I'm the apple of her eyes.

_____ ➡ _____

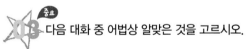다음 빈칸에 들어갈 말로 알맞은 것을 고르시오.

> **A:** I played tennis yesterday.
>
> **B:** So _____ I.

① am   ② was   ③ can
④ do   ⑤ did

다음 대화 중 어법상 알맞은 것을 고르시오.

① A: What instrument can you play? I can play the violin.
  B: So can I.
② A: Are you worried about the exam? I'm so worried about it.
  B: So be I.
③ A: Jack is a diligent student. What about Susan?
  B: So did Susan.
④ A: My friends played soccer yesterday.
  B: Did you?
  A: Yes. So did me.
⑤ A: Being ill, I couldn't join the party.
  B: So could I.

04 다음 빈칸에 들어갈 말이 나머지와 다른 하나를 고르시오.

① A: I had some sandwiches yesterday.
  B: So _____ I.
② A: I was very happy yesterday.
  B: So _____ I.
③ A: She preferred history to math.
  B: So _____ I.
④ A: He wanted to be a singer in the future.
  B: So _____ my sister.
⑤ A: He looked for a new work.
  B: So _____ my brother.

05 다음 빈칸에 들어갈 말을 쓰시오.

> **A:** Yuna doesn't like making shoes.
>
> **B:** _____

06 다음 중 어법상 어색한 것을 고르시오.

① It is impossible to control the weather.
② This book is easy to understand.
③ It is dangerous to ride horses.
④ The math problem was difficult for solve.
⑤ It is pleasant to listen to his songs.

07 다음 밑줄 친 우리말을 영작하시오.

> **A:** I am not a student.
>
> **B:** 나도 아니야. (3 words)

➡ _____

08 다음 문장과 같은 뜻으로 쓰인 문장을 고르시오.

> The book is so difficult that I can't understand it.

① The book is so difficult to understand.
② The book is so difficult for me to understand.
③ The book is so difficult of me to understand.
④ The book isn't difficult to understand.
⑤ The book isn't difficult for me to understand.

09 다음 빈칸에 알맞은 것을 고르시오.

> A: He is interested in taking care of pets.
> B: _____

① So am I.   ② So do I.
③ So was I.   ④ So did I.
⑤ So be I.

10 다음 중 바꿔 쓴 것이 어색한 것을 고르시오.

① It is pleasant to read this book.
  → This book is pleasant to read.
② It is not easy for me to meet him.
  → He is not easy of me to meet.
③ It is hard to get along with her.
  → She is hard to get along with.
④ It was hard to find the book in the library.
  → The book was hard to find in the library.
⑤ It is easy to remember your name.
  → Your name is easy to remember.

11 빈칸에 들어갈 말이 알맞게 짝지어진 것은?

> • A: I am thirsty.
>   B: _____
> • A: My parents weren't sure of whether I would pass the exam.
>   B: _____

① So am I. – So weren't my parents.
② So do I. – So were my parents.
③ So do. – Neither were my parents.
④ So am I. – Neither were my parents.
⑤ So am I. – Neither weren't my parents.

12 다음 빈칸에 들어갈 말로 알맞은 것을 고르시오.

> A: I want to learn English.
> B: _____

① So do I.
② Neither do I.
③ Either do I.
④ Neither am I.
⑤ Either am I.

서답형

13 우리말에 맞게 괄호 안의 어휘들을 배열하여 영작할 때,

(1) 3번째 단어를 쓰시오.
  • 밤늦게 공부하는 것은 힘들다. (tough, study, night, it, to, is, at, late)
  ➡ _____

(2) 4번째 단어를 쓰시오.
  • 그녀를 기쁘게 하는 것을 불가능하다. (impossible, it, please, is, to, her)
  ➡ _____

(3) 7번째 단어를 쓰시오.
  • 마스킹 테이프는 자르기 쉽다. (easy, the, tape, is, masking, cut, to)
  ➡ _____

서답형

14 다음 빈칸에 들어갈 알맞은 말을 쓰시오.

(1) A: I love swimming.

B: So _____ I.

(2) A: Joel loves swimming.

B: So _____ my sister.

★15 **중요** 다음 우리말을 영작할 때 빈칸에 들어갈 말로 적절한 것을 고르시오.

이 책을 하루에 다 읽는 것은 불가능하다.

→ This book is impossible _____ in a day.

① read ② to read

③ reading ④ reads

⑤ for read

16 다음 밑줄 친 문장이 의미하는 것을 고르시오.

A: I wrote a letter to my grandma.

B: <u>So did a friend of mine.</u>

① A friend of mine wrote a letter to her grandma.

② I wrote a letter to my grandma.

③ I wrote a letter to a friend of mine.

④ You wrote a letter to my grandma.

⑤ You wrote a letter to a friend of mine.

17 다음 빈칸에 들어가기에 <u>어색한</u> 것을 <u>모두</u> 고르시오.

A: My brother cries whenever he visits the dentist.

B: So does _____.

① he ② she

③ him ④ my sister

⑤ I

18 다음 중 밑줄 친 It의 쓰임이 <u>다른</u> 하나를 고르시오.

① <u>It</u> is important to think about our future.

② <u>It</u> is not easy to save money.

③ <u>It</u> is hard for you to jump off the wall.

④ <u>It</u> is mine.

⑤ <u>It</u> is comfortable to lie on this sofa.

★19 **중요** 다음 우리말에 맞게 영작할 때 빈칸에 들어갈 말로 알맞은 것을 고르시오.

그들은 Minji를 길거리에서 보고 깜짝 놀랐다.

→ They were surprised _____ Minji on the street.

① see ② saw

③ seeing ④ that see

⑤ to see

20 다음 빈칸에 들어갈 말로 알맞은 것을 고르시오.

A: She can't sing well.

B: _____

① So can I. ② Neither can I.

③ Either can I. ④ Neither am I.

⑤ Either am I.

01 다음 우리말에 맞게 괄호 안의 어구를 배열하시오.

(1) 이 고기는 씹기 어렵다. (tough, beef, chew, this, is, to)

⇒ _____

(2) 무더운 여름 날 화재 장면을 촬영하는 건 정말 고통스러웠다. (on, shoot, painful, really, to, were, fire scenes, hot summer days)

⇒ _____

_____

(3) 강물의 흐름은 통제할 수 없다. (impossible, control, river, flow, the, is, to)

⇒ _____

(4) 이 설명서는 이해하기 쉽다. (easy, understand, manual, this, is, to)

⇒ _____

(5) 오토바이는 타기에 위험하다. (dangerous, ride, a motorcycle, is, to)

⇒ _____

(6) 물리학은 이해하기 어려웠다. (difficult, understand, physics, was, to)

⇒ _____

(7) 그의 연주는 듣기 좋다. (pleasant, listen, his, to, playing, is, to)

⇒ _____

02 위 문제 1번에서 영작한 각 문장에 대하여 'It ... to부정사'를 활용하여 영작하시오.

(1) 이 고기는 씹기 어렵다.

⇒ _____

(2) 무더운 여름 날 화재 장면을 촬영하는 건 정말 고통스러웠다.

⇒ _____

_____

(3) 강물의 흐름은 통제할 수 없다.

⇒ _____

(4) 이 설명서는 이해하기 쉽다.

⇒ _____

(5) 오토바이는 타기에 위험하다.

⇒ _____

(6) 물리학은 이해하기 어려웠다.

⇒ _____

(7) 그의 연주는 듣기 좋다.

⇒ _____

03 괄호 안의 단어를 활용하여 우리말에 맞게 영작하시오.

(1) 나는 그를 정말로 좋아한다. 그와 이야기 나누기가 매우 편하다. (comfortable)

⇒ I really like him. He _____ _____ talk with.

(2) 나는 수영장에서 수영하고 싶었다. 그도 그랬다. (do)

⇒ I wanted to swim in the pool. _____.

04 각 문장에서 틀린 곳을 찾아 바르게 고쳐 다시 쓰시오.

(1) If she is happy, so do I.

⇒ _____

(2) She likes a cat, and so is he.

⇒ _____

(3) I will not tell about the problem, and neither does she.

⇒ _____

05 우리말에 맞게 괄호 안의 단어를 활용하여 영작하시오.

(1) 음악을 듣는 것은 즐겁다. (pleasant, listen)

➡ _____

➡ _____

(2) 우리가 시험을 통과하는 것은 어렵지 않다. (it, difficult)

➡ _____

(3) 그 지역 방언은 알아듣기가 어려웠다. (difficult, local, dialect)

➡ _____

➡ _____

06 다음 문장을 같은 뜻이 되도록 바꿔 쓸 때 빈칸을 알맞게 채우시오.

John is hard to persuade.
➡ _____ John.

07 다음 각 문장에 동의하는 문장을 주어를 'I'로 하여 쓰시오.

(1) She will not go.

➡ _____

(2) Hearing this breaking news, she became gloomy.

➡ _____

(3) Mr. Smith can't drive a bus.

➡ _____

(4) My cousin will go shopping this Saturday with my aunt.

➡ _____

08 다음 문장을 같은 뜻이 되도록 바꿔 쓰시오.

It is difficult for us to understand his English.

➡ _____

09 다음 밑줄 친 우리말을 3 단어로 영작하시오.

(1) I liked to play the piano, and 너도 피아노 치는 것을 좋아했다.

➡ _____

(2) I could decide our meeting time, and 그도 그럴 수 있었다.

➡ _____

(3) I like her, and 그도 그녀를 좋아한다.

➡ _____

(4) Because of Covid-19, I took distance learning class in my house, and Paul도 원격수업을 했다.

➡ _____

10 다음 문장을 같은 뜻이 되도록 바꿔 쓰시오.

This river is dangerous for him to swim in.

➡ _____

Reading

교과서

Welcome to Careers Day!

Welcome to our Careers Day! These days, jobs are hard to come by.
= 'It is hard to come by jobs.' 목적어 자리에 있던 'jobs'가 주어 자리로 이동되었다.

But if you keep on trying your best, you will succeed in your career.
조건의 부사절에서는 미래를 나타낼 때 미래 시제 대신 현재 시제(keep)를 사용

Today, we will welcome back some of the graduates of our school,

and listen to them talk about their jobs. Are you excited about meeting
지각동사의 목적보어(원형부정사)

them? So am I. As you listen to their talks, think about what you would
앞 문장에 대해 동의하거나 동사구를 반복할 때 부사 'so'를 사용하여 표현할 수 있다. = I am excited about meeting them. too.

like to do in the future. Please welcome our first speaker, Ilkem, the
~하기를 원하다(= want to)

weather controller.

Hello, everyone. I'm Ilkem. I'm a scientist studying the weather. Just
겨우, 단지

a few years ago, people thought the weather was impossible to control.
= it was impossible to control the weather

So did I. Thanks to modern technology, however, my fellow scientists
앞 문장에 대해 동의하거나 동사구를 반복할 때 부사 'so'를 사용하여 표현할 수 있다.

and I can change the weather as we want. For example, we can control

the rain, using a cloud seeding system.
= if we use a cloud seeding system

career 직업
these days 요즘에는
come by (힘쓴 끝에) ~을 얻다
control 조절하다
modern 현대의, 근대의
fellow 동료의
seeding 씨 뿌리기
system 체제, 시스템

 확인문제

● 다음 문장이 본문의 내용과 일치하면 T, 일치하지 않으면 F를 쓰시오.

1 These days, it is hard to come by jobs. ☐

2 Today, the students will listen to the celebrities of their community talk about their jobs. ☐

3 Ilkem is the weather controller. ☐

4 Ilkem is a teacher who teaches science. ☐

5 Just a few years ago, people thought it was impossible to control the weather. ☐

6 At present, scientists can't change the weather as they want. ☐

We spray dry ice into clouds to make them rain. In China, they made
rain in another city instead of Beijing during the opening event of the
Olympics and its closing event as well. We can also reduce the side
effects of global warming by controlling the climate. We can't control
the weather perfectly yet, but may be able to do so soon. Then, we
could prevent many kinds of natural disasters like floods and storms.
So you will be able to live in a better and safer environment. Why
don't you join us in making a better environment by controlling the
weather?

Hi, I'm Eva. I'm an architect, and I design net-zero energy houses.
Many people are worried about using too much energy at home. So
were my parents. When I was young, my parents often said, "Eva!
How many times do I have to tell you? Turn off the TV when you're
not watching it!" Since then, I have wanted to design energy-saving
houses. I studied architecture and environmental engineering to make
my dream come true. Now, I design houses that use wind power or
other alternative energy sources. The houses make more energy than
they use. You don't need to worry about wasting energy anymore. If
you are interested in designing net-zero energy houses, please come
and talk to me.

instead of ~ 대신에
side effect 부작용
global warming 지구 온난화
climate 기후
disaster 재난, 재해
storm 폭풍
architect 건축가
architecture 건축학, 건축 양식
alternative 대체 가능한
source 원천, 근원

 확인문제

● 다음 문장이 본문의 내용과 일치하면 T, 일치하지 <u>않으면</u> F를 쓰시오.

1 Scientists studying the weather can reduce the side effects of global warming by
controlling the climate. ☐

2 At present, scientists studying the weather can control the weather perfectly. ☐

3 Eva is an architect, and she designs net-zero energy houses. ☐

4 Eva's parents were not worried about using too much energy at home. ☐

5 Eva studied architecture and environmental engineering to make her dream come
true. ☐

6 Net-zero energy houses make less energy than they use. ☐

Hello. My name is Jiwon, and I'm an end-of-life planner. As the
~함에 따라(접속사)
number of old people is increasing, people are interested in how to

be happy and wealthy in their old age. I help people not only to live
not only A but also B(= B as well as A)는 'A뿐만 아니라 B도'
a healthy life but also to plan for their death. For example, I help

them exercise regularly. I also give them some tips on how to invest
준사역동사 help는 목적어(them) 다음에 목적격 보어로서 동사원형이나 to부정사가 온다.
for retirement and get along well with their family. And I even teach
전치사 on의 목적어   심지어
them how to make a will! This helps their family members avoid a lot

of problems after the person dies. I feel proud of what I'm doing.
자랑스럽게 느끼다

Teacher: Let's give a big hand to the speakers. I hope today's talks

have been helpful for you. I see many students having a hard
'지각동사+목적어+목적격보어'(목적어와 목적격보어가 능동의 관계일 때 원형이나 현재분사)
time learning something new, while worrying about their

future. They are worried that they are slow learners. So was

I. I was a late bloomer. I tried to find what I was good at,
= the thing that
and finally became a teacher. So, I want to say, "Believe in

yourself, and you can do it."

---

end-of-life 임종
increase 증가하다, 증가시키다
wealthy 부유한, 재산이 많은
invest 투자하다
retirement 은퇴, 퇴직
avoid 피하다
will 유언장
bloomer 재능을 발휘하는 사람

📎 **확인문제**

● 다음 문장이 본문의 내용과 일치하면 T, 일치하지 <u>않으면</u> F를 쓰시오.

1 Jiwon is an end-of-life planner. ☐

2 Jiwon helps people go to see a doctor when they get sick. ☐

3 Jiwon helps people exercise regularly. ☐

4 To give people some tips on how to invest for retirement isn't what an end-of-life
   planner does. ☐

5 Jiwon gives people some tips on how to get along well with their family. ☐

6 Jiwon writes a will for people. ☐

● 우리말을 참고하여 빈칸에 알맞은 말을 쓰시오.

1 Welcome to _____ _____!

2 _____ _____ our Careers Day!

3 These days, jobs are hard _____ _____ _____.

4 But if you _____ _____ _____ your best, you will succeed in your career.

5 Today, we will welcome back some of _____ _____ of our school, and _____ _____ _____ _____ about their jobs.

6 Are you _____ _____ meeting them?

7 _____ _____ _____.

8 As you listen to their talks, think about what you _____ _____ _____ do in the future.

9 Please welcome our first speaker, Ilkem, _____ _____ _____.

10 Hello, everyone. _____ _____.

11 I'm a scientist _____ _____ _____.

12 Just a few years ago, people thought the weather was _____ _____ _____.

13 So _____ I.

14 _____ _____ modern technology, however, my fellow scientists and I can change the weather as we want.

15 For example, we can control the rain, _____ a cloud seeding system.

1 직업의 날에 온 것을 환영합니다!

2 우리 직업의 날에 온 것을 환영합니다!

3 요즘은 직업을 얻기가 어렵습니다.

4 하지만 여러분이 계속해서 노력한다면, 여러분의 진로에서 성공할 수 있을 것입니다.

5 오늘, 우리는 우리 학교 졸업생 몇몇을 맞이하고, 그들의 직업에 관해 이야기를 들을 거예요.

6 그들을 만나는 게 신나나요?

7 저도 그렇습니다.

8 그들의 이야기를 들으면서 여러분이 미래에 무엇을 하고 싶은지 생각해 보세요.

9 첫 번째 연설자인 날씨 조절자 Ilkem을 환영합시다.

10 안녕하세요, 여러분. 저는 Ilkem입니다.

11 저는 날씨를 연구하는 과학자입니다.

12 몇 년 전까지만 해도, 사람들은 날씨를 조절하는 것이 불가능하다고 생각했어요.

13 저도 그랬습니다.

14 그러나 현대 기술 덕분에 저의 동료 과학자들과 저는 원하는 대로 날씨를 바꿀 수 있습니다.

15 예를 들어, 우리는 구름 씨 뿌리기 기술을 이용해 강우를 조절할 수 있습니다.

16 We spray dry ice into clouds to _____ _____ _____.

17 In China, they made rain in another city _____ _____ Beijing _____ the opening event of the Olympics and its closing event as well.

18 We can also reduce _____ _____ _____ of global warming by controlling the climate.

19 We can't _____ _____ _____ perfectly yet, but may be able to do so soon.

20 Then, we could prevent many kinds of _____ _____ _____ floods and storms.

21 So you will be able to live _____ _____ _____ _____ _____.

22 _____ _____ _____ us in making a better environment by controlling the weather?

23 Hi, I'm Eva. I'm an architect, and I design _____ _____ _____.

24 Many people are worried about _____ _____ _____ _____ at home.

25 So _____ my parents.

26 When I was young, my parents often said, "Eva! How many times _____ _____ _____ _____ _____ you?

27 _____ _____ the TV when you're not watching it!"

28 Since then, I have wanted to design _____ _____.

29 I studied architecture and environmental engineering to make my dream _____ _____.

30 Now, I design houses that use wind power or other _____ _____ _____.

31 The houses _____ _____ _____ than they use.

32 You don't need to worry about _____ _____ anymore.

33 If you _____ _____ _____ designing net-zero energy houses, please come and talk to me.

16 우리는 구름 속에 드라이아이스를 뿌려 구름을 비로 만듭니다.

17 중국에서는 올림픽의 개막식과 폐막식에 북경 대신 다른 도시에 비가 오게끔 했습니다.

18 또한 우리는 기후를 조절함으로써 지구 온난화의 부작용들을 줄일 수 있습니다.

19 아직은 날씨를 완벽하게 조절할 수 없지만, 곧 그렇게 할 수 있을 것입니다.

20 그러면 홍수나 폭풍 같은 다양한 자연재해를 예방할 수 있을 것입니다.

21 그래서 여러분이 좀 더 안전하고 좋은 환경에서 살 수 있을 거예요.

22 여러분도 날씨를 조절하여 더 나은 환경을 만드는 데에 함께하는 게 어때요?

23 안녕하세요, 저는 Eva입니다. 저는 건축가로, net-zero 에너지 집을 설계합니다.

24 많은 사람들이 집에서 너무 많은 에너지를 사용하는 것에 대해 걱정합니다.

25 저희 부모님도 그랬습니다.

26 제가 어릴 때 부모님께서는 "Eva! 내가 몇 번을 말해야 하니?

27 TV를 보지 않을 때는 꺼!"라고 자주 말씀하셨습니다.

28 그때부터 저는 에너지를 절약하는 집을 설계하고 싶었습니다.

29 저의 꿈을 실현하기 위해 저는 건축과 환경 공학을 공부했습니다.

30 이제 저는 풍력이나 다른 대체 에너지 자원을 사용하는 집들을 설계합니다.

31 그 집들은 사용하는 것보다 더 많은 에너지를 만들어 냅니다.

32 더 이상 에너지를 낭비하는 것을 걱정할 필요가 없습니다.

33 여러분이 net-zero 에너지 집을 설계하는 것에 관심이 있다면, 저에게 와서 얘기하세요.

34 Hello. My name is Jiwon, and I'm an _____ _____.

35 _____ the number of old people _____ _____, people are interested in how to be happy and wealthy in their old age.

36 I help people _____ _____ to live a healthy life _____ _____ to plan for their death.

37 For example, I help them _____ _____.

38 I also give them some tips on how to _____ _____ _____ and _____ _____ _____ _____ their family.

39 And I even teach them how to _____ _____!

40 This helps their family members _____ _____ _____ _____ after the person dies.

41 I _____ _____ what I'm doing.

42 Teacher: Let's _____ _____ _____ _____ _____ the speakers.

43 I hope today's talks have been _____ _____ you.

44 I see many students _____ _____ _____ _____ _____ something new, while worrying about their future.

45 They are worried that they are _____ _____.

46 So _____ I.

47 I was _____ _____ _____.

48 I tried to find _____ _____ _____ _____ _____, and finally became a teacher.

49 So, I want to say, "_____ _____ _____, and you can do it."

● 우리말을 참고하여 본문을 영작하시오.

1 직업의 날에 온 것을 환영합니다!

➡ _____

2 우리 직업의 날에 온 것을 환영합니다!

➡ _____

3 요즘은 직업을 얻기가 어렵습니다.

➡ _____

4 하지만 여러분이 계속해서 노력한다면, 여러분의 진로에서 성공할 수 있을 것입니다.

➡ _____

5 오늘, 우리는 우리 학교 졸업생 몇몇을 맞이하고, 그들의 직업에 관해 이야기를 들을 거예요.

➡ _____

6 그들을 만나는 게 신나나요?

➡ _____

7 저도 그렇습니다.

➡ _____

8 그들의 이야기를 들으면서 여러분이 미래에 무엇을 하고 싶은지 생각해 보세요.

➡ _____

9 첫 번째 연설자인 날씨 조절자 Ilkem을 환영합시다.

➡ _____

10 안녕하세요, 여러분. 저는 Ilkem입니다.

➡ _____

11 저는 날씨를 연구하는 과학자입니다.

➡ _____

12 몇 년 전까지만 해도, 사람들은 날씨를 조절하는 것이 불가능하다고 생각했어요.

➡ _____

13 저도 그랬습니다.

➡ _____

14 그러나 현대 기술 덕분에 저의 동료 과학자들과 저는 원하는 대로 날씨를 바꿀 수 있습니다.

➡ _____

15 예를 들어, 우리는 구름 씨 뿌리기 기술을 이용해 강우를 조절할 수 있습니다.

➡ _____

16 우리는 구름 속에 드라이아이스를 뿌려 구름을 비로 만듭니다.

➡ _____

17 중국에서는 올림픽의 개막식과 폐막식에 북경 대신 다른 도시에 비가 오게끔 했습니다.

➡ _____

_____

18 또한 우리는 기후를 조절함으로써 지구 온난화의 부작용들을 줄일 수 있습니다.

➡ _____

19 아직은 날씨를 완벽하게 조절할 수 없지만, 곧 그렇게 할 수 있을 것입니다.

➡ _____

20 그러면 홍수나 폭풍 같은 다양한 자연재해를 예방할 수 있을 것입니다.

➡ _____

21 그래서 여러분이 좀 더 안전하고 좋은 환경에서 살 수 있을 거예요.

➡ _____

22 여러분도 날씨를 조절하여 더 나은 환경을 만드는 데에 함께하는 게 어때요?

➡ _____

23 안녕하세요, 저는 Eva입니다. 저는 건축가로, net-zero 에너지 집을 설계합니다.

➡ _____

24 많은 사람들이 집에서 너무 많은 에너지를 사용하는 것에 대해 걱정합니다.

➡ _____

25 저희 부모님도 그랬습니다.

➡ _____

26 제가 어릴 때 부모님께서는 "Eva! 내가 몇 번을 말해야 하니?

➡ _____

27 TV를 보지 않을 때는 꺼!"라고 자주 말씀하셨습니다.

➡ _____

28 그때부터 저는 에너지를 절약하는 집을 설계하고 싶었습니다.

➡ _____

29 저의 꿈을 실현하기 위해 저는 건축과 환경 공학을 공부했습니다.

➡ _____

30 이제 저는 풍력이나 다른 대체 에너지 자원을 사용하는 집들을 설계합니다.

➡ _____

31 그 집들은 사용하는 것보다 더 많은 에너지를 만들어 냅니다.

➡ _____

32 더 이상 에너지를 낭비하는 것을 걱정할 필요가 없습니다.

➡ _____

33 여러분이 net-zero 에너지 집을 설계하는 것에 관심이 있다면, 저에게 와서 얘기하세요.

➡ _____

34 안녕하세요. 제 이름은 지원이고, 저는 임종 설계사입니다.

➡ _____

35 고령 인구가 증가함에 따라 사람들은 어떻게 하면 노년에 행복하고 부유하게 살 수 있는지에 대해 관심을 가집니다.

➡ _____

_____

36 저는 사람들이 건강한 삶을 사는 것을 도울 뿐만 아니라 그들의 죽음을 계획할 수 있게 돕습니다.

➡ _____

37 예를 들어, 저는 그들이 규칙적으로 운동하도록 돕습니다.

➡ _____

38 또한 은퇴 후에 투자를 하는 방법이나 그들의 가족과 잘 어울려 지내는 것에 대한 조언을 합니다.

➡ _____

39 그리고 저는 심지어 그들에게 유언장 쓰는 법을 가르칩니다!

➡ _____

40 이것은 그가 죽고 난 후 가족들이 많은 문제들을 피하는 데에 도움을 줍니다.

➡ _____

41 저는 제가 하는 일이 자랑스럽습니다.

➡ _____

42 선생님: 연설자들에게 큰 박수를 보냅시다.

➡ _____

43 오늘 이야기들이 여러분에게 도움이 되었기를 바랍니다.

➡ _____

44 저는 많은 학생들이 새로운 것을 배우는 데에 어려움을 겪고 그들의 미래에 대해 걱정하는 것을 봅니다.

➡ _____

45 그들은 배우는 속도가 느리다고 걱정합니다.

➡ _____

46 저 또한 그랬습니다.

➡ _____

47 저는 늦게 꽃피우는 사람이었죠.

➡ _____

48 내가 무엇을 잘하는지 찾기 위해 노력했고, 결국은 선생님이 되었습니다.

➡ _____

49 그래서 여러분에게 이렇게 말하고 싶습니다. "여러분 자신을 믿으세요, 그러면 할 수 있습니다."

➡ _____

[01~03] 다음 글을 읽고 물음에 답하시오.

Welcome to our Careers Day! These days, jobs are hard to come by. But if you keep on trying your best, you will succeed ⓐ your career. Today, we will welcome back some of the graduates of our school, and listen to (A) them talk about their jobs. Are you excited ⓑ meeting them? So am I. As you listen to their talks, think about what you would like to do in the future. Please welcome our first speaker, Ilkem, the weather controller.

01 위 글의 빈칸 ⓐ와 ⓑ에 들어갈 전치사가 바르게 짝지어진 것은?

	ⓐ	ⓑ		ⓐ	ⓑ
①	for	about	②	in	of
③	in	about	④	for	of
⑤	on	at			

서답형

02 위 글의 밑줄 친 (A)them이 가리키는 것을 본문에서 찾아 쓰시오.

➡ _____

중요

03 According to the passage, which is NOT true?

① On Careers Day, some of the graduates visit the school and talk about their jobs.
② It isn't easy to get a job these days.
③ Keeping trying your best will lead to your successful career.
④ The guests of the Careers Day are the experts in various fields.
⑤ Ilkem is a weather controller.

[04~06] 다음 글을 읽고 물음에 답하시오.

Hello, everyone. I'm Ilkem. I'm a scientist studying the weather. Just a few years ago, people thought the weather was impossible to control. So did I. Thanks to modern technology, ⓐ , my fellow scientists and I can change the weather ⓑas we want. For example, we can control the rain, using a cloud seeding system. We spray dry ice into clouds to make them rain. In China, they made rain in another city instead of Beijing during the opening event of the Olympics and its closing event as well. We can also reduce the side effects of global warming by controlling the climate. We can't control the weather perfectly yet, but may be able to do so soon. Then, we could prevent many kinds of natural disasters like floods and storms. So you will be able to live in a better and safer environment. Why don't you join us in making a better environment by controlling the weather?

04 위 글의 빈칸 ⓐ에 들어갈 알맞은 말을 고르시오.

① in addition   ② for example
③ however   ④ similarly
⑤ in other words

05 위 글의 밑줄 친 ⓑas와 같은 의미로 쓰인 것을 고르시오.

① She sang as she walked.
② Woman as she was, my aunt was brave.
③ As we go up, the air grows colder.
④ As I was tired, I soon fell asleep.
⑤ Do as you would be done by.

⭐️06 위 글의 제목으로 알맞은 것을 고르시오.

① Controlling the Weather? Impossible!
② Some Good Points about Controlling the Weather
③ How to Make Rain Using a Cloud Seeding System
④ The Side Effects of Global Warming
⑤ Remove Natural Disaster and Make a Better Environment

07 주어진 글 다음에 이어질 글의 순서로 가장 적절한 것은?

> Hi, I'm Eva. I'm an architect, and I design net-zero energy houses. Many people are worried about using too much energy at home. So were my parents.

> (A) Since then, I have wanted to design energy-saving houses. I studied architecture and environmental engineering to make my dream come true. Now, I design houses that use wind power or other alternative energy sources.
> (B) When I was young, my parents often said, "Eva! How many times do I have to tell you? Turn off the TV when you're not watching it!"
> (C) The houses make more energy than they use. You don't need to worry about wasting energy anymore. If you are interested in designing net-zero energy houses, please come and talk to me.

① (A)–(C)–(B) ② (B)–(A)–(C)
③ (B)–(C)–(A) ④ (C)–(A)–(B)
⑤ (C)–(B)–(A)

[08~09] 다음 글을 읽고 물음에 답하시오.

> Hello. My name is Jiwon, and I'm an end-of-life planner. As the number of old people is increasing, people are interested in how to be happy and wealthy in their old age. I help people not only to live a healthy life but also to plan for their death. For example, ⓐI help them exercising regularly. I also give them some tips on how to invest for retirement and get along well with their family. And I even teach them how to make a ⓑwill! This helps their family members avoid a lot of problems after the person dies. I feel proud of what I'm doing.

서답형
08 위 글의 밑줄 친 ⓐ에서 어법상 틀린 부분을 찾아 고치시오.

➡ _____

09 위 글의 밑줄 친 ⓑwill과 같은 의미로 쓰인 것을 고르시오.

① She has a strong will.
② Will you send this letter for me, please?
③ My father left me the house in his will.
④ If it's made of wood, it will float.
⑤ How long will you be staying in Paris?

[10~13] 다음 글을 읽고 물음에 답하시오.

> Hello, everyone. I'm Ilkem. I'm a scientist studying the weather. Just a few years ago, people thought the weather was impossible to control. ⓐNeither did I. Thanks to modern technology, however, my fellow scientists and I can change the weather as we want. For example, we can control the rain, ⓑusing a

cloud seeding system. We spray dry ice into clouds to make them rain. In China, they made rain in another city instead of Beijing during the opening event of the Olympics and its closing event as well. ⓒ또한 우리는 기후를 조절함으로써 지구 온난화의 부작용들을 줄일 수 있습니다. We can't control the weather perfectly yet, but may be able to do so soon. Then, we could prevent many kinds of natural disasters like floods and storms. So you will be able to live in a better and safer environment. Why don't you join us in making a better environment by controlling the weather?

서답형

10 위 글의 밑줄 친 ⓐ에서 어법상 틀린 부분을 찾아 고치시오.

➡ _____

11 위 글의 밑줄 친 ⓑusing과 문법적 쓰임이 같은 것을 모두 고르시오.

① The boy sleeping under the tree is my brother.
② She stood there looking at the bill.
③ I enjoy spending time with my parents.
④ I saw Tom crossing the street.
⑤ I can express my emotions by writing.

서답형

12 위 글의 밑줄 친 ⓒ의 우리말에 맞게 주어진 어휘를 알맞게 배열하시오.

global warming / by / can / the climate / also / reduce / we / the side effects / controlling / of

➡ _____

_____

중요

13 Which question CANNOT be answered after reading the passage?

① What is Ilkem?
② At present, is it possible to control the weather?
③ How long does it take to control the rain, using a cloud seeding system?
④ Why did China use the cloud seeding system during the Olympics?
⑤ What natural disasters could we prevent by controlling the weather?

[14~17] 다음 글을 읽고 물음에 답하시오.

Welcome to our Careers Day! (①) These days, jobs are hard ⓐto come by. (②) But if you keep on trying your best, you will succeed in your career. (③) ⓑToday, we will welcome back some of the graduates of our school, and listen to them to talk about their jobs. (④) ⓒSo am I. (⑤) As you listen to their talks, think about what you would like to do in the future. Please welcome our first speaker, Ilkem, the weather controller.

14 위 글의 흐름으로 보아, 주어진 문장이 들어가기에 가장 적절한 곳은?

Are you excited about meeting them?

① ② ③ ④ ⑤

서답형

15 위 글의 밑줄 친 ⓑ에서 어법상 틀린 부분을 찾아 고치시오.

➡ _____

16 위 글의 밑줄 친 ⓐto come과 to부정사의 용법이 같은 것을 <u>모두</u> 고르시오.

① I want you <u>to be</u> a doctor.
② My father lived <u>to be</u> one hundred years old.
③ I don't have any friends <u>to talk</u> with.
④ His job is <u>to sing</u> a song.
⑤ She stood up <u>to go</u> out.

서답형
17 다음 빈칸에 알맞은 말을 넣어, 위 글의 밑줄 친 문장 ⓒ가 내 포하는 의미를 완성하시오.

➡ I am excited about meeting them, _____.
또는 I am _____ excited about meeting them.

[18~19] 다음 글을 읽고 물음에 답하시오.

Hi, I'm Eva. I'm an architect, and I design net-zero energy houses. Many people are worried about using too much energy at home. So were my parents. When I was young, my parents often said, "Eva! How many times do I have to tell you? Turn off the TV when you're not watching it!" Since then, I have wanted to design energy-saving houses. I studied architecture and environmental engineering to make my dream come true. Now, I design houses that use wind power or other alternative energy sources. The houses make more energy than they use. You don't need to worry about wasting energy anymore. If you are interested in designing net-zero energy houses, please come and talk to me.

중요
18 위 글의 주제로 알맞은 것을 고르시오.

① the history of designing net-zero energy houses
② the importance of saving energy
③ to design the houses that can save energy
④ the efficiency of solar power generation
⑤ the side effects of wasting energy

19 위 글을 읽고 알 수 <u>없는</u> 것을 고르시오.

① What is Eva?
② What has Eva wanted to design?
③ What did Eva study to make her dream come true?
④ How many alternative energy sources do net-zero energy houses use?
⑤ Do net-zero energy houses make more energy than they use?

[20~22] 다음 글을 읽고 물음에 답하시오.

Hi, I'm Eva. I'm an architect, and I design net-zero energy houses. Many people are worried about using too much energy at home. So were my parents. When I was young, my parents often said, "Eva! How many times do I have to tell you? Turn off the TV when you're not watching it!" Since then, I (A)<u>have wanted</u> to design energy-saving houses. I studied architecture and environmental engineering to make my dream ⓐ_____ _____. Now, I design houses that use wind power or other alternative energy sources. The houses make more energy than they use. You don't need to worry about wasting energy anymore. If you are interested in designing net-zero energy houses, please come and talk to me.

서답형

20 위 글의 빈칸 ⓐ에 become a reality와 같은 뜻의 두 단어를 쓰시오.

➡ _____

21 위 글의 밑줄 친 (A)have wanted와 현재완료의 용법이 같은 것을 <u>모두</u> 고르시오.

① He <u>has been</u> dead for 15 years.

② I <u>have</u> never <u>met</u> a student like him before.

③ She <u>hasn't eaten</u> her hamburger yet.

④ How long <u>have</u> you <u>worn</u> this shirt?

⑤ I <u>have been</u> to London many times.

서답형

22 다음 빈칸 (A)~(C)에 알맞은 단어를 넣어 'net-zero energy houses'에 대한 소개를 완성하시오.

> They are the houses that use wind power or other (A)_____ _____ _____, and they make (B)_____ _____ than they use, so you don't need to worry about (C)_____ _____ anymore.

[23~24] 다음 글을 읽고 물음에 답하시오.

Teacher: Let's give a big hand ⓐ<u>to</u> the speakers. I hope today's talks have been helpful ⓑ<u>for</u> you. I see many students having a hard time learning something new, while worrying ⓒ<u>about</u> their future. (①) They are worried that they are slow learners. (②) I was a late bloomer. (③) I tried to find what I was good ⓓ<u>for</u>, and finally became a teacher. (④) So, I want to say, "Believe ⓔ<u>in</u> yourself, and you can do it." (⑤)

서답형

23 밑줄 친 ⓐ~ⓔ 중에서 전치사가 옳지 <u>않은</u> 것을 찾아 고치시오.

➡ _____

중요

24 위 글의 흐름으로 보아, 주어진 문장이 들어가기에 가장 적절한 곳은?

> So was I.

①   ②   ③   ④   ⑤

[25~26] 다음 글을 읽고 물음에 답하시오.

> Hello. My name is Jiwon, and I'm an end-of-life planner. As the number of old people is increasing, people are interested in how to be happy and wealthy in their old age. I help people not only to live a healthy life but also to plan for their death. ___ⓐ___, I help them exercise regularly. I also give them some tips on ⓑ<u>how to invest</u> for retirement and get along well with their family. And I even teach them how to make a will! This helps their family members avoid a lot of problems after the person dies. I feel proud of what I'm doing.

25 위 글의 빈칸 ⓐ에 들어갈 알맞은 말을 고르시오.

① Therefore   ② For example

③ In fact   ④ That is

⑤ Furthermore

서답형

26 위 글의 밑줄 친 ⓑ를 다음과 같이 바꿔 쓸 때 빈칸에 들어갈 알맞은 말을 두 단어로 쓰시오.

➡ how _____ _____ invest

[01~04] 다음 글을 읽고 물음에 답하시오.

Welcome to our Careers Day! These days, ⓐjobs are hard to come by. But if you keep on trying your best, you will succeed in your career. Today, we will welcome back some of the graduates of our school, and listen to them talk about their jobs. Are you excited about meeting them? ⓑ저도 그렇습니다. As you listen to their talks, think about what you would like to do in the future. Please welcome our first speaker, Ilkem, the weather controller.

01 주어진 영영풀이에 해당하는 단어를 본문에서 찾아 쓰시오.

It's an event where students learn about different careers by bringing the graduates of the school or community members into the school to discuss their jobs.

➡ _____

02 위 글의 밑줄 친 ⓐ를 다음과 같이 바꿔 쓸 때 빈칸에 들어갈 알맞은 말을 두 단어로 쓰시오.

➡ _____ _____ hard to come by jobs

03 위 글의 밑줄 친 ⓑ의 우리말에 맞게 3 단어로 영작하시오.

➡ _____

04 본문의 내용과 일치하도록 다음 빈칸 (A)와 (B)에 알맞은 단어를 쓰시오.

Today, some of the graduates are going to talk about (A)_____ _____.
Students can think about (B)_____
_____ _____ _____ _____
_____ in the future while listening to their talks.

[05~07] 다음 글을 읽고 물음에 답하시오.

Hello, everyone. I'm Ilkem. I'm a scientist studying the weather. Just a few years ago, people thought the weather was impossible to control. ⓐSo did I. Thanks to modern technology, however, my fellow scientists and I can change the weather as we want. For example, we can control the rain, using a cloud seeding system. We spray dry ice into clouds to make them rain. In China, they made rain in another city instead of Beijing during the opening event of the Olympics and its closing event as well. We can also reduce the side effects of global warming by controlling the climate. We can't control the weather perfectly yet, but may be able to do so soon. Then, we could prevent many kinds of natural disasters ⓑlike floods and storms. So you will be able to live in a better and safer environment. Why don't you join us in making a better environment by controlling the weather?

05 위 글의 밑줄 친 문장 ⓐSo did I가 내포하는 의미를 완전한 문장으로 쓰시오.

➡ _____
_____

06 위 글의 밑줄 친 ⓑlike와 바꿔 쓸 수 있는 말을 두 단어로 쓰시오.

➡ _____

07 다음 빈칸 (A)와 (B)에 알맞은 단어를 넣어 인공 강우의 원리에 대한 소개를 완성하시오.

> The scientists studying the weather can control the rain, using (A)_____ _____ _____, and during the process, they spray (B)_____ _____ into clouds to make them rain.

[08~10] 다음 글을 읽고 물음에 답하시오.

> Hi, I'm Eva. I'm an architect, and I design net-zero energy houses. Many people are worried about using too much energy at home. So ⓐ_____ my parents. When I was young, my parents often said, "Eva! How many times do I have to tell you? Turn off the TV when you're not watching it!" Since then, I have wanted to design energy-saving houses. I studied architecture and environmental engineering to make my dream come true. Now, I design houses that use wind power or other alternative energy sources. The houses make more energy than ⓑthey use. You don't need to worry about wasting energy anymore. If you are interested in designing net-zero energy houses, please come and talk to me.

08 위 글의 빈칸 ⓐ에 들어갈 알맞은 한 단어를 쓰시오.

➡ _____

09 위 글의 밑줄 친 ⓑthey가 가리키는 것을 본문에서 찾아 쓰시오.

➡ _____

10 How can net-zero energy houses save energy? Fill in the blanks with suitable words.

> Net-zero energy houses _____ _____ than they make using wind power or other alternative energy sources, so they can save energy.

[11~12] 다음 글을 읽고 물음에 답하시오.

> **Teacher:** Let's give a big hand to the speakers. I hope today's talks have been helpful for you. ⓐI see many students having a hard time learning something new, while worrying about their future. They are worried that they are slow learners. So was I. I was ⓑa late bloomer. I tried to find what I was good at, and finally became a teacher. So, I want to say, "Believe in yourself, and you can do it."

11 위 글의 밑줄 친 ⓐ를 다음과 같이 바꿔 쓸 때 빈칸에 들어갈 알맞은 말을 (1) 한 단어로, (2) 두 단어로 쓰시오.

➡ (1) I see many students having _____ learning something new
(2) I see many students having _____ _____ learning something new

12 다음 빈칸에 알맞은 단어를 넣어 위 글의 밑줄 친 ⓑ의 의미를 완성하시오.

➡ a person who achieves proficiency or success in a field comparatively _____ in life

구석구석

Everyday English 2 C. Communication Activity

A: How do you feel about classical music?
'~에 대해 어떻게 생각하니?'라는 뜻으로 상대방의 의견을 묻는 표현

B: I don't like it, because it's too boring. How about you?
대명사 it은 앞서 언급된 classical music을 지칭   상대방의 의견을 되묻는 표현

A: I think it's very good. I feel calm when I listen to classical music.
'~라고 생각한다'라는 뜻으로 의견을 나타내는 표현

B: Then why don't you become a musician in the future?
'~하는 게 어떠니'라는 뜻으로 상대방에게 제안하는 표현

A: That's a good idea.

구문해설 · classical music 클래식 음악 · boring 지루하게 하는 · calm 차분한 · musician 음악가
· in the future 미래에

A: 클래식 음악에 대해서 어떻게 생각하니?
B: 난 그것을 좋아하지 않아. 너무 지루하기 때문이야. 너는 어떠니?
A: 난 그게 매우 좋다고 생각해. 클래식 음악을 들을 때 차분해지거든.
B: 그럼, 미래에 음악가가 되는 건 어떠니?
A: 그거 좋은 생각이다.

After You Read A

Ilkem

· I can control the rain, using a cloud seeding system.
분사구문

· By controlling the climate, I can reduce the side effects of global warming.
By ~ing: ~함으로써

Eva

· I design net-zero energy houses.

· I make houses that use wind power or other alternative energy sources.
주격 관계대명사

Jiwon

· I help people not only to live a healthy life but also to plan for their death.
not only A but also B = B as well as A: A뿐만 아니라 B도

· This job helps their family avoid a lot of problems after the person dies.
help+목적어+동사원형 또는 to부정사

구문해설 · seeding: 씨 뿌리기 · system: 체제, 시스템 · climate: 기후 · side effect: 부작용
· global warming: 지구 온난화 · alternative: 대체 가능한 · source: 원천, 근원
· healthy: 건강한 · avoid: 피하다

Ilkem
· 저는 구름 씨 뿌리기 기술을 이용해 강우를 조절할 수 있습니다.
· 저는 기후를 조절함으로써 지구 온난화의 부작용들을 줄일 수 있습니다.

Eva
· 저는 net-zero 에너지 집을 설계합니다.
· 저는 풍력이나 다른 대체 에너지 자원을 사용하는 집들을 설계합니다.

Jiwon
· 저는 사람들이 건강한 삶을 사는 것을 도울 뿐만 아니라 그들의 죽음을 계획할 수 있게 돕습니다.
· 이 직업은 그 사람이 죽고 난 후 가족들이 많은 문제들을 피하는 데에 도움을 줍니다.

Culture & Project Step 1

Our group has made a poster to look for space tour guides. In the future, we
to부정사의 형용사적 용법

will be able to travel to space. So, we need someone to guide us around space.
조동사 will과 can 두 개를 겹쳐 쓸 수 없으므로 will be able to로 표현   to부정사의 형용사적 용법

The space tour guides should know a lot about planets and space so that they

can explain many things about space to tourists. Also, they should be healthy
explain+목적어+to 사람: 목적어를 사람에게 설명하다

and help people travel safely and comfortably.
help+목적어+목적격보어(원형부정사)

구문해설 · look for: ~을 찾다 · so that: ~하기 위해서

우리 모둠은 우주여행 가이드를 찾는 포스터를 만들었다. 미래에, 우리는 우주를 여행할 수 있을 것이다. 그래서 우리는 우주를 우리에게 안내해 줄 누군가가 필요하다. 우주여행 가이드는 우주에 대하여 여행자들에게 많은 것을 설명할 수 있어야 해서 우주와 행성들에 대해 많이 알아야 한다. 또한, 그들은 건강해야 하고 사람들이 안전하고 편안하게 여행하는 것을 도와야 한다.

영역별 핵심문제

Words & Expressions

01 다음 짝지어진 단어의 관계가 같도록 빈칸에 알맞은 말을 쓰시오.

> reduce : increase = regularly : _____

02 다음 중 밑줄 친 부분의 뜻풀이가 바르지 <u>않은</u> 것은?

① He was unwell. <u>However</u>, he went to work. (그러나)
② This machine is worked by <u>wind power</u>. (풍력)
③ She <u>graduated</u> from Harvard law school last semester. (졸업생)
④ They live in a <u>wealthy</u> suburb of LA. (부유한, 재산이 많은)
⑤ John is going to take early <u>retirement</u>. (은퇴, 퇴직)

03 다음 주어진 문장의 밑줄 친 season과 같은 의미로 쓰이지 <u>않은</u> 것은?

> The hotels are always full during the peak <u>season</u>.

① How many goals has the team missed this <u>season</u>?
② Harry has just earned his fourth MVP award this <u>season</u>.
③ You need to <u>season</u> steak strips with salt and pepper.
④ The menu in the famous restaurant varies with the <u>season</u>.
⑤ We need extra help during the peak <u>season</u>.

04 다음 우리말을 주어진 단어를 이용하여 영작하시오.

> 전 세계적으로 10월에는 관광객의 수가 차츰 줄어든다. (the number of)

➡ _____

_____

05 다음 영영풀이에 해당하는 단어로 알맞은 것은?

> the air, water, and land in or on which people, animals, and plants live

① operation
② occupation
③ disaster
④ catastrophe
⑤ environment

Conversation

06 다음 대화의 밑줄 친 부분과 바꿔 쓸 수 <u>없는</u> 것은? (2개)

> A: Which one do you prefer, eating out or ordering in?
> B: <u>I prefer ordering in over eating out.</u>

① I like ordering in more than eating out.
② I like ordering in better than eating out.
③ I prefer ordering in better over eating out.
④ I prefer ordering in to eating out.
⑤ I prefer ordering in more than eating out.

[07~09] 다음 대화를 읽고 물음에 답하시오.

> B: I got a ticket for the Coolboys concert.
> G: ① You're so lucky! When is it?
> B: ② I'm thinking of going there with my friends.

G: ③ By the way, (A)그들의 새 앨범에 대해 어떻게 생각하니?

B: I like it. ④ All the songs are so exciting, aren't they?

G: Yes, but I prefer their last album to the new one. ⑤

B: Why?

G: It has more songs of different genres.

07 위 대화의 ①~⑤ 중에서 주어진 문장이 들어가기에 가장 적절한 곳은?

| It's next Saturday. |

①   ②   ③   ④   ⑤

08 위 대화의 밑줄 친 (A)를 우리말에 맞게 feel을 이용해 영작하시오. (8 words)

➡ _____

09 다음 중 위 대화의 내용과 일치하지 <u>않는</u> 것은?

① B is going to go to the concert with his friends.

② B likes the boy band's new album very much.

③ B thinks all the songs in the new album are exciting.

④ G thinks the new album is better than the last one.

⑤ G thinks the last album has more songs of different genres.

10 다음 대화의 밑줄 친 우리말을 바르게 영작하시오. (10 words)

A: How do you feel about taking a trip around the world?

B: 나는 전 세계를 여행하는 게 좋다고 생각해. It helps us experience different cultures.

➡ _____

[11~13] 다음 글을 읽고 물음에 답하시오.

M: Have you heard about the new STARS camera? It is a smart camera (A)[who/which] will catch your best moments. It is very small, but very strong. It's very easy (B)[taking / to take] good pictures with this camera. All you have to do is just talk to the camera without (C)[having / to have] to use your fingers. Oh, and this is the last chance to get one at a good price. It's 30 percent off at the moment. (a)우리 상점에 방문하셔서 카메라를 둘러보는 것에 대해서 어떻게 생각하시나요?(our store / do / how / visiting / you / about / to see / feel / one)

11 위 글의 괄호 (A)~(C)에서 어법상 적절한 것을 골라 쓰시오.

➡ (A) _____
    (B) _____
    (C) _____

12 위 글의 밑줄 친 (a)의 우리말에 맞게 주어진 단어를 바르게 나열하시오.

➡ _____

13 다음 중 위 글의 목적으로 가장 적절한 것은?

① to criticize   ② to advertise

③ to promote   ④ to recommend

⑤ to encourage

Grammar

14 다음 중 빈칸에 들어갈 단어로 알맞은 것을 고르시오.

> A: My tooth hurts, but I hate going to the dentist.
> B: So _____ my younger sister.

① do   ② did   ③ am
④ does   ⑤ are

15 다음 중 밑줄 친 It의 쓰임이 다른 하나를 고르시오.

① It is exciting to see a boxing game.
② It is impossible for him to live alone in a big city.
③ It is a big size T-shirt.
④ It is amazing to meet a movie star.
⑤ It is boring to go fishing.

16 다음 빈칸 (A)~(C)에 들어갈 말이 바르게 짝지어진 것을 고르시오.

> (1) A: I went to Africa last summer.
>   B: So __(A)__ she.
> (2) A: I have been to Paris.
>   B: So __(B)__ my sister.
> (3) A: I had gone to bed when they came home.
>   B: So __(C)__ I.

	(A)	(B)	(C)
①	did	has	had
②	do	have	had
③	did	have	have
④	do	has	have
⑤	did	had	had

17 괄호 안의 단어를 활용하여 우리말에 맞도록 영작하시오.

> 프랑스어를 공부하는 것은 나에게 어렵다.
> (difficult)

➡ _____ (8 단어)

18 다음 문장에 동의하는 문장을 쓰시오.

> I didn't like to sing a song when I was young.

➡ _____

19 다음 우리말을 영작할 때 빈칸에 들어갈 말을 쓰시오.

> 그는 과학자이고 그녀 역시 그렇다.
> ➡ He is a scientist, and so is _____.

20 다음 중 빈칸에 들어갈 단어로 어색한 것을 고르시오.

> It is more convenient for _____ to go by car.

① her   ② us   ③ him
④ me   ⑤ she

21 다음 문장을 주어진 말로 시작하는 문장으로 바꿔 쓰시오.

> Some robots are dangerous to handle.

➡ It _____.

Reading

[22~24] 다음 글을 읽고 물음에 답하시오.

Welcome to our Careers Day! These days, jobs are hard to come by. But if you keep on ____ⓐ____ your best, you will succeed in your career. Today, we will welcome back some of the graduates of our school, and listen to them talk about their jobs. Are you excited about meeting them? ⓑSo do I. As you listen to their talks, think about what you would like to do in the future. Please welcome our first speaker, Ilkem, the weather controller.

22 위 글의 빈칸 ⓐ에 try를 알맞은 형태로 쓰시오.

➡ _____

23 위 글의 밑줄 친 ⓑ에서 어법상 틀린 부분을 찾아 고치시오.

➡ _____

24 위 글의 제목으로 알맞은 것을 고르시오.

① Welcome to School Open Day!
② The Difficulty of Getting Jobs
③ Let's Listen to the Graduates Talk about Jobs
④ Keep Trying Your Best
⑤ In the Future, It Will Be Easy to Succeed in Your Career

[25~26] 다음 글을 읽고 물음에 답하시오.

Hello, everyone. I'm Ilkem. I'm a scientist studying the weather. Just a few years ago, people thought the weather was impossible to control. So did I. Thanks to modern technology, however, my fellow scientists and I can change the weather as we want. ⓐ_____, we can control the rain, using a cloud seeding system. We spray dry ice into clouds to make them rain. In China, they made rain in another city instead of Beijing during the opening event of the Olympics and its closing event as well. We can also reduce the side effects of global warming by controlling the climate. We can't control the weather perfectly yet, but may be able to do so soon. Then, we could prevent many kinds of natural disasters like floods and storms. So you will be able to live in a better and safer environment. Why don't you join us in making a better environment by controlling the weather?

25 위 글의 빈칸 ⓐ에 들어갈 알맞은 말을 고르시오.

① That is   ② However
③ Whereas   ④ Additionally
⑤ For example

26 What was the weather like in Beijing during the opening and closing events of the Olympics? Fill in the blanks (A) and (B) with suitable words.

It (A)_____ rain in Beijing during the opening and closing events of the Olympics by making rain in (B)_____ _____ instead of Beijing, using a cloud seeding system.

[27~28] 다음 글을 읽고 물음에 답하시오.

Hi, I'm Eva. I'm an architect, and I design net-zero energy houses. Many people are worried about ⓐ<u>using</u> too much energy at home. So were my parents. When I was young, my parents often said, "Eva! How many times do I have to tell you? Turn off the TV when you're not watching it!" Since then, I have wanted to design energy-saving houses. (①) I studied architecture and environmental engineering to make my dream come true. (②) The houses make more energy than they use. (③) You don't need to worry about wasting energy anymore. (④) If you are interested in designing net-zero energy houses, please come and talk to me. (⑤)

27 위 글의 밑줄 친 ⓐusing과 문법적 쓰임이 <u>다른</u> 것을 <u>모두</u> 고르시오.

① The man kept <u>looking</u> at me.
② He was <u>planting</u> some flowers.
③ He watched TV <u>eating</u> some snacks.
④ <u>Drinking</u> a lot of water is good for your health.
⑤ My hobby is <u>playing</u> baseball.

28 위 글의 흐름으로 보아, 주어진 문장이 들어가기에 가장 적절한 곳은?

> Now, I design houses that use wind power or other alternative energy sources.

　①　　　②　　　③　　　④　　　⑤

[29~30] 다음 글을 읽고 물음에 답하시오.

Friday, Oct 30th, 2020
Today was Careers Day, and some graduates visited our school. I went to the student hall to listen to their talks. They had many different kinds of jobs. The weather controller can control the climate and prevent natural disasters such as storms. The net-zero energy house architect designs houses that save energy by using alternative energy sources. The end-of-life planner helps people live a happy and wealthy life after retirement. After the talks, I thought about what I want to do in the future. I like science, and there are lots of things I can do using modern technology. It was a great chance to think about my future.

29 위 글의 종류로 알맞은 것을 고르시오.

① e-mail　　　② article
③ essay　　　④ diary
⑤ review

30 According to the passage, which is NOT true?

① The weather controller can control the climate.
② The weather controller can prevent natural disasters such as storms.
③ The net-zero energy house architect designs houses that waste energy.
④ The net-zero energy house uses alternative energy sources.
⑤ The end-of-life planner helps people live a happy and wealthy life after retirement.

출제율 90%

01 다음 영영풀이가 가리키는 것을 고르시오.

> offering a choice between two or more things

① alternative   ② imperfect

③ impossible   ④ irreplaceable

⑤ classical

출제율 100%

02 〈보기〉에서 알맞은 단어를 골라 문장을 완성하시오.

> ┤ 보기 ├
> succeed in / these days / get along well with / feel proud of / good at

(1) Henry will _____ climbing the mountain.

(2) I _____ my supervisor and colleagues.

(3) Good self-esteem helps you _____ yourself.

[03~05] 다음 대화를 읽고 물음에 답하시오.

G: What are you doing?

B: I'm making a new soup. Would you like to taste it?

G: Sure. Um...(*Tasting the soup*)

B: Do you like it? (A)이 새 요리법에 대해서 어떻게 생각하세요? (feel)

G: Well, I think you need to put some salt in (B)it.

B: You're right. Thank you.

출제율 90%

03 주어진 단어를 이용해서 밑줄 친 (A)를 영작하시오.

➡ _____

출제율 95%

04 위 대화의 밑줄 친 (B)it이 가리키는 것을 찾아 쓰시오.

➡ _____

출제율 100%

05 위 대화에 이어질 B의 행동으로 가장 적절한 것은?

① B is going to make a new soup.

② B is going to taste the new soup.

③ B is going to teach G the new recipe.

④ B is going to throw away the soup.

⑤ B is going to put some salt in the soup.

[06~07] 다음 대화를 읽고 물음에 답하시오.

M: How can I help you?

G: I'd like to buy a hat for my mother.

M: How do you feel about this red one? It's very popular.

G: It looks good. I'll take it.

출제율 95%

06 What is G looking for? (6 words)

➡ _____

출제율 100%

07 위 대화에 나타난 M과 G의 관계로 가장 적절한 것을 고르시오.

① student – teacher   ② chef – customer

③ doctor – patient   ④ clerk – customer

⑤ mother – daughter

B: Mom, can you come to my room?

W: Yes. What are you doing?

B: I'm getting ready for a date. It's Jina's birthday.

W: Aha! So, you're trying your clothes on several times.

B: Yes. Mom, how do I look in this blue shirt?

W: It looks good on you, but are you going to wear those blue jeans, too?

B: I think so. I prefer jeans to my other pants.

W: How do you feel about wearing a white shirt instead?

B: I think the white one and the jeans match better. Thanks for your advice.

W: No problem.

출제율 95%

08 Whose birthday is B getting ready for? (7 words)

➡ _____

출제율 90%

09 What does the mom suggest B to wear? (8 words)

➡ _____

출제율 100%

10 다음 중 위 대화의 내용과 일치하지 <u>않는</u> 것은?

① B is going to meet Jina.

② B is trying on his clothes several times.

③ B is very fond of jeans.

④ B prefers other pants over jeans.

⑤ B is thankful for his mom's advice.

출제율 90%

11 다음 대화의 밑줄 친 부분이 의도하는 바로 가장 적절한 것은?

> A: Which day do you prefer, Saturday or Sunday?
> B: <u>I prefer Saturday rather than Sunday.</u>

① 선호 표현하기   ② 의견 나타내기

③ 감정 표현하기   ④ 가능성 나타내기

⑤ 감사 표현하기

출제율 95%

12 다음 문장을 어법에 맞게 고치시오.

> I'm impossible to be there before eight.

➡ _____

출제율 90%

13 다음 빈칸에 들어갈 말로 알맞은 것을 고르시오.

> A: She watched the movie *Avengers* yesterday.
> B: _____

① So do we.   ② So did we.

③ So do us.   ④ So did us.

⑤ So are we.

출제율 95%

14 다음 밑줄 친 우리말에 맞게 영작한 것을 고르시오.

> A: Miju won't be ready until 7 o'clock.
> B: <u>Jack도 그럴 거야.</u>

① So will Jack   ② So won't Jack.

③ Neither will Jack.   ④ Neither won't Jack.

⑤ Neither be Jack.

[15~16] 다음 글을 읽고 물음에 답하시오.

Welcome to our Careers Day! These days, jobs are hard to come by. But if you keep on trying your best, you will succeed in your career. Today, we will welcome back some of the ⓐgraduates of our school, and listen to them talk about their jobs. Are you excited about meeting them? So am I. ⓑAs you listen to their talks, think about what you would like doing in the future. Please welcome our first speaker, Ilkem, the weather controller.

출제율 95%

15 위 글의 밑줄 친 ⓐgraduates와 같은 의미로 쓰인 것을 고르시오.

① He will get a job after he graduates from Oxford.
② The dawn graduates into day.
③ The university graduates 1,000 students every year.
④ They are Yale graduates.
⑤ I'll work with him if he graduates from Oxford.

출제율 90%

16 위 글의 밑줄 친 ⓑ에서 어법상 틀린 부분을 찾아 고치시오.

➡ _____

[17~19] 다음 글을 읽고 물음에 답하시오.

Hello, everyone. I'm Ilkem. I'm a scientist studying the weather. Just a few years ago, people thought the weather was impossible to control. So did I. Thanks to modern technology, however, my fellow scientists and I can change the weather as we want. For example, we can control the rain, using a cloud seeding system.

We spray dry ice into clouds to make ⓐthem rain. In China, they made rain in another city instead of Beijing during the opening event of the Olympics and its closing event as well. We can also reduce the side effects of global warming by controlling the climate. We can't control the weather perfectly yet, but may be able to do so soon. Then, we could prevent many kinds of natural disasters like floods and storms. So you will be able to live in a better and safer environment. ⓑWhy don't you join us in making a better environment by controlling the weather?

출제율 90%

17 위 글의 밑줄 친 ⓐthem이 가리키는 것을 본문에서 찾아 쓰시오.

➡ _____

출제율 95%

18 위 글의 밑줄 친 ⓑWhy don't you join us와 뜻이 같지 않은 것을 고르시오.

① How about joining us
② Why can't you join us
③ Why not join us
④ What about joining us
⑤ What do you say to joining us

출제율 100%

19 위 글의 주제로 알맞은 것을 고르시오.

① the benefits we can have by controlling the weather
② the difficulty of controlling the weather
③ the way to use a cloud seeding system
④ what enabled the opening event of the Beijing Olympics
⑤ how to prevent many kinds of natural disasters

[20~22] 다음 글을 읽고 물음에 답하시오.

Hello. My name is Jiwon, and I'm an end-of-life planner. As the number of old people is increasing, people are interested in how to be happy and wealthy in their old age. I help people not only to live a healthy life but also to plan for their death. (①) For example, I help them exercise regularly. (②) I also give them some tips on how to invest for retirement and get along well with their family. (③) And I even teach them how to make a will! (④) I feel proud of ___ⓐ___ I'm doing. (⑤)

출제율 90%

20 위 글의 빈칸 ⓐ에 들어갈 알맞은 말을 고르시오.

① that   ② what
③ which   ④ how
⑤ why

출제율 95%

21 위 글의 흐름으로 보아, 주어진 문장이 들어가기에 가장 적절한 곳은?

> This helps their family members avoid a lot of problems after the person dies.

①   ②   ③   ④   ⑤

출제율 100%

22 다음 중 '임종 설계사'가 하는 일에 해당하지 않는 것을 고르시오.

① 사람들이 규칙적으로 운동하도록 돕는다.
② 사람들에게 은퇴 후에 투자를 하는 방법에 대한 조언을 한다.
③ 사람들이 아플 때 그들을 병원에 데리고 간다.
④ 사람들이 그들의 가족과 잘 어울려 지내는 것에 대한 조언을 한다.
⑤ 사람들에게 유언장 쓰는 법을 가르친다.

[23~24] 다음 글을 읽고 물음에 답하시오.

When I grow up, I want to be a train operator on the Trans-Siberian-Railroad(TSR) because I think trains are fun to operate. I want to operate the train from Busan to Moscow in the future. When I was 13 years old, I went to Busan by train which my uncle operated. My uncle was proud of helping people travel comfortably. ___ⓐ___ were his colleagues. Since then, I have wanted to be a train operator. To achieve my dream, I will study hard and exercise regularly. Also, I will read a lot of books about trains.

출제율 90%

23 위 글의 빈칸 ⓐ에 들어갈 알맞은 말을 고르시오.

① As   ② Neither
③ Such   ④ Nor
⑤ So

출제율 100%

24 Which question CANNOT be answered after reading the passage?

① What does the writer want to be in the future?
② Why does the writer want to work in that area?
③ Does the writer have any special experience for choosing the job?
④ When will the writer be able to achieve the dream?
⑤ What will the writer prepare to do the work?

[01~02] 다음 대화를 읽고 물음에 답하시오.

B: I'm looking forward to the music festival.
(A) I prefer dancing than singing.
(B) I like singing. It would be very fun if we can sing and dance together.
(C) Me too. Which do you prefer, singing or dancing?

01 위 대화가 자연스럽게 이어지도록 배열하시오.

➡ _____

02 위 대화에서 어법상 어색한 것을 찾아 바르게 고치시오.

➡ _____

[03~04] 다음 대화를 읽고 물음에 답하시오.

I got a ticket for the Coolboys concert.
G: You're so lucky! When is it?
B: It's next Saturday. I'm thinking of going there with my friends.
G: By the way, how do you feel about their new album?
B: I like it. All the songs are so exciting, aren't they?
G: Yes, but I prefer their last album to the new one.
B: Why?
G: It has more songs of different genres.

03 When is B going to go to the concert?

➡ _____

04 What does B think about the Coolboys's new album?

➡ _____

05 다음 문장에서 어법상 어색한 부분을 찾아 바르게 고쳐 쓰시오.

(1) You are not mad, and neither will he.

➡ _____

(2) She hates black nail color, and so am I.

➡ _____

(3) My father doesn't like pizza, and neither is my mother.

➡ _____
_____

(4) His Airpot is gorgeous. So are yours, Jihye.

➡ _____

(5) If you don't care about this class, then neither am I.

➡ _____
_____

(6) She was relieved to hear that, and so is he.

➡ _____

06 다음 문장을 조건에 맞게 바꿔 쓰시오.

(1) 누군가를 미워하는 것은 쉽지 않다. (hate, easy, 7 단어)

➡ _____

(2) 진정한 사랑을 찾는 것은 어렵다. (difficult)
➡ (8 단어) _____
➡ (7 단어) _____

(3) 월식을 관찰하는 것은 어렵다. (hard, observe) *a lunar eclipse: 월식
➡ (8 단어) _____
➡ (7 단어) _____

[07~09] 다음 글을 읽고 물음에 답하시오.

Hello, everyone. I'm Ilkem. I'm a scientist studying the weather. Just a few years ago, people thought ⓐthe weather was impossible to control. So did I. Thanks to modern technology, however, my fellow scientists and I can change the weather as we want. For example, we can control the rain, using a cloud seeding system. We spray dry ice into clouds to make them rain. In China, they made rain in another city instead of Beijing during the opening event of the Olympics and its closing event as well. We can also reduce the side effects of global warming by controlling the climate. We can't control the weather perfectly yet, but may be able to do so soon. Then, we could prevent many kinds of natural disasters like floods and storms. So you will be able to live in a better and safer environment. ⓑ여러분도 날씨를 조절하여 더 나은 환경을 만드는 데 함께하는 게 어때요?

07 위 글의 밑줄 친 ⓐ를 it으로 시작하여 고쳐 쓰시오.

➡ _____

08 위 글의 밑줄 친 ⓑ의 우리말에 맞게 주어진 어휘를 이용하여 14 단어로 영작하시오.

why, in making, by controlling

➡ _____
_____

09 본문의 내용과 일치하도록 다음 빈칸 (A)와 (B)에 알맞은 단어를 쓰시오.

Thanks to modern technology, the scientists studying the weather can (A)_____ _____ _____ as they want and they can reduce the side effects of global warming by (B)_____ _____ _____.

[10~12] 다음 글을 읽고 물음에 답하시오.

Hello. My name is Jiwon, and I'm an end-of-life planner. ⓐAs the number of old people are increasing, people are interested in how to be happy and wealthy in their old age. ⓑI help people not only to live a healthy life but also to plan for their death. For example, I help them exercise regularly. I also give them some tips on how to invest for retirement and get along well with their family. And I even teach them how to make a will! ⓒThis helps their family members avoid a lot of problems after the person dies. I feel proud of what I'm doing.

10 위 글의 밑줄 친 ⓐ에서 어법상 틀린 부분을 찾아 고치시오.

➡ _____

11 위 글의 밑줄 친 ⓑ를 as well as를 사용하여 고치시오.

➡ _____
_____

12 위 글의 밑줄 친 ⓒThis가 가리키는 것을 본문에서 찾아 쓰시오.

➡ _____

01 다음 글을 읽고 Nara의 일기를 완성하시오.

M: Have you heard about the new STARS camera? It is a smart camera which will catch your best moments. It is very small, but very strong. It's very easy to take good pictures with this camera. All you have to do is just talk to the camera without having to use your fingers. Oh, and this is the last chance to get one at a good price. It's 30 percent off at the moment. How do you feel about visiting our store to see one?

Yesterday, I was walking on the street and then I saw a flyer in front of a shop. It says, they have a new STARS camera, which is _____ that catches your best moment. It's very small, but _____. Moreover, it's very easy to take good pictures with it. Without having to _____, I can take pictures by talking to the camera. In addition, it's 30 _____ at the moment. I really want to buy the camera.

02 다음 내용을 바탕으로 자신의 장래 희망에 관한 글을 쓰시오.

Q1: What do you want to be in the future?
A: I want to be a train operator on the Trans-Siberian-Railroad.
Q2: Why do you want to work in that area?
A: Because I think trains are fun to operate.
Q3: Do you have any special experience for choosing the job?
A: When I was 13 years old, I went to Busan by train which my uncle operated. My uncle was proud of helping people travel comfortably. So were his colleagues.
Q4: What will you prepare to do the work?
A: To achieve my dream, I will study hard and exercise regularly. Also, I will read a lot of books about trains.

When I grow up, I want to be (A)_____ on the Trans-Siberian-Railroad(TSR) because I think (B)_____. I want to operate the train from Busan to Moscow in the future. When I was 13 years old, I went to Busan by train which (C)_____. My uncle was proud of (D)_____. So were his colleagues. Since then, I have wanted to be a train operator. To achieve my dream, I will (E)_____ _____. Also, I will (F)_____.

단원별 모의고사

01 다음 영영풀이가 가리키는 것은?

> the act of leaving your job and stopping working, usually because you are old

① investment ② management
③ withdrawal ④ payment
⑤ retirement

02 다음 빈칸에 알맞은 단어를 고르시오.

> There are several cultural practices related to food. Seaweed soup, _____, is believed to help the pregnant women make a quick recovery in Korea.

① therefore ② for example
③ in other words ④ nonetheless
⑤ consequently

03 다음 우리말에 맞게 빈칸에 알맞은 말을 쓰시오.

> 3월 이후로 생필품 값이 계속 오르고 있다.
> ➡ The prices of commodities _____
> _____ _____ rising since March.

[04~06] 다음 글을 읽고 물음에 답하시오.

W: Are you looking for a job? And are you an animal lover? If you are, here is the best job for you. We need someone to take care of some pets ___(A)___ their family is on vacation. You will need to wash the pets, feed them regularly, and play with them. By the way, we prefer people ___(B)___ can work with us for a long time to those who

can only work for a short time. You will work from 9 to 5, Monday to Friday. If you are interested in taking care of pets, please call 567-1234.

04 위 글의 빈칸 (A)와 (B)에 들어갈 적절한 말을 쓰시오.

➡ (A)_____ (B)_____

05 위 글을 읽고 답할 수 <u>없는</u> 질문을 고르시오.

① What kind of person is the speaker looking for?
② What kind of job position is the speaker hiring?
③ What kind of pets does the speaker mention?
④ How many hours does the sitter have to work in a day?
⑤ How can the sitter contact to the speaker?

06 위 글에서 주어진 영영풀이가 가리키는 단어를 찾아 쓰시오.

> to give food to a person, group, or animal

➡ _____

[07~08] 다음 대화를 읽고 물음에 답하시오.

(Phoue rings.)
B: Hello?
G: Hello, Minwoo. This is Yena.
B: Hi, Yena. What's up?
G: I received your present for my birthday today. Thank you so much.

B: Do you like it? (A)그것의 밝은 색깔에 대해서는 어떻게 생각하니?

G: I really like it. It can help drivers see me well in the rain.

B: I'm glad to hear that.

G: Thank you again. I hope it rains soon so that I can use it.

B: Haha. I hope so. See you soon!

07 위 대화의 밑줄 친 (A)를 영작한 것으로 적절하지 <u>않은</u> 것은?

① How did you feel about its bright color?

② How do you feel about its bright color?

③ What about its bright color?

④ What do you think of its bright color?

⑤ What do you think about its bright color?

08 Why does G hope it will rain soon? (Answer in English with 8 words beginning with "It's because.")

➡ _____

09 주어진 두 문장 사이에 대화가 자연스럽게 이어지도록 순서대로 배열하시오.

> A: How do you feel about classical music?
>
> (A) I think it's very good. I feel calm when I listen to classical music.
>
> (B) I don't like it, because it's too boring. How about you?
>
> (C) Then why don't you become a musician in the future?
>
> A: That's a good idea.

➡ _____

[10~12] 다음 대화를 읽고 물음에 답하시오.

Jisu: Hello, Mr. Brown. Are you busy now?

Mr. Brown: Not really. ①

Jisu: ② Then, can I talk to you for a minute?

Mr. Brown: Of course. Jisu, what's wrong? You look worried.

Jisu: ③ I don't know what I want to be in the future.

Mr. Brown: (A)작가가 되는 것에 대해서는 어떻게 생각하니? You like literature, don't you?

Jisu: ④ Well, no. I prefer science to literature. But I don't know what kinds of jobs I could do.

Mr. Brown: Why don't you come to the student hall tomorrow? Our graduates will talk about their jobs.

Jisu: ⑤ That will be very helpful. Thank you.

Mr. Brown: No problem.

10 위 대화의 ①~⑤ 중에서 주어진 문장이 들어가기에 가장 적절한 곳은?

I'm worried about my future.

①   ②   ③   ④   ⑤

11 위 대화의 밑줄 친 (A)의 우리말을 바르게 영작하시오.
(Answer in English with 8 words beginning with "How.")

➡ _____

12 다음 중 위 대화의 내용과 일치하지 <u>않는</u> 것은?

① Jisu wanted to have a conversation with Mr. Brown.

② Jisu is worried about her future.

③ Jisu likes literature better than science.

④ Jisu does not know what she wants to do in the future.

⑤ Jisu is going to go to the student hall tomorrow.

13 다음 문장과 뜻이 같은 것을 고르시오.

It was difficult for him to understand the news.

① It was difficult to understand the news.

② He was difficult that understand the news.

③ He was difficult to understanding the news.

④ The news was difficult for him to understand it.

⑤ The news was difficult for him to understand.

14 다음 우리말을 바르게 영작한 것을 <u>모두</u> 고르시오.

이 문제를 푸는 것은 쉬워.

① This problem is easy solving.

② This problem is easy to solve.

③ It is easy to solve this problem.

④ It is easy that solve this problem.

⑤ It is easy solving this problem.

15 다음 문맥상 빈칸에 들어갈 말로 알맞은 것은?

Once you have removed the virus, _____ to the Internet.

① it is safe reconnect

② it is safe to reconnect

③ it is safely to reconnect

④ it is safety to reconnect

⑤ it is safe reconnecting

16 다음 그림을 참고하여 밑줄 친 우리말을 알맞게 영작하시오.

• Scientist: I can control the rain, using a cloud seeding system. By controlling the climate, I can reduce the side effects of global warming.

• Teacher: I think that (A)<u>날씨를 조절하는 것은 불가능했다.</u>

• Life planner: I help people not only to live a healthy life but also to plan for their death. This job helps their family avoid a lot of problems after the person dies.

• Teacher: It is very helpful to people, and (B)<u>건축가 역시 그러합니다.</u>

• Architect: I design net-zero energy houses. I make houses that use wind power or other alternative energy sources.

➡ (A) _____

_____

(B) _____

17 It is hard to와 각 문장의 괄호 안의 단어를 활용하여 우리말에 맞게 영작하시오.

(1) 얼마나 많은 아동들이 난독증에 시달리는지는 추정하기가 어렵다. (estimate, suffer, 난독증: dyslexia)

➡ _____

_____

(2) 그러한 고충을 참는 것은 어렵다. (endure, pain)

➡ _____

(3) 직업을 찾는 것이 너무 힘들다. (find, job)

➡ _____

(4) 그와 그의 형을 비교하는 것은 어렵다. (comparison, between)

➡ _____

_____

(5) 모든 사람의 비위를 맞추기는 어렵다. (suit everybody)

➡ _____

(6) 때로는 새로운 일을 시작하는 것이 힘들어요. (start, job)

➡ _____

[18~20] 다음 글을 읽고 물음에 답하시오.

Hello, everyone. I'm Ilkem. I'm a scientist studying the weather. Just a few years ago, people thought the weather was impossible ⓐto control. So did I. (①) Thanks to modern technology, however, my fellow scientists and I can change the weather as we want. (②) We spray dry ice into clouds to make them rain. (③) In China, they made rain in another city instead of Beijing during the opening event of the Olympics and its closing event as well. (④) We can also reduce the side effects of global warming by controlling the climate. (⑤) We can't control the weather perfectly yet, but may be able to do so soon. Then, we could prevent many kinds of natural disasters like floods and storms.

So you will be able to live in a better and safer environment. Why don't you join us in making a better environment by controlling the weather?

18 아래 〈보기〉에서 위 글의 밑줄 친 ⓐto control과 to부정사의 용법이 다른 것의 개수를 고르시오.

┌─── 보기 ───┐
① He can't be rich to ask me for some money.
② He was sad to get "F".
③ It is important to use your time well.
④ He grew up to be a cook.
⑤ They came here to ask a question.
└─────────┘

① 1개 ② 2개 ③ 3개 ④ 4개 ⑤ 5개

19 위 글의 흐름으로 보아, 주어진 문장이 들어가기에 가장 적절한 곳은?

┌─────────────────────┐
For example, we can control the rain, using a cloud seeding system.
└─────────────────────┘

①   ②   ③   ④   ⑤

20 다음 빈칸 (A)와 (B)에 알맞은 단어를 넣어 날씨 조절이 환경에 미치는 영향을 완성하시오.

┌─────────────────────┐
By controlling the climate, we can (A)_____ the side effects of global warming and prevent many kinds of (B)_____ _____ like floods and storms. As a result, we can make a better environment.
└─────────────────────┘

[21~23] 다음 글을 읽고 물음에 답하시오.

Hi, I'm Eva. I'm an architect, and I design net-zero energy houses. Many people are worried about using too much energy at home. (A)So were my parents. When I was young, my parents often said, "Eva! How many times do I have to tell you? Turn off the TV when you're not watching it!" Since then, I have wanted to design energy-saving houses. I studied architecture and environmental engineering to make my dream come true. Now, I design houses that use wind power or other ⓐ_____ energy sources. The houses make more energy than they use. You don't need to worry about wasting energy anymore. If you are interested in designing net-zero energy houses, please come and talk to me.

21 주어진 영영풀이를 참고하여 빈칸 ⓐ에 철자 a로 시작하는 단어를 쓰시오.

different from the one that you already have, and can be done or used instead

➡ _____

22 위 글의 밑줄 친 문장 (A)가 내포하는 의미를 영어로 쓰시오.

➡ _____
_____
_____

23 According to the passage, which is NOT true?

① Eva is an architect who designs net-zero energy houses.
② When young, Eva often forgot to turn off the TV when she was not watching it.
③ Eva studied architecture and environmental engineering to design energy-saving houses.
④ Net-zero energy houses use wind power or other alternative energy sources.
⑤ Net-zero energy houses use more energy than they make.

[24~25] 다음 글을 읽고 물음에 답하시오.

Teacher: ⓐ큰 박수를 보냅시다 to the speakers. I hope today's talks have been helpful for you. I see many students having a hard time learning something new, while worrying about their future. They are worried that they are slow learners. So was I. I was a late bloomer. I tried to find what I was good at, and finally became a teacher. So, I want to say, "ⓑBelieve in yourself, and you can do it."

24 위 글의 밑줄 친 ⓐ의 우리말에 맞게 5 단어로 영작하시오.

➡ _____

25 위 글의 밑줄 친 ⓑ를 다음과 같이 바꿔 쓸 때 빈칸에 들어갈 알맞은 말을 두 단어로 쓰시오.

➡ _____ _____ believe in yourself, you can do it.

MEMO

Lesson 8

What People Live By

 의사소통 기능

- 비난 수용 및 거부하기
  It's all my fault. / It was not my fault.
- 의무 표현하기
  You're supposed to make up with him as soon as possible.

 언어 형식

- 접속사 whether
  I'm not sure **whether** he is dead **or not**.

- It's time 가정법
  It's about **time** I **left** here.

Words & Expressions

Key Words

- **adopt**[ədápt] 동 입양하다
- **argument**[á:rgjumənt] 명 논쟁
- **blame**[bleim] 동 탓하다
- **certainly**[sə́:rtnli] 부 분명히
- **conflict**[kɑnflíkt] 명 싸움, 다툼
- **confused**[kənfjú:zd] 형 혼란스러운
- **convey**[kənvéi] 동 전달하다, 나르다
- **copy**[kápi] 명 복사본
- **cross**[krɔ:s] 동 건너다
- **death**[deθ] 명 죽음
- **disabled**[diséibld] 형 장애를 가진
- **disability**[dìsəbíləti] 명 장애
- **discount**[dískaunt] 명 할인
- **drunk**[drʌŋk] 형 술에 취한
- **dwell**[dwel] 동 거주하다
- **explain**[ikspléin] 동 설명하다
- **fault**[fɔ:lt] 명 잘못
- **feed**[fi:d] 동 먹이를 주다
- **fine**[fain] 형 질 좋은, 정교한
- **gain**[gein] 동 (무게를) 늘리다, 얻다
- **greet**[gri:t] 동 인사하다
- **happen**[hǽpən] 동 발생하다, 일어나다
- **heart attack** 심장마비
- **human beings** 인류
- **hurt**[hə:t] 동 다치게 하다, 아프게 하다
- **hurry**[hə́:ri] 동 서두르다
- **judge**[dʒʌdʒ] 동 판단하다
- **last**[læst] 동 지속하다, 계속되다
- **learn**[lə:rn] 동 배우다, 깨우치다
- **leather**[léðər] 명 가죽
- **leave**[li:v] 동 떠나다
- **little**[lítl] 형 거의 없는
- **master**[mǽstər] 명 주인
- **mess**[mes] 명 쓰레기
- **needs**[ni:dz] 명 요구, 욕구
- **neighbor**[néibər] 명 이웃
- **nobleman**[nóublmən] 명 귀족
- **novel**[návəl] 명 소설
- **order**[ɔ́:rdər] 동 주문하다
- **pity**[píti] 명 동정, 연민, 유감
- **proud**[praud] 형 자랑스러워하는
- **punish**[pʌ́niʃ] 동 처벌하다
- **punishment**[pʌ́niʃmənt] 명 처벌
- **regret**[rigrét] 동 후회하다
- **save**[seiv] 동 구하다
- **secret**[sí:krit] 명 비밀
- **servant**[sə́:rvənt] 명 하인
- **serve**[sə:rv] 동 음식을 차려내다
- **shine**[ʃain] 동 빛나다
- **sudden**[sʌ́dn] 형 갑작스러운
- **suddenly**[sʌ́dnli] 부 갑자기
- **support**[səpɔ́:rt] 동 부양하다
- **truth**[tru:θ] 명 진실, 진리
- **twin**[twin] 명 쌍둥이
- **volunteer**[vàləntíər] 명 자원봉사자 동 자원하다
- **while**[hwail] 접 ~하는 동안에
- **without**[wiðáut] 전 ~ 없이

Key Expressions

- **at first** 처음에는
- **be ready to** ~할 준비가 되다
- **bring up** 양육하다
- **die of** ~로 죽다
- **each other** 서로
- **each time** 매번
- **earn a living** 생계를 유지하다
- **fail to** ~하지 못하다, ~을 실패하다
- **figure out** 알아내다
- **for oneself** 스스로, 자기를 위하여
- **for the first time** 처음으로
- **give birth to** ~을 출산하다
- **in advance** 먼저, 앞서
- **instead of** ~ 대신에
- **in surprise** 놀라서
- **live by** ~에 따라 살다
- **now that** 이제 ~이므로, ~이기 때문에
- **one day** 어느날
- **on one's way back** 돌아오는 길에
- **put simply** 간단히 말해
- **stop ~ing** ~하는 것을 멈추다
- **thanks to** ~ 덕분에
- **think back** 돌이켜 생각하다
- **walk away from** ~에게서 멀어지다
- **with a blank face** 무표정으로

Word Power

※ 서로 비슷한 뜻을 가진 어휘

☐ **certainly** 분명히 – **definitely** 명확히, 분명히
☐ **dwell** 거주하다 – **reside** 거주하다, 주재하다
☐ **fault** 잘못 – **mistake** 실수, 잘못
☐ **hurry** 서두르다 – **rush** 서두르다
☐ **judge** 판단하다 – **evaluate** 평가하다, 감정하다

☐ **regret** 후회하다 – **repent** 후회하다, 뉘우치다
☐ **save** 구하다 – **rescue** 구하다, 구조하다
☐ **support** 부양하다 – **maintain** 먹여 살리다, 부양하다
☐ **truth** 진실, 진리 – **reality** 진실

※ 서로 반대의 뜻을 가진 어휘

☐ **certainly** 분명히 ↔ **uncertainly** 자신 없게
☐ **death** 죽음 ↔ **birth** 탄생
☐ **gain** (무게를) 늘리다, 얻다 ↔ **lose** 잃다, 상실하다
☐ **leave** 떠나다 ↔ **arrive** 도착하다, 닿다
☐ **save** 구하다 ↔ **endanger** 위험에 빠뜨리다

☐ **conflict** 싸움, 다툼 ↔ **agreement** 일치, 조화, 동의
☐ **drunk** 술에 취한 ↔ **sober** 술 취하지 않은
☐ **hurt** 다치게 하다, 아프게 하다 ↔ **heal** 상처를 치료하다
☐ **little** 거의 없는 ↔ **much** 많은

※ 접두사 un- + 형용사

☐ **un-** + **attractive** → **unattractive** 매력적이지 못한
☐ **un-** + **conventional** → **unconventional** 비관습적인
☐ **un-** + **fortunate** → **unfortunate** 불행한
☐ **un-** + **intelligent** → **unintelligent** 우둔한
☐ **un-** + **usual** → **unusual** 특이한, 흔치 않은

☐ **un-** + **comfortable** → **uncomfortable** 불편한
☐ **un-** + **educated** → **uneducated** 무지한
☐ **un-** + **healthy** → **unhealthy** 건강하지 못한
☐ **un-** + **predictable** → **unpredictable** 예상할 수 없는
☐ **un-** + **wise** → **unwise** 현명하지 못한

English Dictionary

☐ **adopt** 입양하다
→ to legally take another person's child into your own family and take care of him or her as your own child
합법적으로 다른 사람의 아이를 본인의 가족으로 데려와 친자식처럼 보살피다

☐ **argument** 논쟁
→ a disagreement, or the process of disagreeing
의견 충돌 또는 의견이 충돌하는 과정

☐ **disability** 장애
→ an illness, injury, or condition that makes it difficult for someone to do the things that other people do
어떤 사람이 다른 사람들이 하는 일들을 못하게 하는 조건이나 질병 또는 부상

☐ **dwell** 거주하다
→ to live in a place or in a particular way
어느 장소에 또는 특정한 방식으로 살다

☐ **explain** 설명하다
→ to make something clear or easy to understand by describing or giving information about it
묘사하거나 정보를 제공함으로써 이해하기 쉽고 분명하게 하다

☐ **fault** 잘못
→ a mistake, especially something for which you are to blame
잘못, 특히 비난 받을 만한 실수

☐ **judge** 판단하다
→ to form, give, or have as an opinion, or to decide about something or someone, especially after thinking carefully
어떤 일이나 사람에 대해 주의 깊이 생각한 다음 의견을 결정 또는 형성, 제공하다

☐ **last** 지속하다, 계속되다
→ to continue to exist 계속해서 존재하다

☐ **needs** 요구, 욕구
→ the things you must have for a satisfactory life
만족스러운 삶을 위해 반드시 가져야 할 것들

☐ **punish** 처벌하다
→ to cause someone who has done something wrong or committed a crime to suffer, by hurting them, forcing them to pay money, sending them to prison, etc.
잘못을 한 사람 또는 범죄를 저지른 사람을 다치거나 돈을 내거나 감옥에 보냄으로써 고통 받게 하다

☐ **save** 구하다
→ to stop someone or something from being killed, injured, or destroyed
어떤 사람이나 사물이 살해 당하거나 다치거나 파괴되는 것을 막다

☐ **secret** 비밀
→ a piece of information that is only known by one person or a few people and should not be told to others
한 사람이나 몇몇의 사람에게만 알려지고 다른 사람들에게 말해서는 안 되는 정보

서답형

01 다음 짝지어진 단어의 관계가 같도록 빈칸에 알맞은 말을 쓰시오.

> certainly : definitely = judge : _____

중요

02 다음 중 밑줄 친 부분의 뜻풀이가 바르지 <u>않은</u> 것은?

① The hotel has special facilities for <u>disabled</u> people. (장애를 가진)
② Colours like red <u>convey</u> a sense of energy and strength. (전달하다, 나르다)
③ She <u>gained</u> confidence when she went to college. (늘렸다, 얻었다)
④ You'll be on time if you <u>hurry</u>. (서두르다)
⑤ The team was unbeaten in their <u>last</u> four games. (지속하다, 지속되다)

서답형

03 다음 우리말을 주어진 어휘를 이용하여 영작하시오.

(1) 그들 모두에게 개별적으로 인사하는 것은 거의 불가능하다. (greet, them)
➡ _____

_____

(2) 학교들은 학생들을 시험 결과에 의해서만 평가 해서는 안 된다. (should, judge)
➡ _____

_____

(3) 좋은 이웃이 먼 사촌보다 낫다. (better, distant)
➡ _____

04 다음 영영풀이가 가리키는 것을 고르시오.

> to legally take another person's child into your own family and take care of him or her as your own child

① avoid　　② adopt　　③ dwell
④ cross　　⑤ happen

서답형

05 다음 문장의 빈칸에 들어갈 말을 〈보기〉에서 골라 쓰시오.

> ── 보기 ├──
> each time / figure out / live by /
> put simply / at first

(1) Ashley is still trying to _____ what to wear for tomorrow.
(2) Man cannot _____ bread alone.
(3) I found the job tiring _____ but I soon got used to it.

중요

06 다음 문장의 (A)와 (B)에 각각 공통으로 들어갈 말이 바르게 짝지어진 것은?

> • He shouted ____(A)____ surprise as if he weren't expecting it.
> • They handed ____(A)____ their resignation as a group.
> • When I think ____(B)____, people's lives were much more peaceful.
> • She just managed to hold ____(B)____ her anger.

① at – back　　　② at – about
③ in – back　　　④ in – about
⑤ to – back

01 다음 짝지어진 단어의 관계가 같도록 빈칸에 알맞은 말을 쓰시오.

> conflict : agreement = gain : _____

02 다음 우리말에 맞게 빈칸에 알맞은 말을 쓰시오.

> 내가 말하고 있을 때 딴 데 가지 마라.
> ➡ Don't _____ _____ _____ me when I'm talking to you.

03 다음 문장의 빈칸에 들어갈 말을 〈보기〉에서 골라 쓰시오. (필요하면 어형 변화를 할 것)

> ┌─ 보기 ─┐
> proud / novel / volunteer / leather / servant

(1) Are there any _____ to help clear up?

(2) _____ are now almost extinct in modern society.

(3) Polish shoes regularly to protect the _____ .

04 우리말과 일치하도록 주어진 어구를 배열하여 영작하시오.

(1) 그녀는 논쟁에서 이기는 것을 아주 좋아한다.
(loves / an argument / she / to / win)
➡ _____

(2) John은 종종 그의 상사와 갈등을 빚곤 한다.
(comes into / often / with / conflict / his boss / John)
➡ _____

(3) 그는 수술 도중에 심장 마비로 사망했다.
(a heart attack / during / died of / he / an operation)
➡ _____

05 다음 우리말에 맞게 주어진 단어를 사용하여 영작하시오.

(1) 그 처벌은 매우 타당했다. (punishment, fair)
➡ _____

(2) 내 생각엔 네가 많은 귀족들을 만나본 적이 없는 것 같다. (suppose, noblemen)
➡ _____

(3) 인간에게는 의식주가 필요하다. (human beings, shelter)
➡ _____

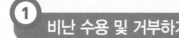

Conversation

교과서

① 비난 수용 및 거부하기

> A: Our team lost by one point. 우리 팀이 1점 차로 졌어.
>
> B: It's not your fault. We did our best. Cheer up! 네 잘못이 아니야. 우리는 최선을 다했잖아. 힘내!

■ 'It's one's fault.'는 '~의 잘못이다'라는 의미로 책임이나 비난에 대해 인정하는 표현이다. 누군가를 탓하는 표현으로 'This[It] is your fault.'라는 문장을 쓸 수 있다. 이때 fault는 '잘못, 책임'이라는 뜻으로 사용된다. 반면 'It's not one's fault.'는 '~의 잘못이 아니다'라는 의미로 책임이나 비난에 대해 부인하는 표현이다.

■ 비난, 책임을 묻는 표현

- accuse A of B A를 B로 고발하다, 고소하다
  His parents were accused of child abuse. 그의 부모는 아동학대로 고발당했다.

- blame A for B A를 B 때문에 비난하다
  Don't blame yourself. 네 자신을 탓하지 마.
  = It's not your fault. 네 탓이 아니야.
  = Don't be so hard on yourself. 자책하지 마.

핵심 Check

1. 다음 대화의 밑줄 친 우리말을 바르게 영작하시오.

> A: Our team lost by one point.
> B: 네 잘못이 아니야. We did our best. Cheer up!

➡ _____

2 의무 표현하기

> A: I'm late for school. 나 학교에 늦었어.
>
> B: You should not cross the street now. 지금 길을 건너서는 안 돼.

■ 의무를 나타내는 표현으로는 조동사 had better/should/ought to/have to/must 등이 있다. 이 표현들은 모두 '~해야 한다'라는 뜻을 지닌다. 조동사 must와 have to 모두 '꼭 ~해야 한다'는 강한 의무를 나타낸다. 그러나 must는 공식적인 문서나 규칙 등에 사용되는 반면에 have to는 강한 의무를 나타내기는 하지만 좀 더 일상적인 의미로 사용된다. 한편 should와 ought to는 '~하는 게 좋겠다'라는 의미로 개인적인 충고나 조언 등에 쓰이는 표현이다.

■ 의무를 나타내는 표현들
had better ~하는 게 좋겠다
had better not ~하지 않는 게 좋겠다
should ~하는 게 좋겠다/해야 한다
should not ~하지 않는 게 좋겠다/하지 말아야 한다
ought to ~하는 게 낫다
ought not to ~하지 않는 게 낫다
have to 꼭 ~해야 한다
don't/doesn't have to ~할 필요 없다
must 꼭 ~해야만 한다
must not ~해서는 안 된다

■ 의무를 나타내는 다른 표현으로는 'be supposed to ~'가 있다. '~하기로 되어 있다', '~해야 한다'라는 의미이며, 약속이나 규칙 등 예정된 일에 대해 묻고 답할 때 쓸 수 있다.
I'm supposed to keep it a secret. 난 그걸 비밀로 해야 돼.
I'm supposed to go fishing with my kids. 난 아이들과 낚시 가기로 했어.
You're not supposed to walk on the grass. 잔디밭 위를 걸어서는 안 된다.

핵심 Check

2. 다음 대화의 밑줄 친 부분과 바꿔 쓸 수 <u>없는</u> 것은?

> A: I'm late for the meeting.
> B: You <u>should not</u> cross the street on a red light.

① must not   ② don't have to

③ ought not to   ④ had better not

⑤ are not supposed to

Everyday English 1 B Listening Activity

G: My dog ❶got sick this morning. I'm so worried about him.

B: What did you ❷feed him yesterday?

G: I ❸gave him some milk last night.

B: Oh, you ❹should not feed a dog milk.

G: I was not sure ❺whether or not it is safe for him to drink milk. ❻It was all my fault.

B: Don't worry too much. Did you take him to the animal doctor?

G: Yes, I did. ❼I hope he'll get better soon.

B: He'll certainly ❽get better with your care and love.

G: 오늘 아침에 우리집 개가 아 팠어. 개가 너무 걱정돼.
B: 어제 개한테 뭘 먹였는데?
G: 어젯밤에 우유를 좀 줬어.
B: 오, 개한테는 우유를 먹이면 안 돼.
G: 난 개가 우유를 먹으면 안전 한지 아닌지 확신하지 못 했거 든. 다 내 잘못이야.
B: 너무 걱정하지 마. 수의사에 게 데려갔었니?
G: 응, 데려갔었어. 개가 빨리 나 아지길 바랄 뿐이야.
B: 네 보살핌과 사랑으로 분명히 회복할 거야.

❶ get sick 병에 걸리다, 병이 나다 ❷ feed 먹이를 주다 ❸ give + 간접목적어(~에게) + 직접목적어 (~을/를) ~에게 …를 주다 ❹ should not 은 '~해서는 안 된다', '~하지 않는 게 좋겠다'라는 뜻으로 의무를 나타내는 표현이다. ❺ whether A or not 인지 아닌지 ❻ 잘못을 인정하는 표 현으로 fault는 '잘못, 책임'이라는 뜻으로 사용되었다. ❼ 'I hope ~'는 실현 가능한 일에 대해 기원하는 표현이다. ❽ get better 나아지다, 호전 되다

Check(√) True or False

(1) G's dog is sick because he ate what he should not yesterday.   T ☐ F ☐

(2) G didn't take her dog to the animal doctor.   T ☐ F ☐

Everyday English 2 B Listening Activity

B: Jina, what are you ❶planning to do this winter vacation?

G: I'm thinking of doing some ❷volunteer work for people with ❸disabilities. Would you like to join me?

B: Oh, that's a good idea. But I'm ❹a bit worried about it.

G: What makes you feel like that?

B: I'm not sure ❺whether I am ready to help ❻them. Could you give me some advice?

G: ❼You're supposed to respect their needs.

B: What do you mean by their needs?

G: You ❽should help them only when they ask you to do so.

B: Jina야, 이번 겨울 방학에 무엇 을 할 계획이니?
G: 난 장애가 있는 사람들을 위해 자원봉사를 할 생각을 하고 있 어. 너도 같이 할래?
B: 오, 그거 좋은 생각이다. 그런데 난 좀 걱정이 돼.
G: 왜 그렇게 느끼니?
B: 내가 그 사람들을 도울 준비가 되어 있는지 확신하지 못하겠어. 네가 조언 좀 해 줄래?
G: 넌 그 사람들의 요구를 존중해 야 돼.
B: 그 사람들의 요구라는 게 무슨 의미니?
G: 그들이 너에게 그렇게 해 달라 고 요청할 때에만 도움을 줘야 해.

❶ plan to ~를 계획하다 ❷ volunteer work 자원봉사 활동 ❸ disability (신체적, 정신적) 장애 ❹ a bit 조금, 다소, 약간 ❺ whether ~인지 아닌 지 ❻ 대명사 them은 people with disabilities를 가리킨다. ❼ 'be supposed to ~'는 의무를 나타내는 표현으로, '~하기로 되어 있다', '~해야 한 다'라는 의미이다. ❽ should는 '~해야 한다'는 뜻으로 개인적인 충고나 조언 등에 쓰이는 표현이다.

Check(√) True or False

(3) Jina is going to do some volunteer work in the winter vacation.   T ☐ F ☐

(4) B is sure that he will be able to do volunteer work very well.   T ☐ F ☐

Everyday English 1 A Listen and Check (1)

B: Who made this ❶mess? It was clean this morning.

G: ❷It's not my fault. Your dog did it.

B: Oh, my goodness! It will ❸take a lot of time to ❹clear it up.

G: Let's do ❺it together. I'll help you.

❶ mess 쓰레기 ❷ '내 잘못이 아니다.'라는 의미로 책임이나 비난에 대해 부인하는 표현이다. ❸ take (시간이) 걸리다 ❹ clear up 정리하다 ❺ 대명사 it은 to clear up을 의미한다.

Everyday English 1 A Listen and Check (2)

G: Minsu, why were you late for school today?

B: ❶It was all my fault.

G: What happened?

B: I ❷got up late this morning, so I ❸missed the bus.

❶ '나의 잘못이었다.'라는 의미로 책임이나 비난에 대해 인정하는 표현이다. ❷ get up late 늦게 일어나다 ❸ miss 놓치다

Everyday English 1 A Listen and Check (3)

(*Phone rings.*)

W: Hello, ❶this is the shoe shop. ❷How may I help you?

M: I ❸have a problem with the boots ❹that I bought there yesterday.

W: What's the problem with them?

M: They're a bit dirty. But ❺it is not my fault. ❻ I've never worn them.

W: Sorry about that. Please visit our shop this week.

❶ 전화 표현에서 '전 ~입니다'라고 말할 때 'I am' 대신 'this is'를 쓴다.
❷ '어떻게 도와드릴까요?'라는 의미로, 'How can I help you?'라는 표현과 바꿔 쓸 수 있다.
❸ have a problem with ~에 문제가 있다
❹ 관계대명사 that으로 앞의 the boots를 수식하는 문장을 이끈다.
❺ '내 잘못이 아니다'라는 의미로 책임이나 비난에 대해 부정하는 표현이다.
❻ 현재완료 용법이 사용된 문장으로, '입은 적이 없다'라고 해석한다.

Everyday English 2 A Listen and Check (1)

B: Did you hear that Minsu is in the hospital?

G: Oh, I didn't know ❶that. ❷Aren't we supposed to visit him?

B: No, he doesn't ❸want anyone to visit him. He is just worried about ❹missing classes.

G: Then should I ❺make a copy of my notes for him?

B: That's a good idea.

❶ that은 지시대명사로 민수가 병원에 입원했다는 소식을 의미한다.
❷ 'be supposed to ~'는 의무를 나타내는 표현으로, '~하기로 되어 있다', '~해야 한다'라는 의미이다.
❸ want A to B A가 B하기를 원하다.
❹ missing classes는 be worried about의 목적어로 동명사 형태로 쓰였다.
❺ make a copy 복사본을 만들다, 복사하다

Everyday English 2 A Listen and Check (2)

B: Jina, you look ❶confused. ❷What's the matter?

G: My partner cannot hear anything. I don't know ❸how to communicate with her.

B: ❹Have you tried communicating with her by writing?

G: Yes, I have. But the problem is ❺that we do not ❻always have a pencil.

B: Then, ❼you are supposed to learn how to use ❽sign language.

❶ confused 혼란스러운
❷ '무슨 일이니?'라는 뜻으로, 'What's wrong?'과 바꿔 쓸 수 있다.
❸ how to ~하는 방법
❹ try ~ing 시험 삼아 ~해 보다
❺ 접속사 that으로 두 문장을 연결해준다.
❻ 빈도 부사 always는 조동사 뒤, 일반동사 앞에서 쓰인다.
❼ 'be supposed to ~'는 의무를 나타내는 표현으로, '~하기로 되어 있다', '~해야 한다'라고 해석한다.
❽ sing language 수화

In Real Life

Inho: Lina, you look so ❶depressed. What's the matter?

Lina: Oh, Inho. I ❷had an argument with Ryan.

Inho: Was it your fault?

Lina: No, ❸it wasn't my fault! There was just a misunderstanding between us.

Inho: ❹In that case, you're supposed to ❺make up with him ❻as soon as possible.

Lina: Well, Ryan got ❼so angry that he wouldn't talk with me.

Inho: But ❽who knows? He might regret it now, just like you.

Lina: Do you think so?

Inho: Yes, everyone wants to ❾maintain good friendships.

Lina: Thanks for your advice. I hope I can make up with him soon.

❶ depressed 우울한, 침체된 ❷ have an argument with ~와 말다툼하다 ❸ '내 잘못이 아니다'라는 의미로 책임이나 비난에 대해 부인하는 표현이다. ❹ in that case 그런 경우에 ❺ make up with ~와 화해하다 ❻ as soon as possible 가능한 한 빨리 ❼ so... that ~ 구문이 사용된 문장으로, '너무 …해서 ~하다'라고 해석한다. ❽ 'who knows?'는 '누가 알겠어?', '혹시 모르지'라는 뜻이다. ❾ maintain 유지하다

 Check Your Progress 2

W: Thank you for watching "Play World." Are you ❶looking forward to this month's play? This month's play is *Hamlet*. ❷There are two interesting points about this play. ❸First, it is a 21st century version of Shakespeare's *Hamlet*. ❹It has changed the costumes and the dead language of the 16th century ❺that most of today's audiences might feel uncomfortable with. Second, the famous actor, Park Mujin, ❻appears in this play. His performance shows a deep ❼understanding of the main character, Hamlet. Please ❽bear in mind that you will

need to ❾book your ticket online. It won't be your fault if you miss this play. But you'll certainly ❿regret missing it.

❶ look forward to ~를 학수고대하다 ❷ There is/are 구문에서 동사의 단/복수는 뒤에 오는 주어에 따라 결정된다. ❸ first 첫번째로 ❹ 대명사 It은 연극 Hamlet을 가리킨다. ❺ 관계대명사 that으로 앞에 있는 the costumes and the dead language of the 16th century를 가리킨다. ❻ appear 출연하다, 나타나다 ❼ understanding 이해 ❽ bear in mind ~을 명심하다, 유념하다 ❾ book 예매하다, 예약하다 ❿ regret ~ing ~한 것을 후회하다

 Check Your Progress 3

(Phone rings.)

W: Hello. This is the Culture Theater. ❶How may I help you?

B: I'd like to ❷book four seats for *Sleeping Beauty* this Friday.

W: Okay, ❸let me check. The performances are at 6 p.m., and 8 p.m. ❹Which one do you prefer?

B: 6 p.m. please.

W: Oh, I'm sorry but we only have two seats ❺left for that time.

B: ❻Never mind. It's all my fault for calling so late. What about 8 p.m.?

W: There are enough seats at 8 p.m. That will be 60 dollars ❼in total.

B: Can I get a student discount? We are all students.

W: Sure, it's ❽30% off.

B: What ❾should I do to get the discount?

W: ❿You're supposed to bring your student ID card.

❶ '무엇을 도와드릴까요?'라는 의미로 'How can I help you?'와 바꿔 쓸 수 있다. ❷ book 예매하다, 예약하다 ❸ 동사 let은 목적보어로 동사원형을 취한다. ❹ 상대방의 선호를 물어보는 문장으로, '어느 것을 선호하십니까?'라고 해석한다. ❺ two seats와 left 사이에 '관계대명사 + be동사(that are)'가 생략되어 있다. ❻ '괜찮아요.' 또는 '신경 쓰지 마세요.'라는 뜻으로 'Forget it.'으로 바꿔 쓸 수 있다. ❼ in total 총합으로 ❽ 30% off 30프로 할인 ❾ '~해야 한다'라는 뜻으로 'have to'로 바꿔 쓸 수 있다. ❿ 'be supposed to ~'는 '~하기로 되어 있다', '~해야 한다'라는 의미로 의무를 나타내는 표현이다.

● 다음 우리말과 일치하도록 빈칸에 알맞은 말을 쓰시오.

Everyday English 1 A Listen and Check

(1) **B:** Who _____ this mess? It was _____ this morning.

   G: It's not my fault. Your dog _____ it.

   B: Oh, my _____! It will _____ a lot of time to clear it up.

   G: Let's do it _____. I'll help you.

(2) **G:** Minsu, _____ were you late _____ school today?

   B: It was _____ my fault.

   G: What _____?

   B: I got up late this morning, so I _____ the bus.

(3) (*Phone rings.*)

   W: Hello, _____ is the shoe shop. _____ may I help you?

   M: I have a _____ with the boots that I _____ there yesterday.

   W: What's the _____ with them?

   M: They're a bit _____. But it is not my _____. I've _____ worn them.

   W: Sorry _____ that. Please _____ our shop this week.

해석

(1) B: 누가 이렇게 엉망으로 만들었니? 오늘 아침에는 깨끗했는데.
   G: 내 잘못이 아니야. 너의 개가 그랬어.
   B: 맙소사! 이걸 다 치우려면 시간이 많이 걸리겠다.
   G: 같이 해. 내가 도와 줄게.

(2) G: 민수야, 오늘 왜 학교에 늦었니?
   B: 다 내 잘못이야.
   G: 무슨 일이 있었는데?
   B: 오늘 아침에 늦게 일어나서 버스를 놓쳤어.

(3) (전화가 울린다.)
   W: 여보세요, 신발 가게입니다. 어떻게 도와드릴까요?
   M: 제가 어저께 거기서 산 부츠에 문제가 있는데요.
   W: 문제가 무엇입니까?
   M: 조금 더러워서요. 근데 제 잘못은 아니에요. 신어 보지도 않았거든요.
   W: 죄송합니다. 이번 주에 저희 가게에 들러 주세요.

Everyday English 1 B Listening Activity

G: My dog got _____ this morning. I'm so _____ about him.

B: What did you _____ him yesterday?

G: I _____ him some milk last night.

B: Oh, you _____ not feed a dog milk.

G: I was not sure _____ or not it is _____ for him to drink milk. It was _____ my _____.

B: Don't _____ too much. Did you take him to the animal _____?

G: Yes, I did. I hope he'll _____ better soon.

B: He'll _____ get better _____ your care and love.

G: 오늘 아침에 우리집 개가 아팠어. 개가 너무 걱정돼.
B: 어제 개한테 뭘 먹였는데?
G: 어젯밤에 우유를 좀 줬어.
B: 오, 개한테는 우유를 먹이면 안 돼.
G: 난 개가 우유를 먹으면 안전한지 아닌지 확신하지 못 했거든. 다 내 잘못이야.
B: 너무 걱정하지 마. 수의사에게 데려갔니?
G: 응, 데려갔었어. 개가 빨리 나아지길 바랄 뿐이야.
B: 네 보살핌과 사랑으로 분명히 회복할 거야.

Everyday English 2 A Listen and Check

(1) **B:** Did you hear that Minsu is in the _____?

G: Oh, I didn't know that. Aren't we _____ to visit him?

B: No, he doesn't want _____ to visit him. He is just _____ about _____ classes.

G: Then should I make a _____ of my notes for him?

B: That's a good _____.

(2) **B:** Jina, you look _____. What's the matter?

G: My partner _____ hear _____. I don't know how to _____ with her.

B: Have you _____ communicating with her by writing?

G: Yes, I have. But the problem is that we do not _____ have a pencil.

B: Then, you are _____ to learn how to use _____ language.

Everyday English 2 B Listening Activity

B: Jina, what are you _____ to do this winter vacation?

G: I'm thinking of doing some _____ work for people with _____. Would you like to _____ me?

B: Oh, that's a good idea. But I'm a bit _____ about it.

G: What _____ you feel like that?

B: I'm not sure _____ I am ready to help them. Could you give me some _____?

G: You're supposed to _____ their needs.

B: What do you _____ by their _____?

G: You should help them _____ when they _____ you to do so.

In Real Life

Inho: Lina, you look so _____. What's the _____?

Lina: Oh, Inho. I had an _____ with Ryan.

Inho: Was it your _____?

Lina: No, it wasn't my fault! There was just a _____ between us.

Inho: In that _____, you're supposed to _____ up with him as soon as _____.

해석

(1) **B:** 민수가 병원에 입원했다는 소식 들었니?

G: 오, 난 몰랐어. 우리 민수에게 병문안 가야 하지 않을까?

B: 아니, 민수가 병문안 오는 걸 원치 않아. 민수는 그저 수업을 놓치는 게 걱정스러운가봐.

G: 그럼, 내가 그를 위해 내 노트를 복사해 줄까?

B: 좋은 생각이야.

(2) **B:** 지나야, 혼란스러워 보인다. 무슨 일이니?

G: 내 파트너가 아무것도 들을 수가 없어. 그녀와 어떻게 의사소통해야 할지 모르겠어.

B: 글을 써서 의사소통하려고 시도해 봤니?

G: 응, 해 봤어. 근데 문제는 우리가 연필을 항상 갖고 있는 건 아니라는 거야.

B: 그럼, 너는 수화를 사용하는 법을 배워야 해.

B: Jina야, 이번 겨울 방학에 무엇을 할 계획이니?

G: 난 장애가 있는 사람들을 위해 자원봉사를 할 생각을 하고 있어. 너도 같이 할래?

B: 오, 그거 좋은 생각이다. 그런데 난 좀 걱정이 돼.

G: 왜 그렇게 느끼니?

B: 내가 그 사람들을 도울 준비가 되어 있는지 확신하지 못하겠어. 네가 조언 좀 해 줄래?

G: 넌 그 사람들의 요구를 존중해야 돼.

B: 그 사람들의 요구라는 게 무슨 의미니?

G: 그들이 너에게 그렇게 해 달라고 요청할 때에만 도움을 줘야 해.

Inho: Lina야, 너 너무 우울해 보인다. 무슨 일 있니?

Lina: 오, 인호야. 나 Ryan과 말다툼을 했어.

Inho: 네 잘못이었니?

Lina: 아니, 내 잘못이 아니었어! 단지 우리 사이에 오해가 있었거든.

Inho: 그런 경우라면, 최대한 빨리 Ryan과 화해를 해야 돼.

Lina: Well, Ryan got so _____ that he wouldn't talk with me.

Inho: But who _____? He might regret it now, just like you.

Lina: Do you think _____?

Inho: Yes, everyone wants to _____ good _____.

Lina: Thanks for your _____. I hope I can _____ _____ with him soon.

Lina: 글쎄, 그 애는 화가 너무 나서 나랑 이야기하려고 하지 않을 거야.

Inho: 그렇지만, 누가 알겠어? 그 애도 지금 너처럼 후회하고 있을지.

Lina: 그렇게 생각하니?

Inho: 응, 모두들 좋은 우정을 유지하고 싶어하거든.

Lina: 네 조언 고마워. 나도 곧 그 애랑 화해하기를 바라.

Check Your Progress 2

W: Thank you for _____ "Play World." Are you looking _____ to this month's play? This month's play is *Hamlet* There are two _____ points about this play. First, it is a 21st _____ version of Shakespeare's *Hamlet*. It has _____ the _____ and the dead language of the 16th century that most of today's _____ might feel uncomfortable with. _____, the famous actor, Park Mujin, appears in this play. His _____ shows a deep understanding of the main character, Hamlet. Please _____ in mind that you will need to _____ your ticket online. It won't be your _____ if you miss this play. But you'll certainly _____ missing it.

W: "연극 세상"을 시청해 주셔서 감사합니다. 이 달의 연극을 기대하고 계신가요? 이 달의 연극은 "햄릿"입니다. 이 연극에는 두 가지 흥미로운 점이 있습니다. 첫째, 셰익스피어가 쓴 햄릿의 21세기 버전이라는 점입니다. 오늘날의 관객들 대부분이 불편하다고 느끼실 16세기 의상과 사장된 고어를 변화시켰습니다. 둘째, 유명한 배우인 박무진이 이 연극에 출연합니다. 그의 연기는 주연인 햄릿에 대한 깊은 이해를 반영합니다. 티켓은 인터넷으로 예매하셔야 한다는 점을 숙지해 주시기 바랍니다. 이 연극을 놓치게 되더라도 여러분의 책임은 아닐 겁니다. 그러나 연극을 놓치게 된다면 분명 후회하게 되실 겁니다.

Check Your Progress 3

(*Phone rings.*)

W: Hello. This is the Culture Theater. _____ may I help you?

B: I'd like to book four _____ for *Sleeping Beauty* this Friday.

W: Okay, let me _____. The _____ are at 6 p.m., and 8 p.m. Which one do you _____?

B: 6 p.m. please.

W: Oh, I'm sorry but we only have two seats _____ for that time.

B: _____ mind. It's all my fault for calling so late. What about 8 p.m.?

W: There are _____ seats at 8 p.m. That will be 60 dollars in _____.

B: Can I get a student _____? We are all students.

W: Sure, it's 30% off.

B: What _____ I do to get the _____?

W: You're _____ to bring your student ID card.

(전화가 울린다)

W: 여보세요. 컬쳐 극장입니다. 무엇을 도와드릴까요?

B: 이번 주 금요일에 하는 '잠자는 미녀' 네 좌석을 예매하고 싶은데요.

W: 네, 확인해 보겠습니다. 공연은 저녁 6시와 8시에 있습니다. 어느 걸 선호하십니까?

B: 6시 걸로 해주세요.

W: 오, 죄송하지만, 그 시간은 두 석만 남아 있습니다.

B: 괜찮습니다. 제가 늦게 전화한 것이 잘못인 걸요. 8시는 어떤가요?

W: 저녁 8시 좌석은 충분히 있습니다. 총 60달러입니다.

B: 학생 할인을 받을 수 있을까요? 저희 모두 학생이라서요.

W: 그럼요. 30프로 할인이 됩니다.

B: 할인을 받으려면 뭘 해야 하나요?

W: 학생증을 가져 오셔야 합니다.

01 다음 대화가 자연스럽게 이어지도록 순서대로 배열하시오.

> B: Who made this mess? It was clean this morning.
> (A) Let's do it together. I'll help you.
> (B) Oh, my goodness! It will take a lot of time to clear it up.
> (C) It's not my fault. Your dog did it.

➡ _____

02 다음 대화의 밑줄 친 부분을 바르게 영작한 것은?

> A: My sister cried.
> B: Was it your fault?
> A: Yes, <u>모두 내 잘못이야</u>. I lost her cap.

① it is all my fault　　② it isn't all my fault

③ it was all my fault　　④ it wasn't all my fault

⑤ it has been all my fault

[03~04] 다음 대화를 읽고 물음에 답하시오.

> B: Did you hear that Minsu is in the hospital?
> G: Oh, I didn't know that. Aren't we supposed to visit him?
> B: No, he doesn't want anyone to visit him. He is just worried about missing classes.
> G: (A)<u>그럼 내가 그를 위해 내 노트를 복사해 줄까?</u> (should, copy, notes)
> B: That's a good idea.

03 위 대화의 밑줄 친 (A)를 주어진 단어를 사용해 영작하시오. (11 words)

➡ _____

04 다음 중 위 대화를 읽고 대답할 수 <u>없는</u> 질문은?

① Why is Minsu in the hospital?

② Are B and G going to visit Minsu?

③ Does Minsu want his friends to visit him?

④ What is Minsu worried about?

⑤ What are B and G going to do for Minsu?

[01~03] 다음 대화를 읽고 물음에 답하시오.

G: My dog ⓐgot sick this morning. I'm so worried about him.

B: What did you feed him yesterday?

G: I gave ⓑto him some milk last night.

B: Oh, you ⓒshould not feed a dog milk.

G: I was not sure ⓓwhether or not it is safe for him to drink milk. It was all my fault.

B: Don't worry too much. Did you take him to the animal doctor?

G: Yes, I did. I hope he'll ⓔget better soon.

B: He'll certainly get better with your care and love.

서답형

01 위 대화의 밑줄 친 ⓐ~ⓔ 중 어법상 어색한 것을 찾아 바르게 고치시오.

➡ _____

02 위 대화에 나타난 G의 심정으로 가장 적절한 것은?

① concerned
② astonished
③ disappointed
④ touched
⑤ impressed

03 위 대화를 읽고 대답할 수 없는 질문은?

① When did G's dog get sick?
② How does G feel about her dog?
③ What did G give to her dog?
④ Where did G take her dog to?
⑤ What is safe and unsafe for dogs?

[04~06] 다음 대화를 읽고 물음에 답하시오.

B: Jina, what are you (A)[planned/planning] to do this winter vacation?

G: I'm thinking of (B)[doing/to do] some volunteer work for people with disabilities. Would you like to join me?

B: Oh, that's a good idea. But I'm a bit worried about it.

G: What (C)[makes/made] you feel like that?

B: I'm not sure whether I am ready to help them. Could you give me some advice?

G: (a)You're supposed to respect their needs.

B: What do you mean by their needs?

G: You should help them only when they ask you to do so.

04 위 대화의 (A)~(C)에 들어갈 말이 바르게 짝지어진 것은?

	(A)	(B)	(C)
①	planned	to do	made
②	planned	doing	makes
③	planning	to do	made
④	planning	doing	makes
⑤	planning	to do	makes

05 위 대화의 밑줄 친 (a)와 바꿔 쓸 수 없는 것은?

① You must respect their needs.
② You don't need to respect their needs.
③ You should respect their needs.
④ You have to respect their needs.
⑤ You ought to respect their needs.

06 위 대화에서 주어진 영영풀이가 가리키는 것을 찾아 쓰시오. (단수형으로 쓸 것)

> an illness, injury, or condition that makes it difficult for someone to do the things that other people do

➡ _____

09 위 대화의 밑줄 친 (A)them이 가리키는 것을 쓰시오. (7 words)

➡ _____

[07~09] 다음 대화를 읽고 물음에 답하시오.

> (*Phone rings.*)
> W: Hello, this is the shoe shop. How may I help you?
> M: I have a problem with the boots who I bought there yesterday.
> W: What's the problem with (A)them?
> M: They're a bit dirty. But it is not my fault. I've never worn them.
> W: Sorry about that. Please visit our shop this week.

[10~11] 다음 대화를 읽고 물음에 답하시오.

> B: Jina, you look confused. What's the matter?
> G: My partner cannot hear anything. I don't know how to communicate with her.
> B: Have you tried communicating with her by writing?
> G: Yes, I have. But the problem is that we do not always have a pencil.
> B: Then, you _____(A)_____ learn how to use sign language.

07 위 대화에서 어법상 어색한 것을 하나 찾아 바르게 고치시오.

➡ _____

10 위 대화의 빈칸 (A)에 들어갈 말로 적절하지 <u>않은</u> 것은?

① should
② might
③ ought to
④ had better
⑤ have to

08 위 대화의 W와 M의 관계로 가장 적절한 것은?

① shop assistant – customer
② doctor – patient
③ teacher – student
④ father – daughter
⑤ coach – athlete

11 What does B advise G to do? (10 words)

➡ _____

[01~02] 다음 대화를 읽고 물음에 답하시오.

Inho: Lina, you look so depressed. What's the matter?

Lina: Oh, Inho. I had an argument with Ryan.

Inho: Was it your fault?

Lina: No, it wasn't my fault! There was just a misunderstanding between us.

Inho: In that case, you're supposed to make up with him as soon as possible.

Lina: Well, Ryan got so angry that he wouldn't talk with me.

Inho: But who knows? He might regret (A)it now, just like you.

Lina: Do you think so?

Inho: Yes, everyone wants to maintain good friendships.

Lina: Thanks for your advice. I hope I can make up with him soon.

01 What did Inho advise Lina to do as soon as possible? (12 words)

➡ _____

_____

02 위 대화의 밑줄 친 (A)it이 가리키는 것을 우리말로 쓰시오.

➡ _____

03 다음 대화의 밑줄 친 우리말을 주어진 단어를 써서 영작하시오. (9 words)

A: What do you think is important for staying healthy?

B: I think taking a regular exercise is important.

A: How can I put that idea into practice? Any suggestions?

B: 너는 매일 한 시간씩 달려야 해. (suppose)

➡ _____

[04~06] 다음 대화를 읽고 물음에 답하시오.

(*Phone rings.*)

W: Hello. This is the Culture Theater. How may I help you?

B: I'd like to book four seats for *Sleeping Beauty* this Friday.

W: Okay, let me check. The performances are at 6 p.m., and 8 p.m. Which one do you prefer?

B: 6 p.m. please.

W: Oh, I'm sorry but we only have two seats left for that time.

B: Never mind. It's all my fault for calling so late. What about 8 p.m.?

W: There are enough seats at 8 p.m. That will be 60 dollars in total.

B: Can I get a student discount? We are all students.

W: Sure, it's 30% off.

B: What should I do to get the discount?

W: You're supposed to bring your student ID card.

04 Why did B call the Culture Theater? (7 words)

➡ _____

05 What time is B going to watch the performance? (10 words)

➡ _____

06 What does B have to do to get a student discount? (8 words)

➡ _____

Grammar

1 접속사 whether

> I'm not sure **whether** he is dead or not. 그가 죽은 건지 아닌 건지 모르겠군.

■ 접속사 whether는 '~인지 아닌지'라는 뜻으로 문장에서 주어, 목적어 또는 보어 역할을 하는 명사절을 이끈다. 'whether+주어+동사+or not'으로 쓰며 'or not'은 생략되기도 하고 'whether' 바로 뒤에 쓰이기도 한다.
  - **Whether** he will attend the meeting (or not) is uncertain. (주어) 그가 그 모임에 참석할지는 확실하지 않다.
    = **Whether** (or not) he will attend the meeting is uncertain.
  - I don't remember **whether** I locked the door (or not). (목적어) 나는 문을 잠갔는지 어떤지 기억이 안 난다.
  - The question is **whether** he will come to the party (or not). (보어) 문제는 그가 파티에 오느냐 오지 않느냐이다.

■ whether A or B의 경우 양자택일의 문제가 될 수 있다.
  - **Whether** Peter goes swimming **or** shopping is his choice. 피터가 수영하러 갈지 쇼핑을 할지는 그의 선택이다.

■ 'whether' 절이 타동사의 목적어를 이끌 때에는 의문사가 없는 간접의문문이다.
  - The clerk wonders **whether** I will buy the clock or not. 점원은 내가 시계를 살지 안 살지 의아해 한다.

■ 'whether'는 'if'로 바꿔 쓸 수 있다. 'if'가 명사절을 이끌 경우에는 전치사의 목적어로 쓰일 수 없고, 동사의 목적어로만 쓰이며, 'or not'과 붙여 쓸 수 없다. 또한 'if' 다음에 'to부정사'가 나올 수 없다.
  - I asked **whether[if]** she solved the problem or not. 나는 그녀가 문제를 풀었는지 아닌지를 물었다.
  - Mr. Kim called to ask **whether[if]** the upcoming seminar on September 10th could be postponed until next week. 김 선생은 곧 있을 9월 10일 세미나를 다음 주까지 연기할 수 있을지 묻기 위해 전화했다.
  - She can't decide **whether** to buy the house or not. 그녀는 집을 살지 말지 결정하지 못한다.

핵심 Check

1. 다음 괄호 안에서 알맞은 말을 고르시오.
  (1) He'll ask me (whether / if) or not you can bake bread.
  (2) (If / Whether) he will take a trip or not depends on the weather tomorrow.

2 It's time that 가정법

It's about **time I left** here. 이제 제가 떠날 때가 왔군요.

- 'It's (about[high]) time (that)+주어+동사의 과거형[should 동사원형]' 형태이고 '~할 때이다'로 해석한다. 현재 일어나지 않은 일에 관한 화자의 불만족이나 재촉 등의 주관적인 감정을 나타낸다.
  - **It's time that** we **studied** English. (우리가 영어 공부를 해야 할 때이다.)
  - = **It's time that** we should study English.
    (현재 공부를 열심히 하지 않고 있기 때문에, 이제부터 열심히 해야 한다는 의미)

- 'It is (about[high]) time (that)+주어+과거형 동사'는 '~할 때인데 왜 안하고 있습니까?'라는 의미를 내포하고, 'It is (about[high]) time (that)+주어+(should) 동사원형'은 당위성을 내포하고 있어 약간의 차이가 있다.
  - **It is high time** that you **stopped** smoking. 담배를 끊어야 할 때이다. (= 끊어야 했는데 왜 아직도 피우니?)
  - = **It is high time that** you should stop smoking. 담배를 당장 끊어야 한다.
  - = **It is high time that** you stop smoking. [당위성을 나타낼 때 조동사 should 생략 가능]

- 직설법으로 쓰일 때에는 화자의 불만족이나 재촉이 담겨 있지 않다.
  - **It's time that** we study English. (우리가 영어를 공부할 시간이다.) (시간상, 지금이 영어를 공부할 시간이 되었다는 의미)
  - * '~할 시간이다.'라는 표현은 'It's time to 동사원형'이다. 무언가를 할 시간이 임박해 있을 때 사용할 수 있다.
    - **It's time to** say good bye. 헤어져야 할 시간이야.
    - **It's time** (for you) **to** go to bed. 잠자리에 들 시간이다.
  * I wish 가정법

- I wish 가정법 과거는 'I wish+주어+과거형 동사' 형태이고 현재에 이룰 수 없는 소망을 표현할 때 사용한다. 해석은 '~라면 좋을 텐데.'이다. 'I'm sorry+현재시제'로 바꿔 쓸 수 있다.
  - **I wish** he **agreed** with her. (그가 그녀에게 동의한다면 좋을 텐데.)
  - = I'm sorry he doesn't agree with her. (그가 그녀에게 동의하지 않다니 유감이다.)

- I wish 가정법 과거완료는 'I wish+주어+had p.p.'로 과거에 이루지 못한 소망을 표현할 때 사용한다. 해석은 '~했더라면 좋았을 텐데.'이다. 'I'm sorry+과거시제'로 바꿔 쓸 수 있다.
  - **I wish** I **had been** at the meeting (내가 모임에 갔더라면 좋을 텐데.)
  - = I'm sorry I was not at the meeting. (내가 모임에 가지 못해 유감이다.)

핵심 Check

2. 다음 문장을 풀어 쓸 때 일치하면 ○, 일치하지 않으면 ×를 고르시오.

(1) It's time that I went home.
→ It's too late. I should go home. ▶ (○, ×)

(2) It's time you learned how to to read.
→ Now you should learn how to read. ▶ (○, ×)

01 다음 문장에서 어법상 <u>어색한</u> 부분을 바르게 고쳐 쓰시오. (없으면 '없음'으로 쓸 것.)

(1) The question is that we are ready for the contest or not.

_____ ➡ _____

(2) If you agree or not is important for our decision.

_____ ➡ _____

(3) It's time what you did your homework.

_____ ➡ _____

(4) It's time that we should work out regularly.

_____ ➡ _____

(5) I'm not sure if or not he can carry this heavy box.

_____ ➡ _____

02 다음 빈칸에 들어갈 말로 적절한 말을 쓰시오. (3 단어)

We should already be at the train station. It's high time
_____. So, hurry up!

03 다음 밑줄 친 우리말에 맞게 주어진 단어를 이용해서 8 단어로 영작하시오.

A: Jimmy, it's already 7 o'clock. It's too late. It's time that <u>우리 강아지랑 산책하러 나가야 할</u>. (take, walk)
B: I'm sorry, Mom.

➡ _____

04 다음 빈칸에 공통으로 들어갈 적절한 단어를 쓰시오.

• I was asked _____ I could drive.
• I wonder _____ she made the bread.

01 밑줄 친 우리말에 맞게 괄호 안의 단어를 이용하여 영작하시오.

> Mom: Somi, you're getting fat.
> Somi: Yes. I think 내가 먹는 정크 푸드를 줄여
> 야 할 때다. (cut down on, junk food)
>
> *cut down on ~을 줄이다

➡ _____

02 다음 빈칸에 어법상 알맞은 것을 고르시오.

> _____ I believe you or not is
> irrelevant now.
>
> *irrelevant 무관한, 상관없는

① If   ② Whatever
③ Whether   ④ What
⑤ Which

03 다음 중 어법상 어색한 것을 고르시오.

① I asked him if he would attend the
   conference.
② I'm not interested in whether he will
   come or not.
③ He tried to see if he could fly.
④ If she had a car or not isn't important to
   me.
⑤ She didn't know whether to laugh or cry.

04 다음 중 어법상 어색한 곳을 고르시오.

> It is time that we should return to our
> country.
> = It ①is time ②that ③we ④have
> returned ⑤to our country.

05 다음 빈칸에 공통으로 들어갈 말로 알맞은 것을 모두 고르
시오.

> • Do you know _____ this bus goes to
>   the CN Tower?
> • I wonder _____ Jack passed this
>   interview.
> • I don't know _____ the next meeting
>   will be in Toronto.

① whether   ② which   ③ what
④ if   ⑤ who

06 괄호 안의 단어를 활용하여 빈칸에 들어갈 말을 쓰시오

> 우리 새 차를 사야 할 때가 되지 않았어? (about)
> ➡ _____ time we got a new car?

07 다음을 읽고 각 빈칸에 들어갈 알맞은 말을 쓰시오.

> My car was broken yesterday, so I
> dropped by the car service center.
> ➡ It's _____ time I _____
> my car.

08 다음 중 어법상 어색한 것을 고르시오.

① I'm not sure if she likes me.
② I'm not sure whether shopping online is cheaper than offline.
③ I'm not sure whether he is sick or not.
④ If his soccer team will win the match or not is not important.
⑤ I'm not sure whether we can get to the theater in time.

09 다음 문장과 같은 뜻으로 쓰인 문장을 모두 고르시오.

> He has got nothing left in the bank, so it's about time he started saving more.

① He has enough money in the bank, so it's time he started saving more.
② He has got nothing left in the bank, so it's time he should start saving more.
③ He has got nothing left in the bank, so it's time he started saving more.
④ He has enough money in the bank, so it isn't time he started saving more.
⑤ He has got nothing left in the bank, so it isn't time he started saving more.

10 다음 빈칸에 들어갈 단어로 알맞은 것을 모두 고르시오.

> I wonder _____ he will come tomorrow.

① if   ② that   ③ which
④ whether   ⑤ what

11 다음 빈칸에 알맞은 것을 모두 고르시오.

> A: Because of Covid-19, we noted we were not very good, especially in education field.
> B: _____

① I think it's about time that our country invested in education.
② I don't think it's about time that our country invest in education.
③ I think it's about time these people were fined for this behavior.
④ I don't think it's about time we should prepare for the next step.
⑤ I think it's about time that our country should offer a nice solution.

서답형
12 우리말에 맞게 괄호 안의 어휘들을 배열하여 영작할 때,

(1) You로 시작하여 8번째 단어를 쓰시오.
 • 넌 좋든 싫든 학교에 다녀야 해. (have, to, go, to, got, you, whether, it, like, school, not, or, you)
(2) If로 시작하여 3번째 단어를 쓰시오.
 • 만약 그녀가 내일 온다면, 나는 행복할 것이다. (tomorrow, I, she, comes, if, be, will, happy)
(3) They로 시작하여 5번째 단어를 쓰시오.
 • 그들은 대화를 이어갈지 심사숙고했다. (deeply, they, thought, whether, continue, to, the talk)

➡ (1) _____ (2) _____ (3) _____

13 다음 빈칸에 들어갈 말끼리 짝지어진 것을 고르시오.

> (1) A: Is she angry?
>
>   B: _____
>
> (2) A: How about joining the leather boots making class?
>
>   B: _____

① We don't know whether she can join us.
– I'm not sure whether I can make fine leather boots or not.

② I don't know whether she is angry. – It's doubtful whether there'll be any seats left.

③ We don't know whether she can join us.
– It's doubtful whether there'll be any seats left.

④ I don't know whether she is angry. – I'm not sure whether I can make fine leather boots or not.

⑤ I don't know whether she is angry. – I'm not sure whether I can make cookies until then.

14 다음 빈칸에 들어갈 말로 알맞은 것을 고르시오.

> 그가 원하든 원하지 않든, 자기 방을 치워야만 할 것이다.
>
> → _____, he'll have to clean his room.

① What he wants

② As he wants

③ If or not he wants

④ Whether he wants or not

⑤ That he wants

15 다음 빈칸에 들어갈 단어로 알맞은 것을 모두 고르시오.

> I wonder _____ Jack will marry Kate.

① that   ② if   ③ what
④ whether   ⑤ which

16 다음 빈칸에 들어갈 알맞은 말을 쓰시오.

> We use Ms rather than Mrs or Miss when we don't know _____ a women is married _____.

17 It's about time과 괄호 안의 단어를 활용하여 우리말에 맞게 영작하시오.

> 이제 그것에서 벗어날 때도 됐잖아. (be, free)

➡ _____

18 다음 빈칸에 들어가기에 적절한 것을 모두 고르시오.

> My laboratory made the Covid-19 Vaccine.
> _____

① It's about time you should tell him.

② It's about time we announced our success.

③ It's about time he should do his homework.

④ It's about time she should know the fact.

⑤ It's about time many companies should invest my lab.

01 다음 조건대로 우리말에 맞게 괄호 안의 어휘를 활용하여 영작하시오.

> ┤ 조건 ├
> 1. 'It's high time+가정법 과거' 구문을 이용할 것.
> 2. 'It's high time ~' 구문과 'should'를 이용할 것.

(1) 아빠가 오실 때가 되었다. (show up)

➡ _____

➡ _____

(2) 우리가 멈춰야 할 때이다. (stop)

➡ _____

➡ _____

(3) 내가 집에 돌아갈 때라고 생각해. (go)

➡ _____

➡ _____

(4) 우리가 소프트웨어를 갱신할 때가 되었다. (update)

➡ _____

➡ _____

(5) 지금은 우리가 지구 온난화를 심각하게 고려하기 시작할 때이다. (start, take global warming seriously)

➡ _____
_____

➡ _____
_____

(6) 당신은 사실을 직면하는 법을 배워야겠군요. (learn to, face the facts)

➡ _____

➡ _____
_____

(7) 날씨가 시원해질 때가 되었다. (start cooling off)

➡ _____

➡ _____
_____

(8) 우리가 중대한 조처를 강구해야 할 때이다. (take serious steps)

➡ _____

➡ _____

02 우리말에 맞게 괄호 안의 단어와 'whether' 및 'or not'을 활용하여 영작하시오.

(1) 그녀가 결혼을 했는지 안 했는지 우리는 모른다. (marry)

➡ _____

(2) 그것은 그녀가 돈이 있는지 없는지에 달려 있다. (depend on)

➡ _____

(3) 그것이 작동할지 의문스럽다. (doubt, work)

➡ _____

(4) 네가 그것을 좋아할지 확신할 수 없었다. (sure, would)

➡ _____

(5) 우리는 우리가 가야 하는지 말아야 하는지에 대해 이야기했다. (talk)

➡ _____

03 다음 빈칸에 공통으로 들어갈 말을 쓰시오.

> • And _____ you want this ring, please help me find the poor missing otter.   *otter: 수달
> • Just call me _____ you ever need anything. Okay?
> • Tell me _____ this story sounds familiar.
> • Check _____ the seat is set at the right height.

04 다음 문장의 간접의문문을 직접의문문으로 고치시오.

(1) I want to find out if the house has a garden.

➡ _____

(2) She is not sure whether they will go camping this weekend.

➡ _____

05 괄호 안의 단어를 활용하여 우리말에 맞게 빈칸을 채우시오.

> 고등학교는 학생들에게 은행 업무와 재정 (banking and finance)에 대해 가르쳐야 할 때이다. (teach)

➡ It's about time that _____

_____.

06 다음 우리말에 맞게 괄호 안의 단어를 활용하여 영작하시오.

> 그 헌 신발은 이제 그만 버릴 때도 됐잖아.
> (throw away, high, you, those old shoes)

➡ _____

_____

07 다음 문장에서 어법상 <u>어색한</u> 곳을 찾아 바르게 고치시오.

> We can't say either tourism is harmful or beneficial.

➡ _____

08 우리말을 참고하여 빈칸에 들어갈 알맞은 말을 쓰시오.

> 그녀가 떠나야 할 때입니다.
> ➡ It's time that she _____.

09 우리말을 괄호 안의 어휘를 활용하여 주어진 조건에 맞게 영작할 때 빈칸에 알맞은 말을 쓰시오.

(1) 우리가 임금 인상을 요청할 때다. (ask for a raise) (주관적 감정을 나타내는 문장으로 쓸 것.)

➡ It's about time _____.

(2) 우리가 결판을 지어야 할 때다. (settle the matter) (당위성을 나타내는 문장으로 쓸 것.)

➡ It's about time _____.

(3) 시험이 쉽다면 좋을 텐데. (be) ('I wish 가정법' 문장으로 쓸 것.)

➡ I wish _____.

Three Mysterious Smiles

Scene #1.

It's winter. A poor shoe maker, Simon, fails to buy a warm coat.
'fail'은 to부정사만을 목적어로 취하는 동사다.

On his way back home, he finds a man, Michael, lying in the street

without any clothes.

Simon: I'm not sure whether he is dead or not. But I don't think I can
'I'm not sure of whether he is dead or not.'에서 'of'가 생략된 문장. whether ~ or not: ~인지 아닌지

save him because I'm drunk and have little money. (*walking away from*

Michael at first, but coming back again) Poor man. Are you okay?

Why are you lying here?

Michael: I can't tell you everything. Put simply, I am being punished.
간단히 말해서 = To put it simply   'am being punished': 진행형 수동태(벌을 받고 있는 중이다)

Simon: But it's cold outside. Let's go home together.

Scene #2.

Simon comes home and greets Matrena, his wife. She finds he has
'finds'와 'he' 사이에 명사절을 이끄는 접속사 'that'이 생략

brought nothing.

Matrena: (*surprised and angry*) Simon, you were supposed to buy a coat

for our family. But there's nothing. And who is this man?

Simon: I did not have enough money to buy the coat. I'm sorry.
to부정사의 형용사적 용법

And I know nothing about this man. But it wasn't my fault. I had to

bring him home. I mean just look at him. Don't you think he needs

help?

Matrena: (*looking at Michael with pity*) Okay, Simon.

(Michael smiles for the first time.)

For a week, Michael does no work to support himself.

Simon: (*looking at Michael*) Michael, I'm afraid you've been doing

nothing since you came here. It's time you started to earn a living for
It's time (that) 주어+가정법 과거: ~할 때다 (현재 일어나지 않은 일에 관한 화자의 불만족이나 재촉 등의 주관적인 감정을 나타낸다.)

yourself. If you work for me, I will give you food. Would you like to
시간이나 조건의 부사절에서는 미래시제 대신 현재시제를 쓴다.

work with me?

Michael: (*with a blank face*) Yes, I would.

on one's way back 돌아오는 길에
punish 처벌하다
earn a living 생계를 유지하다

Scene #3.

A year later, Simon has become famous, thanks to Michael's great skills in making shoes. One day, a nobleman comes to order his boots.

Nobleman: I'd like to order fine leather boots that have to last for a year. I'm not sure <u>whether</u> you can make them. Can you do that?
~인지 아닌지

(Michael watches the man carefully and smiles for the second time.)

Simon: Yes, sir. Don't worry.

(The nobleman leaves the shop.)

Simon: Michael, please make some thick leather boots.

Michael: Okay.

(However, Michael makes soft slippers instead of boots.)

Simon: (*finding the slippers*) Michael! I told you there should be no mistakes. What do you think you are doing?

Servant: (*running into the shop*) Please stop making boots and start making soft slippers for a dead body instead. My master has died of a heart attack.

Simon: (*looking at Michael in surprise*) How did you know?

Michael: Well …

Scene #4.

A few years later, a woman customer visits the shoe shop with twin girls.

Customer: I'm here to buy some leather shoes for these twin girls.

Simon: (*seeing that one of the girls has a disability*) I'm sorry about
목적어를 이끄는 접속사   'one of the+복수 명사'가 주어일 때, 'one'에 맞춰서 단수 취급

your daughter's foot. May I ask you <u>if</u> she was born with a disability?
~인지 아닌지 = whether

Customer: Oh, I'm not her real mother. Her mother hurt this girl's leg while she was giving birth to her. Their parents are both dead now. I felt sorry for them. I loved these twins <u>so</u> much <u>that</u> I decided to adopt them.
so+형용사/부사+that+주어+동사: 너무 ~해서 …하다

(Michael smiles for the third time.)

nobleman 귀족
leather 가죽
servant 하인
master 주인
heart attack 심장마비
in surprise 놀라서
give birth to ~을 출산하다
adopt 입양하다

 확인문제

● 다음 문장이 본문의 내용과 일치하면 T, 일치하지 <u>않으면</u> F를 쓰시오.

1   A nobleman orders fine leather boots that have to last for a year. ☐

2   The woman is the twin girls' real mother. ☐

Scene #5.
(*Suddenly, a mysterious light shines from Michael.*)
Simon: What's this light <u>shining</u> from you?
_{현재분사}

Michael: It's about time I left here.
_{It's time (that) 주어+가정법 과거: ~할 때다 (현재 일어나지 않은 일에 관한 화자의 불만족이나 재촉 등의 주관적인 감정을 나타낸다.)}

Simon: What do you mean? And why did you just smile?

Michael: Let me explain. I am an angel. I <u>was sent</u> here as a punishment,
_{수동태 구문}

and I was supposed to learn three truths. Every time I learned one of them, I smiled. <u>Now that</u> I have learned all three of them, I am ready to
_{~이기 때문에, ~이므로}
go back.
Simon: I see. What truths have you learned?

Scene #6.
Michael thinks back to each time that he smiled. Simon and Matrena listen carefully to him.
Michael: First, I learned that love dwells in human beings when Matrena pitied me. This was the answer to the first lesson: Learn <u>what</u> dwells in
_{선행사를 포함하는 관계대명사}
human beings. I smiled because I learned the truth.

But I still had two more to figure out.
Simon: What were they?
Michael: The second was, "Learn <u>what</u> is not given to people."
_{선행사를 포함하는 관계대명사}
When the nobleman ordered that his boots <u>were to last</u> for a year, I
_{be+to부정사'의 '가능'}
knew he would die soon. Then I realized people know little about their own future needs.
Simon: What was the last truth?
Michael: It was from the story of the woman and the twin girls. After the death of <u>their</u> mother, the woman <u>brought them up</u> with her love. Then,
_{쌍둥이 자매}   _{'bring up'은 목적어가 인칭대명사인 경우 'bring+목적어(대명사)+up'의 형식}
I learned people live by having true love for each other. That was the third lesson: What people live by.

shine 빛나다
now that ~이기 때문에
be ready to ~할 준비가 되다
dwell 거주하다
figure out 알아내다
bring up 양육하다

📎 **확인문제**

● 다음 문장이 본문의 내용과 일치하면 T, 일치하지 <u>않으면</u> F를 쓰시오.

1 Michael was supposed to learn three truths. ☐

2 When the nobleman ordered that his boots were to last for a year, Michael didn't know he would die soon. ☐

● 우리말을 참고하여 빈칸에 알맞은 말을 쓰시오.

1　Three ＿＿＿＿＿＿ Smiles

Scene #1.

2　*It's winter. A poor shoe maker, Simon, ＿＿＿＿＿ ＿＿＿＿＿ ＿＿＿＿＿ a warm coat. On his way back home, he finds a man, Michael, ＿＿＿＿＿ in the street without any clothes.*

3　Simon: I'm not sure ＿＿＿＿＿ he is dead ＿＿＿＿＿ ＿＿＿＿＿. But I don't think I can save him because I'm ＿＿＿＿＿ and have little money. (*walking away from Michael at first, but coming back again*) Poor man. Are you ＿＿＿＿＿? ＿＿＿＿＿ are you lying here?

4　Michael: I can't tell you everything. ＿＿＿＿＿ ＿＿＿＿＿, I am being punished.

5　Simon: But it's cold ＿＿＿＿＿. Let's go home together.

Scene #2.

6　*Simon comes home and ＿＿＿＿＿ Matrena, his wife. She finds he ＿＿＿＿＿ ＿＿＿＿＿ ＿＿＿＿＿.*

7　Matrena: (*surprised and angry*) Simon, you ＿＿＿＿＿ ＿＿＿＿＿ ＿＿＿＿＿ buy a coat for our family. But there's ＿＿＿＿＿. And who is this man?

8　Simon: I did not have ＿＿＿＿＿ ＿＿＿＿＿ ＿＿＿＿＿ the coat. I'm sorry. And I know nothing about this man. But it wasn't my ＿＿＿＿＿. I had to bring him home. I mean just look at him. ＿＿＿＿＿ ＿＿＿＿＿ ＿＿＿＿＿ he needs help?

9　Matrena: (*looking at Michael ＿＿＿＿＿ ＿＿＿＿＿*) Okay, Simon.

10　(*Michael smiles ＿＿＿＿＿ ＿＿＿＿＿ ＿＿＿＿＿.*)

11　*For a week, Michael does no work to ＿＿＿＿＿ ＿＿＿＿＿.*

12　Simon: (*looking at Michael*) Michael, I'm afraid you've been doing nothing since you came here. ＿＿＿＿＿ ＿＿＿＿＿ ＿＿＿＿＿ ＿＿＿＿＿ to earn a living for yourself. If you work for me, I will give you food. Would you like ＿＿＿＿＿ ＿＿＿＿＿ with me?

13　Michael: (*with a ＿＿＿＿＿ face*) Yes, I would.

1 세 가지의 신비로운 미소
　장면 1.

2 겨울이다. 가난한 구두장이 Simon은 따뜻한 코트를 사는 데 실패한다. 그는 집에 돌아오는 길에 옷도 입지 않고 길거리에 누워 있는 Michael이라는 한 남자를 발견한다.

3 Simon: 저 남자가 죽은 건지 아닌 건지 모르겠군. 하지만 나는 취해 있고, 돈도 거의 없어서 저 남자를 구할 수 없을 것 같아. (처음엔 Michael에게서 발걸음을 돌리지만, 다시 돌아오며) 불쌍한 사람이군. 괜찮으세요? 왜 여기 누워 있는 거요?

4 Michael: 당신에게 말 못할 사정이 있어요. 간단히 말하자면, 저는 벌을 받고 있어요.

5 Simon: 하지만 밖은 추워요. 같이 집으로 갑시다.
　장면 2.

6 Simon은 집으로 와서 그의 아내인 Matrena와 인사한다. 그녀는 그가 아무것도 가져오지 않은 것을 알게 된다.

7 Matrena: (놀라서 화내며) Simon, 당신은 우리 가족을 위해 코트를 사 오기로 했잖아요. 하지만 아무것도 없네요. 그리고 이 남자는 누구예요?

8 Simon: 코트를 살 정도로 충분한 돈이 없었어요. 미안해요. 그리고 이 남자에 관해서는 아무것도 모르지만, 내 잘못은 아니에요. 나는 이 남자를 집에 데려와야만 했어요. 이 남자를 보세요. 도움이 필요해 보이지 않나요?

9 Matrena: (Michael을 불쌍하게 바라보며) 그래요, Simon.

10 (Michael은 처음으로 미소를 짓는다.)

11 1주일간, Michael은 스스로 자신의 생계를 유지하기 위해 아무 일도 하지 않는다.

12 Simon: (Michael을 바라보며) Michael, 당신이 이곳에 와서 계속 빈둥거리고 있어 걱정되네요. 당신 자신을 위해 생계를 꾸려야 할 때예요. 저를 위해서 일해 준다면, 제가 당신에게 음식을 제공할게요. 저랑 같이 일하시겠어요?

13 Michael: (무표정한 얼굴로) 네, 그렇게 할게요.

Scene #3.

14 *A year later, Simon has become famous, _____ _____ Michael's great skills in making shoes. One day, a nobleman comes to _____ his boots.*

15 Nobleman: I'd like to order fine leather boots _____ _____ _____ for a year. _____ _____ _____ _____ you can make them. Can you do that?

16 (*Michael watches the man carefully and smiles _____ _____ _____ _____ .*)

17 Simon: Yes, sir. _____ _____ .

18 (*The nobleman _____ the shop.*)

19 Simon: Michael, please make some thick _____ _____ .

20 Michael: Okay.

21 (*However, Michael makes soft slippers _____ _____ boots.*)

22 Simon: (*finding the slippers*) Michael! I told you _____ _____ _____ no mistakes. What do you think you are doing?

23 Servant: (*running into the shop*) Please _____ _____ boots and start making soft slippers for a dead body _____ . My master has _____ _____ a heart attack.

24 Simon: (*looking at Michael _____ _____*) How did you know?

25 Michael: Well ...

Scene #4.

26 *A few years later, a woman _____ visits the shoe shop with twin girls.*

27 Customer: I'm here _____ _____ some leather shoes for these twin girls.

28 Simon: (_____ *that one of the girls has a disability*) I'm sorry _____ your daughter's foot. May I ask you _____ she was born with a disability?

14 1년 후, Simon은 Michael의 훌륭한 구두 제작 솜씨 덕분에 유명해졌다. 어느 날, 한 귀족이 부츠를 주문하러 가게에 온다.

15 귀족: 나는 1년을 신어도 끄떡없는 튼튼한 가죽 부츠를 주문하고 싶습니다. 당신이 그 부츠를 만들 수 있을지 모르겠네요. 할 수 있겠습니까?

16 (Michael은 귀족을 유심히 살펴보고는 두 번째로 미소 짓는다.)

17 Simon: 네, 나리. 걱정하지 마세요.

18 (귀족은 가게를 떠난다.)

19 Simon: Michael, 두꺼운 가죽 부츠를 만들어 주세요.

20 Michael: 네.

21 (하지만, Michael은 부츠 대신 부드러운 슬리퍼를 만든다.)

22 Simon: (슬리퍼를 발견하며) Michael! 제가 실수하지 말라고 했잖아요. 지금 뭐 하고 있는 겁니까?

23 하인: (가게로 뛰어들며) 부츠는 그만 만들고 대신 죽은 사람에게 신길 부드러운 슬리퍼를 만들어 주세요. 나리가 심장마비로 돌아가셨습니다.

24 Simon: (놀라서 Michael을 바라보며) 당신은 어떻게 알았습니까?

25 Michael: 글쎄요…

26 몇 년 후, 한 여인이 쌍둥이 소녀들과 함께 신발 가게에 방문한다.

27 손님: 이 쌍둥이 소녀들에게 신길 가죽 신발을 사러 왔습니다.

28 Simon: (장애를 가진 한 소녀를 보며) 따님 한쪽 발이 안타깝네요. 실례지만, 태어날 때부터 장애가 있었는지 여쭤 봐도 될까요?

29 Customer: Oh, I'm not her _____ mother. Her mother hurt this girl's leg while she was _____ _____ _____ her. Their parents are both dead now. I felt sorry for them. I loved these twins _____ _____ _____ I decided to adopt them.

30 (*Michael smiles for the third time.*)

Scene #5.

31 (*Suddenly, a mysterious light _____ _____ Michael.*)

32 Simon: What's this light _____ from you?

33 Michael: It's _____ time I _____ here.

34 Simon: What do you mean? And _____ did you _____ _____?

35 Michael: Let me explain. I am an angel. I _____ here as a punishment, and I _____ _____ learn three truths. _____ _____ I learned one of them, I smiled. Now that I have learned all three of them, I _____ _____ _____ go back.

36 Simon: I see. What truths _____ _____ _____ _____?

Scene #6.

37 Michael _____ _____ _____ each time that he smiled. Simon and Matrena listen carefully to him.

38 Michael: First, I learned that love _____ _____ human beings when Matrena _____ me. This was the answer to the first lesson: Learn _____ dwells in human beings. I smiled because I learned the truth. But I still had two more _____ _____ _____.

39 Simon: What were they?

40 Michael: The second was, "Learn _____ is not given to people." When the nobleman ordered that his boots _____ _____ _____ for a year, I knew he would die soon. Then I realized people _____ _____ _____ their own future needs.

41 Simon: What was the _____ truth?

42 Michael: It was from the story of the woman and the twin girls. After the death of their mother, the woman _____ _____ with her love. Then, I learned people live _____ _____ _____ _____ each other. That was the third lesson: _____ _____ _____ _____.

---

29 손님: 오, 저는 이 아이의 생모가 아니에요. 생모가 아이를 낳던 중에 아이가 다리를 다치게 됐어요. 그들의 부모님은 이미 돌아가셨습니다. 나는 이 쌍둥이가 너무 불쌍했어요. 이 아이들을 너무 사랑해서 입양하기로 결정했습니다.

30 (Michael은 세 번째로 미소를 짓는다.)

장면 5.

31 (갑자기 Michael에게서 신비한 빛이 빛난다.)

32 Simon: 당신에게서 나오는 이 빛은 도대체 뭔가요?

33 Michael: 이제 제가 떠날 때가 왔군요.

34 Simon: 무슨 말씀이시죠? 그리고 당신은 왜 미소를 지었던 건가요?

35 Michael: 설명해 드릴게요. 저는 천사입니다. 저는 벌을 받아 여기로 보내졌고, 세 가지 진리를 깨달아야 했습니다. 제가 진리를 하나씩 깨달을 때마다 미소를 지었던 것입니다. 저는 세 가지 진리를 모두 깨달았기 때문에 돌아갈 준비를 마쳤습니다.

36 Simon: 그렇군요. 당신이 깨달은 진리는 무엇이었나요?

장면 6.

37 Michael은 그가 미소 지었을 때를 회상한다. Simon과 Matrena는 그의 말을 주의 깊게 듣는다.

38 Michael: 첫째, Matrena가 저를 가여워했을 때 인간 내면에 사랑이 존재한다는 것을 저는 깨달았습니다. 이는 '인간 내면에 무엇이 존재하는가'라는 첫 번째 교훈에 관한 답이었던 것입니다. 저는 그 진실을 깨달았기 때문에 미소를 지었습니다. 하지만 저는 아직도 두 가지를 더 알아내야만 했어요.

39 Simon: 그것들은 뭐였나요?

40 Michael: 두 번째는 "인간에게 주어지지 않은 것은 무엇인가"였습니다. 그 귀족이 1년을 신어도 끄떡없는 부츠를 주문했을 때, 저는 그가 곧 죽을 것을 알고 있었습니다. 사람은 자신의 미래에 필요한 것을 알지 못한다는 사실을 그때 저는 깨달았습니다.

41 Simon: 마지막 진리는 무엇이었나요?

42 Michael: 쌍둥이 소녀와 여인의 이야기를 듣고 깨달았습니다. 쌍둥이의 생모가 사망한 후, 그 여인은 그들을 사랑으로 키웠습니다. 그때, 저는 사람은 서로를 향한 참된 사랑으로 산다는 점을 알게 됐습니다. 그것이 '사람은 무엇으로 사는가'에 관한 세 번째 교훈이었습니다.

● 우리말을 참고하여 본문을 영작하시오.

1 ▶ 세 가지의 신비로운 미소
➡ _____

Scene #1.: 장면 1.

2 ▶ 겨울이다. 가난한 구두장이 Simon은 따뜻한 코트를 사는 데 실패한다. 그는 집에 돌아오는 길에 옷도 입지
않고 길거리에 누워 있는 Michael이라는 한 남자를 발견한다.
➡ _____

3 ▶ Simon: 저 남자가 죽은 건지 아닌 건지 모르겠군. 하지만 나는 취해 있고, 돈도 거의 없어서 저 남자를
구할 수 없을 것 같아. (처음엔 Michael에게서 발걸음을 돌리지만, 다시 돌아오며) 불쌍한 사람이군.
괜찮으세요? 왜 여기 누워 있는 거요?
➡ _____
_____

4 ▶ Michael: 당신에게 말 못할 사정이 있어요. 간단히 말하자면, 저는 벌을 받고 있어요.
➡ _____

5 ▶ Simon: 하지만 밖은 추워요. 같이 집으로 갑시다.
➡ _____

Scene #2.: 장면 2.

6 ▶ Simon은 집으로 와서 그의 아내인 Matrena와 인사한다. 그녀는 그가 아무것도 가져오지 않은 것을 알게 된다.
➡ _____

7 ▶ Matrena: (놀라서 화내며) Simon, 당신은 우리 가족을 위해 코트를 사 오기로 했잖아요. 하지만 아무것도 없네요.
그리고 이 남자는 누구예요?
➡ _____

8 ▶ Simon: 코트를 살 정도로 충분한 돈이 없었어요. 미안해요. 그리고 이 남자에 관해서는 아무것도 모르지만,
내 잘못은 아니에요. 나는 이 남자를 집에 데려와야만 했어요. 이 남자를 보세요. 도움이 필요해 보이지 않나요?
➡ _____

9 ▶ Matrena: (Michael을 불쌍하게 바라보며) 그래요, Simon.
➡ _____

10 ▶ (Michael은 처음으로 미소를 짓는다.)
➡ _____

11 ▶ 1주일간, Michael은 스스로 자신의 생계를 유지하기 위해 아무 일도 하지 않는다.
➡ _____

12 ▶ Simon: (Michael을 바라보며) Michael, 당신이 이곳에 와서 계속 빈둥거리고 있어 걱정되네요. 당신 자신을 위해
생계를 꾸려야 할 때에요. 저를 위해서 일해 준다면, 제가 당신에게 음식을 제공할게요. 저랑 같이 일하시겠어요?
➡ _____
_____

13 ▶ Michael: (무표정한 얼굴로) 네, 그렇게 할게요.
➡ _____

Scene #3.: 장면 3.

14 1년 후, Simon은 Michael의 훌륭한 구두 제작 솜씨 덕분에 유명해졌다. 어느 날, 한 귀족이 부츠를 주문하러 가게에 온다.

➡ _____

15 귀족: 나는 1년을 신어도 끄떡없는 튼튼한 가죽 부츠를 주문하고 싶습니다. 당신이 그 부츠를 만들 수 있을지 모르겠네요. 할 수 있겠습니까?

➡ _____

16 (Michael은 귀족을 유심히 살펴보고는 두 번째로 미소 짓는다.)

➡ _____

17 Simon: 네, 나리. 걱정하지 마세요.

➡ _____

18 (귀족은 가게를 떠난다.)

➡ _____

19 Simon: Michael, 두꺼운 가죽 부츠를 만들어 주세요.

➡ _____

20 Michael: 네.

➡ _____

21 (하지만, Michael은 부츠 대신 부드러운 슬리퍼를 만든다.)

➡ _____

22 Simon: (슬리퍼를 발견하며) Michael! 제가 실수하지 말라고 했잖아요. 지금 뭐 하고 있는 겁니까?

➡ _____

23 하인: (가게로 뛰어들며) 부츠는 그만 만들고 대신 죽은 사람에게 신길 부드러운 슬리퍼를 만들어 주세요. 나리가 심장마비로 돌아가셨습니다.

➡ _____
   _____

24 Simon: (놀라서 Michael을 바라보며) 당신은 어떻게 알았습니까?

➡ _____

25 Michael: 글쎄요…

➡ _____

Scene #4.: 장면 4.

26 몇 년 후, 한 여인이 쌍둥이 소녀들과 함께 신발 가게에 방문한다.

➡ _____

27 손님: 이 쌍둥이 소녀들에게 신길 가죽 신발을 사러 왔습니다.

➡ _____

28 Simon: (장애를 가진 한 소녀를 보며) 따님 한쪽 발이 안타깝네요. 실례지만, 태어날 때부터 장애가 있었는지 여쭤 봐도 될까요?

➡ _____

29 손님: 오, 저는 이 아이의 생모가 아니에요. 생모가 아이를 낳던 중에 아이가 다리를 다치게 됐어요. 그들의 부모님은 이미 돌아가셨습니다. 나는 이 쌍둥이가 너무 불쌍했어요. 이 아이들을 너무 사랑해서 입양하기로 결정했습니다.

➡ _____
   _____

30 (Michael은 세 번째로 미소를 짓는다.)

➡ _____

Scene #5.: 장면 5.

31 (갑자기 Michael에게서 신비한 빛이 빛난다.)

➡ _____

32 Simon: 당신에게서 나오는 이 빛은 도대체 뭔가요?

➡ _____

33 Michael: 이제 제가 떠날 때가 왔군요.

➡ _____

34 Simon: 무슨 말씀이시죠? 그리고 당신은 왜 미소를 지었던 건가요?

➡ _____

35 Michael: 설명해 드릴게요. 저는 천사입니다. 저는 벌을 받아 여기로 보내졌고, 세 가지 진리를 깨달아야 했습니다. 제가 진리를 하나씩 깨달을 때마다 미소를 지었던 것입니다. 저는 세 가지 진리를 모두 깨달았기 때문에 돌아갈 준비를 마쳤습니다.

➡ _____

_____

_____

36 Simon: 그렇군요. 당신이 깨달은 진리는 무엇이었나요?

➡ _____

Scene #6.: 장면 6.

37 Michael은 그가 미소 지었을 때를 회상한다. Simon과 Matrena는 그의 말을 주의 깊게 듣는다.

➡ _____

38 Michael: 첫째, Matrena가 저를 가여워했을 때 인간 내면에 사랑이 존재한다는 것을 저는 깨달았습니다. 이는 '인간 내면에 무엇이 존재하는가'라는 첫 번째 교훈에 관한 답이었던 것입니다. 저는 그 진실을 깨달았기 때문에 미소를 지었습니다. 하지만 저는 아직도 두 가지를 더 알아내야만 했어요.

➡ _____

_____

_____

_____

39 Simon: 그것들은 뭐였나요?

➡ _____

40 Michael: 두 번째는 "인간에게 주어지지 않은 것은 무엇인가"였습니다. 그 귀족이 1년을 신어도 끄떡없는 부츠를 주문했을 때, 저는 그가 곧 죽을 것을 알고 있었습니다. 사람은 자신의 미래에 필요한 것을 알지 못한다는 사실을 그때 저는 깨달았습니다.

➡ _____

_____

_____

41 Simon: 마지막 진리는 무엇이었나요?

➡ _____

42 Michael: 쌍둥이 소녀와 여인의 이야기를 듣고 깨달았습니다. 쌍둥이의 생모가 사망한 후, 그 여인은 그들을 사랑으로 키웠습니다. 그때, 저는 사람은 서로를 향한 참된 사랑으로 산다는 점을 알게 됐습니다. 그것이 '사람은 무엇으로 사는가'에 관한 세 번째 교훈이었습니다.

➡ _____

_____

_____

[01~03] 다음 글을 읽고 물음에 답하시오.

Scene #1.

It's winter. A poor shoe maker, Simon, fails to buy a warm coat. On his way back home, he finds a man, Michael, lying in the street without any clothes.

Simon: ⓐI'm not sure that he is dead or not. But I don't think I can save him because I'm drunk and have little money. (*walking away from Michael at first, but coming back again*) Poor man. Are you okay? Why are you lying here?

Michael: I can't tell you everything. Put simply, I am being punished.

Simon: But it's cold outside. Let's go home together.

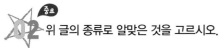

01 위 글의 밑줄 친 ⓐ에서 어법상 틀린 부분을 찾아 고치시오.

➡ _____

02 위 글의 종류로 알맞은 것을 고르시오.

① article   ② play
③ book report   ④ essay
⑤ review

03 According to the passage, which is NOT true?

① Simon is a poor shoe maker.
② Simon doesn't think he can save Michael because he's drunk and has little money.
③ Simon walks away from Michael at first, but comes back again.
④ Michael tells everything to Simon.
⑤ Simon suggests to Michael that they should go home together.

[04~07] 다음 글을 읽고 물음에 답하시오.

Scene #2.

Simon comes home and greets Matrena, his wife. She finds he has brought nothing.

Matrena: (*surprised and angry*) Simon, ①you were supposed to buy a coat for our family. But there's nothing. And who is ②this man?

Simon: I did not have enough money to buy the coat. I'm sorry. And I know nothing about this man. But it wasn't my fault. I had to bring him home. I mean just look at him. Don't you think ③he needs help?

Matrena: (*looking at Michael __ⓐ__ pity*) Okay, Simon.

(*Michael smiles for the first time.*)

For a week, Michael does no work to (A) *support himself.*

Simon: (*looking at Michael*) Michael, I'm afraid you've been doing nothing since you came here. (B)It's time you started to earn a living for yourself. If you work for me, I will give ④you food. Would you like to work with me?

Michael: (__ⓑ__ *a blank face*) Yes, ⑤I would.

04 위 글의 빈칸 ⓐ와 ⓑ에 공통으로 들어갈 전치사를 고르시오.

① for   ② on   ③ at
④ with   ⑤ beyond

05 위 글의 밑줄 친 ①~⑤ 중에서 가리키는 대상이 나머지 넷과 다른 것은?

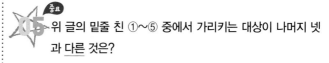

서답형

06 위 글의 밑줄 친 (A)*support himself*와 바꿔 쓸 수 있는 말을 본문에서 찾아 쓰시오. (세 단어)

➡ _____

서답형

07 다음 빈칸에 철자 i로 시작하는 알맞은 부사를 넣어, 위 글의 밑줄 친 문장 (B)의 함축된 의미를 완성하시오.

You should start to earn a living for yourself _____.

[08~10] 다음 글을 읽고 물음에 답하시오.

Scene #3.

A year later, Simon has become famous, thanks to Michael's great skills in making shoes. One day, a nobleman comes to order his boots.

Nobleman: I'd like to order fine leather boots that have to last for a year. (A)I'm not sure whether you can make them. Can you do that?

(Michael watches the man carefully and smiles for the second time.)

Simon: Yes, sir. Don't worry.

(The nobleman leaves the shop.)

Simon: Michael, please make some thick leather boots.

Michael: Okay.

(ⓐ , *Michael makes soft slippers instead of boots.*)

Simon: *(finding the slippers)* Michael! I told you there should be no mistakes. What do you think you are doing?

Servant: *(running into the shop)* Please stop making boots and start making soft slippers for a dead body instead. My master has died of a heart attack.

Simon: *(looking at Michael in surprise)* How did you know?

Michael: Well ...

08 위 글의 빈칸 ⓐ에 들어갈 알맞은 말을 고르시오.

① Moreover   ② Therefore
③ In other words   ④ However
⑤ For example

서답형

09 위 글의 밑줄 친 (A)를 다음과 같이 바꿔 쓸 때 빈칸에 들어갈 알맞은 단어를 쓰시오.

➡ I'm not sure _____ you can make them.

중요

10 위 글의 제목으로 알맞은 것을 고르시오.

① These Boots Must Last for a Year
② Michael's Repeated Mistakes
③ Hey, Why Do You Make Slippers?
④ Sorry, Make Me Slippers, Not Boots
⑤ Michael's Amazing Foresight

[11~13] 다음 글을 읽고 물음에 답하시오.

Scene #4.

A few years later, a woman ___ⓐ___ visits the shoe shop with twin girls.

___ⓐ___ : I'm here to buy some leather shoes for these twin girls.

Simon: *(seeing that one of the girls has a disability)* I'm sorry about your daughter's foot. May I ask you if she was born with a disability?

___ⓐ___ : Oh, I'm not her real mother. Her mother hurt this girl's leg while she was giving birth to her. Their parents are both dead now. I felt sorry for them. ⓑI loved these twins so much that I decided to adopt them.

(Michael smiles for the third time.)

11 위 글의 빈칸 ⓐ에 들어갈 알맞은 말을 고르시오. (대·소문자 무시)

① merchant　　② customer
③ client　　④ hostess
⑤ assistant

서답형
12 위 글의 밑줄 친 ⓑ를 다음과 같이 바꿔 쓸 때 빈칸에 들어갈 알맞은 말을 쓰시오.

➡ I loved these twins _____ much _____ _____ decide to adopt them.

중요
13 Which question CANNOT be answered after reading the passage?

① Why does the woman visit the shoe shop with twin girls?
② Why does one of the twin girls have a disability?
③ Is the woman the twin girls' real mother?
④ Why were the twin girls' parents dead?
⑤ Why did the woman adopt the twin girls?

[14~15] 다음 글을 읽고 물음에 답하시오.

Scene #5.

(Suddenly, a mysterious light shines from Michael.)

Simon: What's this light ⓐ<u>shining</u> from you?

Michael: It's about time I left here.

Simon: What do you mean? And why did you just smile?

Michael: Let me explain. I am an angel. I was sent here as a punishment, and I was supposed to learn three truths. Every time I learned one of them, I smiled.

time I learned one of them, I smiled. Now that I have learned all three of them, I am ready to go back.

Simon: I see. What truths have you learned?

14 위 글의 밑줄 친 ⓐshining과 문법적 쓰임이 <u>다른</u> 것을 고르시오.

① Do you know that boy <u>playing</u> the piano?
② She sat on the bench <u>reading</u> a book.
③ My hobby is <u>listening</u> to music.
④ He kept me <u>waiting</u> all day.
⑤ She isn't <u>listening</u> to music.

중요
15 위 글의 뒤에 올 내용으로 가장 알맞은 것을 고르시오.

① the reason a mysterious light shines from Michael
② the reason Michael smiled
③ the reason Michael is being punished
④ the time Michael has learned three truths
⑤ the truths that Michael has learned

[16~17] 다음 글을 읽고 물음에 답하시오.

Scene #6.

Michael thinks back to each time that he smiled. Simon and Matrena listen carefully to him.

Michael: First, I learned that love dwells in human beings when Matrena pitied me. This was the answer to the first lesson: Learn what dwells in human beings. I smiled because I learned the truth. But I still had two more to figure out.

Simon: What were they?

Michael: The second was, "Learn what is not given to people." When the nobleman ordered that his boots were to last for a year, I knew he would die soon. Then I realized people know little about their own future needs.

Simon: What was the last truth?

Michael: It was from the story of the woman and the twin girls. After the death of their mother, ⓐ그 여인은 그들을 사랑으로 키웠습니다. Then, I learned people live by having true love for each other. That was the third lesson: What people live by.

서답형
16 위 글의 밑줄 친 ⓐ의 우리말에 맞게 주어진 어휘를 알맞게 배열하시오.

> her love / brought / the woman / up / them / with

➡ _____

서답형
17 위 글을 읽고 Michael이 미소를 지은 세 가지 이유를 우리말로 쓰시오.

➡ (1) _____
_____

(2) _____
_____
_____

(3) _____
_____

[18~20] 다음 글을 읽고 물음에 답하시오.

Scene #4.

A few years later, a woman customer visits the shoe shop with twin girls.

Customer: I'm here to buy some leather shoes for these twin girls.

Simon: (*seeing* (A)[*that / whether*] *one of the girls has a disability*) I'm sorry about your daughter's foot. May I ask you ⓐ if she was born with a disability?

Customer: Oh, I'm not her real mother. Her mother hurt this girl's leg (B)[*during / while*] she was giving birth to her. Their parents are both dead now. I felt sorry for them. I loved these twins so much that I decided to (C)[adapt / adopt] them.

(*Michael smiles for the third time.*)

서답형
18 위 글의 괄호 (A)~(C)에서 문맥이나 어법상 알맞은 낱말을 골라 쓰시오.

➡ (A)_____ (B)_____ (C)_____

19 위 글의 밑줄 친 ⓐif와 같은 의미로 쓰인 것을 모두 고르시오.

① I'll only stay if you offer me more money.
② Do you know if he's married?
③ If necessary, I can come at once.
④ You can stay for the weekend if you like.
⑤ I wonder if I should wear a coat.

중요
20 According to the passage, which is NOT true?

① A woman customer visits the shoe shop to buy some leather shoes for the twin girls.
② Simon realizes that one of the girls has a disability.
③ The woman is not the twin girls' real mother.
④ The woman hurt this girl's leg while she was giving birth to her.
⑤ The twin girls' parents are both dead now.

[21~23] 다음 글을 읽고 물음에 답하시오.

Scene #3.

A year later, Simon has become famous, thanks to Michael's great skills in making shoes. One day, a nobleman comes to ⓐorder his boots.

Nobleman: I'd like to order fine leather boots that have to last for a year. I'm not sure whether you can make them. Can you do that?

(Michael watches the man carefully and smiles for the second time.)

Simon: Yes, sir. Don't worry.

(The nobleman leaves the shop.)

Simon: Michael, please make some thick leather boots.

Michael: Okay.

(However, Michael makes soft slippers instead of boots.)

Simon: *(finding the slippers)* Michael! I told you there should be no mistakes. What do you think you are doing?

Servant: *(running into the shop)* ⓑPlease stop to make boots and start making soft slippers for a dead body instead. My master has died of a heart attack.

Simon: *(looking at Michael in surprise)* How did you know?

Michael: Well ⋯

21 위 글의 밑줄 친 ⓐorder와 같은 의미로 쓰인 것을 고르시오.

① The names are listed in alphabetical order.

② He didn't order them to release the prisoner.

③ When did you order the book?

④ The house was kept in good order.

⑤ The general gave the order to advance.

서답형
22 위 글의 밑줄 친 ⓑ에서 어법상 틀린 부분을 찾아 고치시오.

➡ _____

서답형
23 본문의 내용과 일치하도록 다음 빈칸 (A)와 (B)에 알맞은 단어를 쓰시오.

> The nobleman doesn't know he will (A)_____ soon, so he orders fine leather boots that have to last (B)_____ _____ _____.

[24~25] 다음 글을 읽고 물음에 답하시오.

Scene #5.

(Suddenly, a mysterious light shines from Michael.)

Simon: (①) What's this light shining from you?

Michael: (②) It's about time I __ⓐ__ here.

Simon: (③) And why did you just smile?

Michael: (④) Let me explain. (⑤) I am an angel. I was sent here as a punishment, and I was supposed to learn three truths. Every time I learned one of them, I smiled. Now that I have learned all three of them, I am ready to go back.

Simon: I see. What truths have you learned?

서답형
24 위 글의 빈칸 ⓐ에 leave를 알맞은 형태로 쓰시오.

➡ _____

25 위 글의 흐름으로 보아, 주어진 문장이 들어가기에 가장 적절한 곳은?

> What do you mean?

①　　　②　　　③　　　④　　　⑤

[01~03] 다음 글을 읽고 물음에 답하시오.

Scene #1.

It's winter. A poor shoe maker, Simon, fails (A) [to buy / buying] a warm coat. On his way back home, he finds a man, Michael, lying in the street without any (B)[cloths / clothes].

Simon: ⓐ저 남자가 죽은 건지 아닌 건지 모르겠 군. But I don't think I can save him because I'm (C)[drunk / drunken] and have little money. (*walking away from Michael at first, but coming back again*) Poor man. Are you okay? Why are you lying here?

Michael: I can't tell you everything. ⓑPut simply, I am being punished.

Simon: But it's cold outside. Let's go home together.

01 위 글의 괄호 (A)~(C)에서 문맥이나 어법상 알맞은 낱말을 골 라 쓰시오.

➡ (A) _____ (B) _____ (C) _____

02 위 글의 밑줄 친 ⓐ의 우리말에 맞게 주어진 어휘를 이용하 여 9 단어로 영작하시오.

sure, whether, not

➡ _____

03 위 글의 밑줄 친 ⓑ를 다음과 같이 바꿔 쓸 때 빈칸에 들어 갈 알맞은 말을 두 단어로 쓰시오.

➡ _____ _____ it simply

[04~06] 다음 글을 읽고 물음에 답하시오.

Scene #2.

Simon comes home and greets Matrena, his wife. She finds he has brought nothing.

Matrena: (*surprised and angry*) Simon, you were supposed to buy a coat for our family. But there's nothing. And who is this man?

Simon: I did not have enough money to buy the coat. I'm sorry. And I know nothing about this man. But it wasn't my fault. I had to bring him home. I mean just look at him. Don't you think he needs help?

Matrena: (*looking at Michael with pity*) Okay, Simon.

(Michael smiles for the first time.)

For a week, Michael does no work to support himself.

Simon: (*looking at Michael*) Michael, I'm afraid you _____ⓐ_____ nothing since you came here. ⓑIt's time you started to earn a living for yourself. If you work for me, I will give you food. Would you like to work with me?

Michael: (*with a blank face*) Yes, I would.

04 위 글의 빈칸 ⓐ에 do를 알맞은 형태로 쓰시오. (3 단어)

➡ _____

05 위 글의 밑줄 친 ⓑ를 다음과 같이 바꿔 쓸 때 빈칸에 들어갈 알맞은 말을 (1)에는 한 단어로, (2)에는 두 단어로 쓰시오.

➡ (1) It's time you _____ start to earn a living for yourself.
(2) It's time for you _____ _____ to earn a living for yourself.

06 본문의 내용과 일치하도록 다음 빈칸에 들어갈 알맞은 단어를 본문에서 찾아 쓰시오.

> Matrena allows Michael to stay at her house because she feels _____ for him.

[07~09] 다음 글을 읽고 물음에 답하시오.

Scene #4.

A few years later, a woman customer visits the shoe shop with twin girls.

Customer: (A)이 쌍둥이 소녀들에게 신길 가죽 신발을 사러 왔습니다.

Simon: (*seeing that one of the girls has a disability*) I'm sorry about your daughter's foot. May I ask you if she was born with a disability?

Customer: Oh, I'm not her real mother. Her mother hurt this girl's leg while she was giving birth to her. Their parents are both dead now. I felt sorry for them. I loved these twins so much that I decided to ⓐ_____ them.

(*Michael smiles for the third time.*)

07 주어진 영영풀이를 참고하여 빈칸 ⓐ에 철자 a로 시작하는 단어를 쓰시오.

> to legally take another person's child into your own family and take care of him or her as your own child

➡ _____

08 위 글의 밑줄 친 (A)의 우리말에 맞게 주어진 어휘를 알맞게 배열하시오.

> to buy / these twin girls / here / for / I'm / some leather shoes

➡ _____

09 본문의 내용과 일치하도록 다음 빈칸 (A)와 (B)에 알맞은 단어를 쓰시오.

> One of the twin girls has a (A)_____ because her mother hurt the girl's leg while she was (B)_____ _____ _____ her.

[10~11] 다음 글을 읽고 물음에 답하시오.

Scene #5.

(Suddenly, a mysterious light shines from Michael.)

Simon: What's this light shining from you?

Michael: It's ⓐabout time I left here.

Simon: What do you mean? And why did you just smile?

Michael: Let me explain. I am an angel. I was sent here as a punishment, and I was supposed to learn three truths. Every time I learned one of them, I smiled. Now that I have learned all three of them, I am ready to go back.

Simon: I see. What truths have you learned?

10 위 글의 밑줄 친 ⓐabout과 바꿔 쓸 수 있는 한 단어를 쓰시오.

➡ _____

11 다음 빈칸 (A)와 (B)에 알맞은 단어를 넣어 Michael에 대한 소개를 완성하시오.

> Michael is an angel who was sent here as (A)_____ _____. Every time he learned one of (B)_____ _____ that he was supposed to learn, he smiled. Since he has learned all three of them, he is ready to go back.

구석구석

After You Read A

I did not have enough money to buy the coat. I'm sorry.
enough+명사+to부정사: ~할 만큼 충분한 …

And I know nothing about this man. But it wasn't my fault. I had to bring him
= I don't know anything about this man.

home. I mean just look at him! Don't you think he needs help?

→ He looked so pitiful that I couldn't help giving him some help.
so+형용사+that+주어+cannot: 너무 ~해서 …하다   cannot help V-ing ~하지 않을 수 없다

After You Read B

1. Michael was supposed to learn three truths as a punishment.
~으로

2. When Matrena lets Michael stay in her home, he learns that love dwells in
사역동사 let+목적어+원형부정사

human beings.

3. The nobleman orders fine leather boots that have to last for a year.
주격 관계대명사

4. The servant of the nobleman said, "Please stop making boots and start
stop ~ing: ~하기를 그만두다

making soft slippers for a dead body instead. My master has died of a heart
= to make   die of: ~로 죽다

attack."

5. The woman adopted the twin girls, one of whom was disabled.
= and one of them   were(×)

구문해설 · punishment: 벌 · dwell: 거주하다 · nobleman: 귀족 · leather: 가죽 · servant: 하인
· master: 주인 · heart attack: 심장마비 · adopt: 입양하다

Check Your Progress 1

B: Jina, did you hand in your English homework?
제출하다

G: No, I didn't.

B: Why? You're supposed to hand it in today.
~해야 한다, ~하기로 되어 있다

G: It was all my fault. I completed my homework. But just before I was going
완성했다

to save it, the computer broke down.
저장하다   고장 났다

B: What a pity! If I were you, I would tell the teacher why you couldn't hand
불쌍해라!   가정법 과거 If I were you. I would ~.

it in.

G: Yeah, I agree. But I think I'd better do it again as soon as possible.
had better의 줄임말   가능한 한 빨리

B: Can I give you a hand with that?
give+간접목적어(~에게)+a hand ~에게 도움을 주다

G: How kind of you! I'll call you if I need your help.

나는 코트를 살 정도로 충분한 돈이 없었어요. 미안해요. 그리고 이 남자에 관해서는 아무것도 몰라요. 하지만 내 잘못은 아니에요. 나는 이 남자를 집에 데려와야만 했어요. 내 말은, 이 남자를 보세요! 도움이 필요해 보이지 않나요?
→ 그가 너무 불쌍해 보여서 그에게 도움을 주지 않을 수 없었다.

1. Michael은 벌로 세 가지 진리를 깨달아야 했다.
2. Matrena가 Michael을 그녀의 집에 머물게 허락할 때, 그는 인간 내면에 사랑이 존재한다는 것을 깨닫는다.
3. 귀족은 1년을 신어도 끄떡없는 튼튼한 가죽 부츠를 주문한다.
4. 귀족의 하인이 말했다. "부츠는 그만 만들고 대신 죽은 사람에게 신길 부드러운 슬리퍼를 만들어 주세요. 나리가 심장마비로 돌아가셨습니다."
5. 그 여인은 쌍둥이 소녀들을 입양했는데, 그들 중 한 명은 장애가 있었다.

B: Jina야, 너 영어 숙제 제출했니?
G: 아니, 안 냈어.
B: 왜? 오늘까지 내야 하잖아.
G: 다 내 잘못이야. 숙제는 다 했어. 하지만 내가 그걸 저장하기 바로 전에 컴퓨터가 고장나 버렸어.
B: 불쌍해라! 내가 너라면, 선생님께 왜 숙제를 제출 못 했는지 말씀 드릴 거야.
G: 응, 나도 그렇게 생각해. 그렇지만 최대한 빨리 다시 하는 게 더 낫다는 생각이 들어.
B: 내가 좀 도와줄까?
G: 정말 친절하구나! 도움이 필요하면 전화할게.

Words & Expressions

01 다음 짝지어진 단어의 관계가 같도록 빈칸에 알맞은 말을 쓰시오.

> dwell : reside = hurry : _____

02 다음 중 밑줄 친 부분의 뜻풀이가 바르지 않은 것은?

① He stubbornly refuses to admit the truth.
(진실, 진리)

② James left the room abruptly without explanation. (~ 없이)

③ A sudden shower of rain soaked the audiences. (갑작스러운)

④ Have you ever read her new novel? (소설)

⑤ We should try to save water for the future generation. (구하다)

03 다음 주어진 문장의 밑줄 친 cross와 같은 의미로 쓰인 것은?

> Children's lives are in danger every time they cross this road.

① Jane was cross with him for being late.

② You can hold my hand while we cross the road.

③ The cross marks the spot where the gold was found.

④ You had better cross her name off the list.

⑤ A mule is a cross between a horse and a donkey.

04 다음 우리말을 주어진 어구를 이용하여 영작하시오.

> 멀리서 우리는 바다를 처음으로 보았다.
> (ocean, for the first time)

➡ _____

05 다음 영영풀이에 해당하는 단어로 알맞은 것은?

> a mistake, especially something for which you are to blame

① fault   ② truth   ③ novel
④ mess   ⑤ volunteer

Conversation

06 다음 대화의 빈칸에 들어갈 말로 가장 적절한 것은?

> A: I didn't bring my textbook.
> B: Was it your fault?
> A: No, _____. The teacher said we don't need it today.

① it is my fault

② it was my fault

③ it isn't my fault

④ it will be my fault

⑤ it wasn't my fault

[07~09] 다음 대화를 읽고 물음에 답하시오.

B: Jina, did you hand in your English homework?

G: No, I didn't.

B: Why? You're supposed to (A)[hand it in/hand in it] today.

G: It was all my fault. I completed my homework. But just before I was going to save it, the computer broke down.

B: What a pity! If I were you, I (B)[would tell/told] the teacher why you couldn't hand it in.

G: Yeah, I agree. But I think I'd better do it again as soon as possible.

B: Can I give you a (a)hand with that?

G: (C)[How kind/What kind] of you! I'll call you if I need your help.

07 위 대화의 (A)~(C)에 알맞은 말이 바르게 짝지어진 것은?

	(A)	(B)	(C)
①	hand it in	told	How kind
②	hand it in	would tell	What kind
③	hand it in	would tell	How kind
④	hand in it	would tell	What kind
⑤	hand in it	told	How kind

08 위 대화의 밑줄 친 (a)hand와 같은 의미로 쓰인 것은?

① Let me give you a hand with those bags.

② She weighed the stone in her hand.

③ Could you hand these books out, please?

④ Put your hand up if you know the answer.

⑤ The fabric was painted by hand.

09 위 대화의 내용과 일치하지 않는 것은?

① Jina did not submit her homework.

② Jina could not save her homework file.

③ Jina did not tell the teacher why she did not hand in her homework.

④ Jina refuses to get help from her friend.

⑤ Jina is going to do her homework again.

[10~12] 다음 글을 읽고 물음에 답하시오.

W: Thank you for watching "Play World." Are you looking forward to this month's play? This month's play is *Hamlet*. ① There are two interesting points about this play. ② It has changed the costumes and the dead language of the 16th century that most of today's audiences might feel uncomfortable with. ③ Second, the famous actor, Park Mujin, appears in this play. ④ His performance shows a deep understanding of the main character, Hamlet. ⑤ Please bear in mind that you will need to book your ticket online. It won't be your fault if you miss this play. (A)그러나 그것을 놓친 걸 분명 후회하실 겁니다.

10 위 글의 ①~⑤ 중에서 주어진 문장이 들어가기에 가장 적절한 곳은?

> First, it is a 21st century version of Shakespeare's *Hamlet*.

①　　②　　③　　④　　⑤

11 위 글의 밑줄 친 (A)의 우리말을 영작하시오. (6 words)

➡ _____

12 다음 중 위 글의 목적으로 가장 적절한 것은?

① to celebrate　　② to explain

③ to criticize　　④ to promote

⑤ to encourage

Grammar

13 각 문장의 밑줄 친 단어의 뜻으로 알맞은 것을 고르시오.

> a. ~번　　b. ~할 때　　c. 시간

(1) It's time to try your new bike.

　➡ _____

(2) It's time to go now. ➡ _____

(3) It's about time the 9:00 bus came.

　➡ _____

(4) She trained five times a week at her local swimming pool. ➡ _____

(5) I missed the bus two times in a row today. ➡ _____

(6) It's time you grew up. ➡ _____

14 다음 중 어법상 어색한 것을 고르시오.

① It is time you learned it.

② It's time that you went to bed.

③ It's about time that we looked at the point of the matter.

④ It's about time you've gone.

⑤ It's time that we picked up the pieces and make a fresh, new start.

15 주어진 〈조건〉과 괄호 안의 단어를 활용하여 우리말에 맞게 빈칸을 채우시오.

(1) 〈조건〉 'It's time that ~' 구문 활용

> Your room is so messy. _____
> _____ (clean up)
> → 네 방은 너무 지저분해. 청소를 해야 할 때야.

(2) 〈조건〉 'It's time for ~ to ...' 구문 활용

> She has a test tomorrow. _____
> _____ (study)
> → 그녀는 내일 시험이 있다. 그녀가 열심히 공부해야 할 시간이다.

16 괄호 안의 어휘를 활용하여 우리말에 맞도록 영작하시오.

> 네가 멋진 발표를 할 수 있을지 모르겠어.
> (whether, sure, nice presentation, 10 단어)

➡ _____

17 다음 밑줄 친 ①~⑤ 중 어색한 부분을 고르시오.

> I'm ①not ②sure ③if ③to ④get ⑤a new laptop.

①　　②　　③　　④　　⑤

18 빈칸에 들어갈 말로 적절한 것을 모두 고르시오.

> Let me know _____ you will take the subway or not.

① that　　② whether　　③ if

④ what　　⑤ why

19 다음 문장에서 어법상 <u>어색한</u> 것을 골라 바르게 고쳐 쓰시오.

> I'm not sure if to buy a new house or not.

➡ _____

20 괄호 안의 단어를 활용하여 우리말에 맞게 영작하시오.

> 그녀가 화가 났는지 아닌지 알고 싶다. (want, whether)

➡ _____

21 빈칸에 공통으로 들어갈 말을 고르시오.

> • I can't decide _____ to paint the wall green or blue.
> • She didn't know _____ she was laughing or crying.

① that   ② whether   ③ if
④ what   ⑤ why

22 괄호 안의 어구를 사용하여 영작하시오.

> 그녀는 그 일을 승낙해야 할지 말아야 할지를 결정해야만 한다. (accept, going to, has, job, whether)

➡ _____

23 빈칸에 공통으로 들어갈 말을 <u>모두</u> 고르시오.

> • I was just wondering _____ you had any time to grab a coffee with me.
> • I don't know _____ he is Korean.

① that   ② whether   ③ if
④ what   ⑤ why

Reading

[24~26] 다음 글을 읽고 물음에 답하시오.

(A)[Scene / Scenery] #1.

It's winter. A poor (B)[*shoe / shoes*] *maker, Simon, fails to buy a warm coat. On his way back home, he finds a man, Michael,* (C)[*laying / lying*] *in the street without any clothes.*

Simon: I'm not sure whether he is dead or not. But I don't think I can ⓐsave him because I'm drunk and have little money. (*walking away from Michael at first, but coming back again*) Poor man. Are you okay? Why are you lying here?

Michael: I can't tell you everything. Put simply, I am being punished.

Simon: ⓑBut it's cold outside. Let's go home together.

24 위 글의 밑줄 친 ⓐsave와 같은 의미로 쓰인 것을 고르시오.

① You should save a little each week for a new bike.
② Save some food for me.
③ He tried to save a rare species from extinction.
④ You should save data frequently.
⑤ We'll take a taxi to save time.

25 위 글의 괄호 (A)~(C)에서 문맥이나 어법상 알맞은 낱말을 골라 쓰시오.

➡ (A) _____ (B) _____ (C) _____

26 위 글의 마지막 부분 ⓑ에서 알 수 있는 'Simon'의 성격으로 알맞은 것을 **모두** 고르시오.

① merciless ② charitable

③ harsh ④ warm-hearted

⑤ humane

[27~29] 다음 글을 읽고 물음에 답하시오.

Scene #3.

A year later, Simon has become famous, thanks to Michael's great skills in making shoes. One day, a nobleman comes to order his boots.

Nobleman: I'd like to order fine leather boots that have to last for a year. I'm not sure whether you can make (A)them. Can you do that?

(*Michael watches the man carefully and smiles for the second time.*)

Simon: Yes, sir. Don't worry.

(*The nobleman leaves the shop.*)

Simon: Michael, please make some thick leather boots.

Michael: Okay.

(*However, Michael makes soft slippers instead of boots.*)

Simon: (*finding the slippers*) Michael! (B)I told you there should be no mistakes. What do you think you are doing?

Servant: (*running into the shop*) Please stop making boots and start making soft slippers for a dead body instead. My master has died ___ⓐ___ a heart attack.

Simon: (*looking at Michael ___ⓑ___ surprise*) How did you know?

Michael: Well ...

27 위 글의 빈칸 ⓐ와 ⓑ에 들어갈 전치사가 바르게 짝지어진 것은?

　　ⓐ　ⓑ　　　　　　ⓐ　ⓑ
① of – in ② from – by

③ from – at ④ of – at

⑤ for – in

28 위 글의 밑줄 친 (A)them이 가리키는 것을 본문에서 찾아 쓰시오.

➡ _____

29 다음 빈칸 (A)와 (B)에 알맞은 단어를 넣어, 위 글의 밑줄 친 문장 (B)의 함축된 의미를 완성하시오.

You should have made (A)_____ _____ _____ _____ instead of (B)_____ _____.

30 주어진 문장 다음에 이어질 글의 순서로 가장 적절한 것은?

First, I learned that love dwells in human beings when Matrena pitied me.

(A) I smiled because I learned the truth.

(B) But I still had two more to figure out.

(C) This was the answer to the first lesson: Learn what dwells in human beings.

① (A)–(C)–(B) ② (B)–(A)–(C)

③ (B)–(C)–(A) ④ (C)–(A)–(B)

⑤ (C)–(B)–(A)

01 다음 영영풀이가 가리키는 것을 고르시오. *출제율 90%*

> a piece of information that is only known by one person or a few people and should not be told to others

① argument　　② advice
③ secret　　④ report
⑤ punishment

02 〈보기〉에서 알맞은 어구를 골라 문장을 완성하시오. *출제율 100%*

> ─ 보기 ─
> in advance / thanks to / give birth to / die of / one day

(1) Emma will _____ a baby next spring.
(2) Many people mostly _____ malaria in some countries.
(3) It's much cheaper if you book the tickets _____.

[03~04] 다음 대화를 읽고 물음에 답하시오.

G: My dog got sick this morning. I'm so worried about him.
B: What did you feed him yesterday? ①
G: I gave him some milk last night. ②
B: Oh, you should not feed a dog milk. ③
G: (a)그가 우유를 마시는 게 안전한지 아닌지 난 확신하지 못했어. (to drink milk / whether or not / not sure / I / for him / was / it / safe / is) It was all my fault.
B: Don't worry too much. ④ Did you take him to the animal doctor?
G: Yes, I did. ⑤
B: He'll certainly get better with your care and love.

03 위 대화의 ①~⑤ 중 주어진 문장이 들어가기에 가장 적절한 곳은? *출제율 100%*

> I hope he'll get better soon.

①　　②　　③　　④　　⑤

04 위 대화의 밑줄 친 (a)의 우리말에 맞게 주어진 어구를 나열하시오. *출제율 95%*

➡ _____

_____

[05~06] 다음 대화를 읽고 물음에 답하시오.

A: (A)건강을 유지하기 위해서는 무엇이 중요하다고 생각하니?
B: I think healthy eating is important.
A: How can I put that idea into practice? Any suggestions?
B: You _____(B)_____ eat a lot of fruits and vegetables.

05 위 대화의 밑줄 친 (A)의 우리말에 맞게 영작한 것을 고르시오. *출제율 95%*

① Do you think what is important for staying healthy?
② Do you think what important is for staying healthy?
③ What did you think is important for staying healthy?
④ What do you think was important for staying healthy?
⑤ What do you think is important for staying healthy?

06 위 대화의 빈칸 (B)에 들어갈 말로 적절하지 <u>않은</u> 것은?

① would
② ought to
③ have to
④ should
⑤ are supposed to

[07~08] 다음 대화를 읽고 물음에 답하시오.

A: How can I make my parents pleased?
B: (A)넌 아침에 침대를 정리해야 돼. (suppose, make your bed)
A: Why will that make them happy?
B: That's ____(B)____ your parents will be very proud of you for doing a job on your own.

07 위 대화의 밑줄 친 (A)를 주어진 어구를 이용해 영어로 옮기시오.

➡ _____

_____

08 위 대화의 빈칸 (B)에 들어갈 말로 적절한 것은?

① even though
② whether
③ in spite of
④ because
⑤ in addition

09 다음 중 짝지어진 대화가 <u>어색한</u> 것을 고르시오.

① A: I got up late this morning.
   B: Was it your fault?
② A: I'm late for school.
   B: You're supposed to be on time.
③ A: What is important for staying healthy?
   B: You have to sleep for about 8 hours.
④ A: Our team lost by one point.
   B: It's not your fault. We did our best.

⑤ A: Do you want to win the race?
   B: In order to win the race, you must not give up.

10 괄호 안의 단어를 활용하여 빈칸에 들어갈 말을 쓰시오.

It's time that we _____(take) every step to prevent global warming.

11 다음 문장을 어법에 맞게 고치시오.

> I don't know if to buy the blue one or the red one.

➡ _____

_____

12 if를 사용하여 밑줄 친 우리말을 바르게 영작하시오.

> <u>내가 운전을 할 수 있을지 모르겠다.</u> My foot really hurts.

➡ _____

13 다음 빈칸에 들어갈 말로 알맞은 것을 <u>모두</u> 고르시오.

> A: Mom, my jeans wore out.
> B: It's high time I _____ a new pair of jeans.

① should buy
② bought
③ will buy
④ have bought
⑤ to buy

14 다음 빈칸에 들어갈 말로 적절한 것을 고르시오.

> _____ They've been working on it for months.

① It's about time this road was completed.

② It's about time our team won.

③ I'm not certain whether I'll go to hospital.

④ It's about time she got a job.

⑤ It's time you started to earn a living for yourself.

[15~17] 다음 글을 읽고 물음에 답하시오.

Scene #2.

Simon comes home and greets Matrena, his wife. She finds he has brought nothing.

Matrena: (*surprised and angry*) Simon, you were supposed to buy a coat for our family. But there's nothing. And who is this man?

Simon: I did not have enough money to buy the coat. I'm sorry. And I know nothing about this man. But it wasn't my fault. I had to bring him home. I mean just look at him. Don't you think he needs help?

Matrena: (A)(*looking at Michael with pity*) Okay, Simon.

(*Michael smiles for the first time.*)

For a week, Michael does no work to support himself.

Simon: (*looking at Michael*) Michael, I'm afraid you've been doing nothing since you came here. It's time you started to earn a living for yourself. If you work for me, I will give you food. Would you like to work with me?

Michael: (*with a ___ⓐ___ face*) Yes, I would.

15 주어진 영영풀이를 참고하여 빈칸 ⓐ에 철자 b로 시작하는 단어를 쓰시오.

> void of expression

➡ _____

16 위 글의 밑줄 친 (A)에서 알 수 있는 'Matrena'의 성격으로 알맞지 않은 것을 모두 고르시오.

① sympathetic ② cold-blooded

③ cruel ④ compassionate

⑤ arrogant

17 According to the passage, which is NOT true?

① When Matrena finds Simon has brought nothing, she is surprised and angry.

② Simon tells Matrena that he knows nothing about Michael.

③ Matrena agrees that Michael needs help.

④ Simon has been doing nothing since he brought Michael home.

⑤ Michael would like to work with Simon.

[18~19] 다음 글을 읽고 물음에 답하시오.

Scene #6.

Michael thinks back to each time that he smiled. Simon and Matrena listen carefully to him.

Michael: First, I learned that love dwells in human beings when Matrena pitied me. This was the answer to the first lesson: Learn what dwells in human beings. I smiled because I learned the truth. But I still had two more ⓐto figure out.

Simon: What were they?

Michael: The second was, "Learn what is not given to people." When the nobleman ordered that his boots were to last for a year, I knew he would die soon. Then I realized people know little about their own future needs.

Simon: What was the last truth?

Michael: It was from the story of the woman and the twin girls. After the death of their mother, the woman brought them up with her love. Then, I learned people live by having true love for each other. That was the third lesson: What people live by.

출제율 95%

18 아래 〈보기〉에서 위 글의 밑줄 친 ⓐto figure와 to부정사의 용법이 같은 것의 개수를 고르시오.

┌─ 보기 ─┐
① I think it wrong to tell a lie.
② He has many children to look after.
③ I don't know what to do.
④ He awoke to find himself famous.
⑤ Please give me something cold to drink.
└─────┘

① 1개   ② 2개   ③ 3개   ④ 4개   ⑤ 5개

출제율 90%

19 What lesson did Michael learn? Fill in the blanks (A)~(C) with suitable words.

┌─────────────────────┐
The first lesson Michael learned is that (A)_____ dwells in human beings. The second lesson Michael learned is that people know little about (B)_____ _____ _____ _____ . The last lesson Michael learned is that people live by (C)_____ _____ _____ for each other.
└─────────────────────┘

[20~21] 다음 글을 읽고 물음에 답하시오.

TITLE: *What People Live By*

WRITER: Leo Tolstoy

One day, Simon found Michael lying in the street. Simon was not sure whether Michael was dead or not. When Simon took him home, Simon's wife pitied him. Then Michael smiled, as he learned the first lesson: Love dwells in human beings.

A year later, a nobleman asked whether Michael can make some leather boots or not. Michael smiled again because he learned the second lesson: People know little about their own future.

A few years later, a woman who had adopted twin girls visited the shop. Then Michael smiled for the third time because he learned the final lesson: People live by love. As soon as he learned it, he was ready to leave, saying, "It's time I left here."

This book made me think about what people live by. The writer thinks people live by love, but I want to figure out some of the other factors that people live by.

출제율 100%

20 위 글의 종류로 알맞은 것을 고르시오.

① biography   ② diary
③ book report   ④ article
⑤ essay

출제율 95%

21 위 글을 읽고 알 수 <u>없는</u> 것을 고르시오.

① 제목   ② 저자
③ 등장인물   ④ 줄거리
⑤ Michael이 돌아갈 곳

[01~02] 다음 대화를 읽고 물음에 답하시오.

> (*Phone rings.*)
> W: Hello, this is the shoe shop. __(A)__ may I help you?
> M: I have a problem with the boots that I bought there yesterday.
> W: What's the problem with them?
> M: They're a bit dirty. (B)그렇지만 제 잘못은 아니에요. I've never worn them.
> W: Sorry about that. Please visit our shop this week.

01 위 대화의 빈칸 (A)에 알맞은 단어를 쓰시오.

➡ _____

02 위 대화의 밑줄 친 (B)의 우리말을 바르게 영작하시오. (6 words)

➡ _____

[03~04] 다음 대화를 읽고 물음에 답하시오.

> M: Something amazing happened. The tortoise won the race. Congratulations!
> W: Thank you.
> M: How could you win the race?
> W: I didn't give up. In order to win the race, you must not give up.

03 Who won the race? (5 words)

➡ _____

04 What is the reason for the win? (7 words)

➡ _____

05 다음 문장에서 어법상 어색한 부분을 찾아 바르게 고쳐 쓰시오. 없으면 〈없음〉이라고 쓰시오.

(1) I don't like traffic jam! It's high time we arriving at home.

➡ _____
_____

(2) It's time for breakfast.

➡ _____

(3) It's time of us to be on our way.

➡ _____

06 다음 문장의 괄호 안의 단어를 활용하여 주어진 단어 수대로 빈칸을 채우시오.

(1) 이것이 단수 명사인지 아닌지 아세요? (know, 6 단어)

➡ _____
a singular noun or not?

(2) 네가 정답을 알아맞혔는지 확인해 봐. (if, get, 6 단어)

➡ Check _____.

(3) 내일 날씨가 따뜻할지 아닐지 확실하지 않다. (whether, warmer, 5 단어)

➡ I'm not certain _____
_____ or not.

[07~08] 다음 글을 읽고 물음에 답하시오.

> Scene #3.
> *A year later, Simon has become famous, thanks to Michael's great skills in making shoes. One day, a nobleman comes to order his boots.*
> Nobleman: I'd like to order fine leather boots that have to last for a year. I'm not sure whether you can make them. Can you ⓐdo that?

(*Michael watches the man carefully and smiles for the second time.*)

Simon: Yes, sir. Don't worry.

(*The nobleman leaves the shop.*)

Simon: Michael, please make some thick leather boots.

Michael: Okay.

(*However, Michael makes soft slippers instead of boots.*)

Simon: (*finding the slippers*) Michael! ⓑ제가 실수하지 말라고 했잖아요. What do you think you are doing?

Servant: (*running into the shop*) Please stop making boots and start making soft slippers for a dead body instead. My master has died of a heart attack.

Simon: (*looking at Michael in surprise*) How did you know?

Michael: Well ...

07 위 글의 밑줄 친 ⓐdo that이 가리키는 것을 본문에서 찾아 쓰시오. (11 단어)

➡ _____

_____

08 위 글의 밑줄 친 ⓑ의 우리말에 맞게 주어진 어휘를 이용하여 8 단어로 영작하시오.

there, should, no

➡ _____

[09~11] 다음 글을 읽고 물음에 답하시오.

Scene #6.

Michael thinks back to each time that he smiled. Simon and Matrena listen carefully to him.

Michael: First, I learned that love dwells in human beings when Matrena pitied me. This was the answer to the first lesson: Learn ⓐ dwells in human beings. I smiled because I learned the truth. But I still had two more to figure out.

Simon: What were (A)they?

Michael: The second was, "Learn ⓑ is not given to people." When the nobleman ordered that his boots were to last for a year, I knew he would die soon. Then I realized people know little about their own future needs.

Simon: What was the last truth?

Michael: It was from the story of the woman and the twin girls. After the death of their mother, the woman brought them up with her love. Then, I learned people live by having true love for each other. That was the third lesson: What people live by.

09 위 글의 빈칸 ⓐ와 ⓑ에 공통으로 알맞은 한 단어를 쓰시오.

➡ _____

10 위 글의 밑줄 친 (A)they가 가리키는 것을 영어로 쓰시오.

➡ _____

11 Michael이 깨달아야 했던 세 가지 진리를 우리말로 쓰시오.

➡ (1) _____

(2) _____

(3) _____

01 주어진 표현을 이용하여 〈보기〉와 같이 다음 대화의 빈칸에 알맞은 말을 쓰시오.

> A: I'm late for school.
> B: You're supposed to be on time.

┤ 보기 ├

> A: My room is so dirty that I couldn't even step in.
> B: You _____ .

> had better / should / ought to / have to / must / are supposed to
> clean your room / try not to make a mess / clear it up regularly

02 다음 내용을 바탕으로 독후감을 완성하시오.

> • Title: *What People Live By*
> • Writer: Leo Tolstoy
> • Main Character: Simon and Michael
> • The plot of the novel: When Simon found Michael lying in the street, he took Michael home and Simon's wife pitied Michael. A year later, a nobleman asked whether Michael can make some leather boots or not. A few years later, a woman who had adopted twin girls visited the shop. As soon as Michael learned three truths, he was ready to leave, saying, "It's time I left here."
> • Lesson: The first lesson: Love dwells in human beings. The second lesson: People know little about their own future. The final lesson: People live by love.

> TITLE: (A)_____ WRITER: (B)_____
>   One day, Simon found Michael lying in the street. Simon was not sure whether Michael was dead or not. When Simon took him home, (C)_____ pitied him. Then Michael smiled, as he learned the first lesson: (D)_____ dwells in human beings.
>   A year later, a nobleman asked whether Michael can make (E)_____ or not. Michael smiled again because he learned the second lesson: People know little about (F)_____ .
>   A few years later, a woman who (G)_____ visited the shop. Then Michael smiled for the third time because he learned the final lesson: People live by (H)_____ . As soon as he learned it, he was ready to leave, saying, "It's time I left here."
>   This book made me think about what people live by. The writer thinks people live by love, but I want to figure out some of the other factors that people live by.

단원별 모의고사

01 다음 영영풀이가 가리키는 것은?

> the things you must have for a satisfactory life

① needs   ② pity
③ leather   ④ fault
⑤ discount

02 다음 빈칸에 알맞은 단어를 고르시오.

> I try to protect the environment by using a tumbler _____ a paper cup.

① even if   ② in spite of
③ as if   ④ because of
⑤ instead of

03 다음 우리말에 맞게 빈칸에 알맞은 말을 쓰시오. (two words)

> 이제 애들이 집을 떠나서 우리는 여분의 공간이 많아졌다.
> ➡ _____ the kids have left home, we've got a lot of extra space.

[04~06] 다음 대화를 읽고 물음에 답하시오.

Inho: Lina, you look so ⓐdepressed. What's the matter?
Lina: Oh, Inho. I had an argument with Ryan.
Inho: Was it your fault?
Lina: No, it ⓑisn't my fault! There ⓒwas just a misunderstanding between us.
Inho: In that case, you're supposed to make up with him as soon as possible.
Lina: Well, (A)Ryan은 너무 화가 나서 나랑 이야기하려고 하지 않을 거야.
Inho: But who ⓓknows? He might regret it now, just like you.

Lina: Do you think so?
Inho: Yes, everyone wants to maintain good friendships.
Lina: Thanks for your advice. I hope I ⓔcan make up with him soon.

04 위 대화의 밑줄 친 ⓐ~ⓔ 중 어법상 어색한 것은?

① ⓐ   ② ⓑ   ③ ⓒ   ④ ⓓ   ⑤ ⓔ

05 위 대화의 밑줄 친 (A)의 우리말을 바르게 영작하시오.

➡ _____

06 위 대화에 나타난 Lina의 심경 변화로 가장 적절한 것을 고르시오.

① pleased → angry
② impressed → indifferent
③ worried → hopeful
④ tired → satisfied
⑤ surprised → moved

[07~09] 다음 글을 읽고 물음에 답하시오.

W: Thank you for watching "Play World." Are you looking forward to this month's play? This month's play is *Hamlet*. There are two interesting points about this play. (A)첫째로, it is a 21st century version of Shakespeare's *Hamlet*. It has changed the costumes and the dead language of the 16th century that most of today's audiences might feel uncomfortable with. (B)둘째로, the famous actor, Park Mujin, appears in this play. His performance shows a deep understanding of the main character, Hamlet. Please bear in mind that (a)온라인으로 티켓을 예매하셔야 할 것입니다. It won't be your fault if you miss this play. But you'll (C)분명히 regret missing it.

07 위 글의 밑줄 친 (A)~(C)를 영어로 쓰시오.

➡ (A) _____

(B) _____

(C) _____

08 위 글의 밑줄 친 (a)를 영작한 것으로 적절한 것은? (정답 2개)

① You will need to book your ticket online

② You needed to book your ticket online

③ You will book your ticket online

④ You will have to book your ticket online

⑤ You have to book your ticket online

09 다음 중 위 글의 내용과 일치하지 않는 것은?

① This mouth's play is 21st version of the original play.

② This mouth's play has changed the costumes and the old languages.

③ Most of today's audiences might feel uncomfortable with the old version.

④ The famous actor is going to appear in the play.

⑤ Tickets can be purchased online and offline in advance.

[10~12] 다음 대화를 읽고 물음에 답하시오.

B: Jina, did you hand in your English homework?

G: No, I didn't.

B: Why? (A)너 오늘 그것을 제출해야 돼.

G: (B)It was all my fault. I completed my homework. But just before I was going to save it, the computer broke down.

B: What a pity! If I were you, (C)나는 선생님께 네가 왜 제출할 수 없었는지 말씀드릴 거야. (hand it in / why / I / the teacher / would tell / couldn't / you)

G: Yeah, I agree. But I think I'd better do it again as soon as possible.

B: Can I give you a hand with that?

G: How kind of you! I'll call you if I need your help.

10 위 대화의 밑줄 친 (A)를 영작한 것으로 적절하지 않은 것은?

① You're supposed to hand it in today.

② You ought to hand it in today.

③ You could hand it in today.

④ You have to hand it in today.

⑤ You had better hand it in today.

11 위 대화의 밑줄 친 (B)의 의도로 가장 적절한 것은?

① 의무 표현하기　　② 감정 표현하기

③ 감사 표현하기　　④ 물건 추천하기

⑤ 잘못 인정하기

12 위 대화의 밑줄 친 (C)의 우리말에 맞게 주어진 어구를 나열하시오.

➡ _____

_____

13 다음 우리말에 맞게 영작할 때 빈칸에 들어갈 알맞은 접속사를 고르시오.

선생님은 학급에 그 책을 추천할지를 물어볼 것이다.

→ The teachers will ask _____ they would recommend the book to their classes.

① when　　　　② what

③ whether　　　④ why

⑤ that

14 우리말을 바르게 영작한 것을 고르시오.

> 네가 좋은 사람인지 나쁜 사람인지 잘 모르겠다.

① I don't know whether you're good or bad.
② I'm sure you are good.
③ I'm not sure if you have a good relationship.
④ I don't know whether you have a good position or not.
⑤ I'm not sure whether you're right or not.

15 다음은 '애완동물을 위한 법'을 반영할지를 토론하는 장면이다. 〈보기〉의 단어를 활용하여 Kai의 발언을 영작하시오.

> • Teacher: Pets have become an important part in our life, such as for those who live alone. But there are still some people who are rude to their pets. In this situation, what do we do?
> • Kai: 애완동물은 많은 한국인들의 삶의 중요한 일부가 되었기 때문에 이젠 우리의 법이 이런 현실을 반영해야 할 때입니다.

┤ 보기 ├
> about time, should, reflect, this reality

➡ As pets have become an important part of many Koreans' lives, _____ _____.

16 우리말에 맞게 영작할 때 빈칸에 들어갈 말을 고르시오.

> 지금은 우리가 중대한 조처를 강구해야 할 때입니다.
> → _____ we took serious steps.

① It's so critical that
② It's about time that
③ It's too difficult to
④ It's right time enough
⑤ It's critical enough to

17 whether와 각 문장의 괄호 안의 어휘를 활용하여 우리말에 맞게 영작하시오.

(1) 네가 나를 기억할지 못할지 모르겠다. (remember)

➡ _____

(2) 나는 너를 깨워야 할지 말아야 할지 몰랐다. (to wake up)

➡ _____

18 'It's time that' 구문과 주어진 단어를 활용하여 다음 각 문장을 우리말에 맞게 영작하시오.

(1) 한국이 궁핍한 다른 나라를 도와주어야 할 때가 왔다. (about, help)

➡ _____
_____ in need.

(2) 이제 우리가 긍정적인 태도를 가질 때이다. (have)

➡ _____ a positive attitude.

(3) 트랜스 지방과의 전쟁은 점점 확대되고 있고 한국도 이것에 동참할 때이다.

➡ The war against trans fat is getting bigger, and _____.
(join)

[19~20] 다음 글을 읽고 물음에 답하시오.

For a week, Michael does no work to support ⓐ*himself.*

Simon: (*looking at Michael*) Michael, ⓑI'm afraid you've been doing nothing since ⓒyou came here. It's time you started to earn a living for ⓓyourself. If you work for ⓔme, I will give you food. (A) Would you like working with me?

Michael: (*with a blank face*) Yes, I would.

19 밑줄 친 ⓐ~ⓔ 중에서 가리키는 대상이 같은 것을 고르시오.

① ⓐ—ⓑ   ② ⓑ—ⓒ
③ ⓑ—ⓓ   ④ ⓒ—ⓓ
⑤ ⓓ—ⓔ

20 위 글의 밑줄 친 (A)에서 어법상 틀린 부분을 찾아 고치시오.

➡ _____

[21~22] 다음 글을 읽고 물음에 답하시오.

Scene #3.

A year later, Simon has become famous, thanks to Michael's great skills in making shoes. One day, a nobleman comes to order his boots.

Nobleman: I'd like to order fine leather boots that have to ⓐlast for a year. I'm not sure whether you can make them. Can you do that?

(*Michael watches the man carefully and smiles for the second time.*)

Simon: Yes, sir. Don't worry.

(*The nobleman leaves the shop.*)

Simon: Michael, please make some thick leather boots.

Michael: Okay.

(*However, Michael makes soft slippers instead of boots.*)

Simon: (*finding the slippers*) Michael! I told you there should be no mistakes. What do you think you are doing?

Servant: (*running into the shop*) Please stop making boots and start making soft slippers for a dead body instead. My master has died of a heart attack.

Simon: (*looking at Michael in surprise*) How did you know?

Michael: Well ...

21 위 글의 밑줄 친 ⓐlast와 같은 의미로 쓰인 것을 고르시오.

① That is the <u>last</u> thing one would expect.
② We've got enough food to <u>last</u> us for three days.
③ He looked very happy <u>last</u> time I saw him.
④ This is our <u>last</u> bottle of water.
⑤ This weather won't <u>last</u>.

22 According to the passage, which is NOT true?

① A nobleman wants to order fine leather boots that have to last for a year.
② Michael smiles for the second time when he watches the nobleman carefully.
③ Michael makes boots instead of soft slippers.
④ The servant changes the earlier order.
⑤ The nobleman has died of a heart attack.

[23~24] 다음 글을 읽고 물음에 답하시오.

Scene #4.

A few years later, a woman customer visits the shoe shop with twin girls.

Customer: I'm here to buy some leather shoes for these twin girls.

Simon: (*seeing that one of the girls has a disability*) I'm sorry about your daughter's foot. May I ask you if she was born with a disability?

Customer: Oh, I'm not her real mother. Her mother hurt this girl's leg while she was giving birth to her. Their parents are both dead now. I felt sorry for them. ⓐ이 아이들을 너무 사랑해서 입양하기로 결정했습니다.

(*Michael smiles for the third time.*)

23 위 글의 밑줄 친 ⓐ의 우리말에 맞게 주어진 어휘를 이용하여 12 단어로 영작하시오.

> these twins, so, that

➡ _____

_____

24 위 글의 주제로 알맞은 것을 고르시오.

① sympathy for a poor girl who has a disability

② a woman's love for the twin girls

③ difficult lives of the twin orphan girls

④ a girl who was born with a birth defect

⑤ how to overcome a physical disability

[25~26] 다음 글을 읽고 물음에 답하시오.

Scene #6.

Michael thinks back to each time that he smiled. Simon and Matrena listen carefully to him.

Michael: First, I learned that love dwells in human beings when Matrena pitied me. (①) This was the answer to the first lesson: Learn what dwells in human beings. (②) I smiled because I learned the truth. (③)

Simon: What were they? (④)

Michael: The second was, "Learn what is not given to people." (⑤) When the nobleman ordered that his boots were to last for a year, I knew he would die soon. Then I realized people know little about their own future needs.

Simon: What was the last truth?

Michael: It was from the story of the woman and the twin girls. After the death of their mother, the woman ⓐbrought them up with her love. Then, I learned people live by having true love for each other. That was the third lesson: What people live by.

25 위 글의 흐름으로 보아, 주어진 문장이 들어가기에 가장 적절한 곳은?

> But I still had two more to figure out.

①　　②　　③　　④　　⑤

26 위 글의 밑줄 친 ⓐbrought them up과 바꿔 쓸 수 있는 말을 모두 고르시오.

① reared them　　② raised them

③ turned them up　　④ lifted them

⑤ nurtured them

[27~28] 다음 글을 읽고 물음에 답하시오.

Scene #5.

(Suddenly, a mysterious light shines from Michael.)

Simon: What's this light shining from you?

Michael: It's about time I left here.

Simon: What do you mean? And why did you just smile?

Michael: Let me explain. I am an angel. I was sent here as a punishment, and I was supposed to learn three truths. Every time I learned one of them, I smiled. Now that I have learned all three of them, I am ready ⓐto go back.

Simon: I see. What truths have you learned?

27 위 글의 밑줄 친 ⓐto go와 to부정사의 용법이 같은 것을 모두 고르시오.

① I want a chair to sit on.
② I am happy to hear that.
③ My hobby is to collect stamps.
④ He went to the store to buy some fruit.
⑤ It is very important to study English hard.

28 According to the passage, which is NOT true?

① All at once, a mysterious light shines from Michael.
② Michael says it's about time he should arrive here.
③ Michael was supposed to learn three truths.
④ Whenever Michael learned one of three truths, Michael smiled.
⑤ Michael has learned three truths.

[29~30] 다음 글을 읽고 물음에 답하시오.

Scene #6.

Michael thinks back to each time that he smiled. Simon and Matrena listen carefully to him.

Michael: First, I learned that love dwells in human beings when Matrena pitied me. This was the answer to the first lesson: Learn what dwells in human beings. I smiled because I learned the truth. But I still had two more to ⓐfigure out.

Simon: What were they?

Michael: The second was, "Learn what is not given to people." When the nobleman ordered that his boots were to last for a year, I knew he would die soon. Then I realized people know little about their own future needs.

Simon: What was the last truth?

Michael: It was from the story of the woman and the twin girls. After the death of their mother, the woman brought them up with her love. Then, I learned people live by having true love for each other. That was the third lesson: What people live by.

29 위 글의 밑줄 친 ⓐfigure out과 바꿔 쓸 수 없는 말을 고르시오. (3개)

① find out   ② discover
③ analyze   ④ regret
⑤ explain

30 위 글의 제목으로 알맞은 것을 고르시오.

① The Foolishness of Human Beings
② Three Truths about Human Beings
③ What Dwells in Human Beings?
④ What Is Not Given to People?
⑤ What Do People Live by?

INSIGHT
on the textbook

교과서 파헤치기

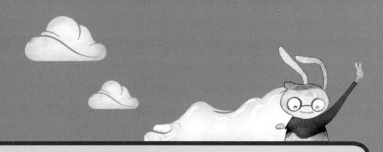

※ 다음 영어를 우리말로 쓰시오.

01 avoid

02 storm

03 regularly

04 calm

05 fellow

06 alternative

07 reduce

08 architect

09 retirement

10 disaster

11 graduate

12 side effect

13 seeding

14 bloomer

15 architecture

16 source

17 personality

18 helpful

19 end-of-life

20 perfectly

21 environment

22 will

23 handle

24 energy-saving

25 invest

26 modern

27 purpose

28 increase

29 career

30 operate

31 prevent

32 literature

33 wealthy

34 control

35 thanks to ~

36 come by

37 instead of

38 give a big hand

39 as well

40 feel proud

41 keep on -ing

42 get along well with

43 succeed in

※ 다음 우리말을 영어로 쓰시오.

01 건축학, 건축 양식

02 정기적으로, 규칙적으로

03 대체 가능한, 대체의

04 피하다, 방지하다

05 은퇴, 퇴직

06 성격, 인격

07 다루다, 처리하다

08 건축가

09 도움이 되는, 유용한

10 인생 말기의

11 줄이다, 낮추다

12 동료의

13 졸업생; 졸업하다

14 에너지를 절약하는

15 목적

16 부유한, 재산이 많은

17 먹이를 주다

18 완벽하게

19 (주변의) 환경

20 방지하다, 막다

21 문학

22 재능을 발휘하는 사람

23 원천, 근원

24 통제하다

25 작동하다, 가동시키다

26 유언장

27 증가하다, 증가시키다

28 투자하다

29 재난, 재해

30 씨 뿌리기

31 부작용

32 현대의, 근대의

33 폭풍

34 경력, 직업

35 ~ 대신에

36 ~를 믿다

37 ~ 덕분에

38 ~에 성공하다

39 계속해서 ~하다

40 크게 박수 치다

41 긍지를 느끼다

42 ~와 잘 지내다

43 A뿐만 아니라 B도

※ 다음 영영풀이에 알맞은 단어를 <보기>에서 골라 쓴 후, 우리말 뜻을 쓰시오.

1 _____ : an unexpected result of a situation: _____

2 _____ : to become greater in amount, number, value, etc.: _____

3 _____ : offering a choice between two or more things: _____

4 _____ : to like, choose, or want one thing rather than another: _____

5 _____ : the general weather conditions usually found in a particular place: _____

6 _____ : to do physical activities to make your body strong and healthy: _____

7 _____ : to order, limit, or rule something, or someone's actions or behavior: _____

8 _____ : to have something happen to you, or to do or feel something: _____

9 _____ : the place something comes from or starts at, or the cause of something: _____

10 _____ : the air, water, and land in or on which people, animals, and plants live: _____

11 _____ : the type of person you are, shown by the way you behave, feel, and think: _____

12 _____ : to buy property, shares in a company, etc. in the hope of making a profit: _____

13 _____ : an event that results in great harm, damage, or death, or serious difficulty: _____

14 _____ : the act of leaving your job and stopping working, usually because you are old: _____

15 _____ : an official statement of what a person has decided should be done with their money and property after their death: _____

16 _____ : the job or series of jobs that you do during your working life, especially if you continue to get better jobs and earn more money: _____

보기			
source	alternative	environment	prefer
career	exercise	disaster	control
personality	increase	invest	side effect
retirement	climate	will	experience

※ 다음 우리말과 일치하도록 빈칸에 알맞은 말을 쓰시오.

Think Back A

W: Miguel! _____ make some shoes _____.

B: Grandma, I don't want to _____ _____.

W: You _____ like it? Then, what do you like _____ _____ _____ making shoes?

B: I like _____ music _____ than _____ shoes! I want to be a _____.

B: _____ do you _____ _____ music?

W: Music is bad! My grandfather left the family _____ of music.

W: Miguel! 함께 신발을 만들자.

B: 할머니, 전 신발을 만들고 싶지 않아요.

W: 그걸 좋아하지 않는 거니? 그럼, 신발 만들기보다 더 좋아하는 건 뭐니?

B: 전 신발 만드는 것보다 음악을 연주하는 게 더 좋아요! 전 음악가가 되고 싶어요.

B: 음악에 대해서 어떻게 생각하세요?

W: 음악은 나쁜 거야! 내 할아버지는 음악 때문에 가족을 떠났단다.

Everyday English 1 Listen and Check

(1) G: Do you like _____?

　　B: Yes, I do. But I _____ soccer _____ basketball.

　　G: Oh, really? Can you _____ me how to _____ soccer?

　　B: Sure.

(2) B: I'm looking _____ to the music festival.

　　G: Me too. _____ do you _____, singing or dancing?

　　B: I _____ dancing _____ singing.

　　G: I like singing. It _____ be very fun _____ we can sing and dance _____.

---

(1) G: 농구 좋아하니?

　　B: 응, 좋아해. 하지만 난 농구보다 축구를 더 좋아해.

　　G: 오, 정말? 축구하는 방법 가르쳐 줄 수 있니?

　　B: 물론이지.

(2) B: 나는 음악 페스티벌을 기대하고 있어.

　　G: 나도 그래. 노래하는 거랑 춤추는 거랑 둘 중에 어느 것을 더 좋아하니?

　　B: 난 노래 부르는 것보다 춤추는 걸 더 좋아해.

　　G: 난 노래하는 게 좋아. 우리 같이 노래하고 춤추면 정말 재밌겠다.

Everyday English 1 B Listening Activity

W: Are you _____ for a job? And are you an animal lover? If you are, _____ is the best job for you. We need _____ to take _____ of some pets _____ their family is on _____. You will need to wash the pets, feed them _____, and play with them. _____ _____ _____, we _____ people who can work with us for a _____ _____ those who can only work for a short time. You will work _____ 9 to 5, Monday _____ Friday. If you are interested in _____ care of pets, please call 567-1234.

W: 일을 찾고 계시나요? 그리고 동물을 사랑하시는 분이신가요? 그렇다면, 여기 당신을 위한 최적의 일이 있습니다. 저희는 애완동물 키우는 가족들이 휴가를 갔을 때 애완 동물을 돌봐줄 사람을 찾고 있습니다. 애완동물들을 씻기고 정기적으로 밥을 주고 놀아 주시면 됩니다. 그건 그렇고, 우리는 단기간만 일할 사람보다는 우리와 장기간 일할 수 있는 사람을 선호합니다. 월요일부터 금요일까지, 9시부터 오후 5시까지 일하게 될 겁니다. 애완동물을 돌보는 데 관심이 있으면, 567-1234로 연락 주세요.

Everyday English 2 A Listen and Check

(1) B: How do you _____ about going on a picnic this _____?

　G: I _____ think it's a good idea. It's _____ to rain this weekend.

　B: _____, _____ _____ going to a concert?

　G: _____ great.

(2) M: _____ can I help you?

　G: I'd _____ to buy a hat for my mother.

　M: How do you feel _____ this red one? It's very _____.

　G: It _____ good. I'll _____ it.

(3) G: What are you _____?

　B: I'm making a new soup. Would you like to _____ it?

　G: Sure. Um... (*Tasting the soup*)

　B: Do you _____ it? How do you _____ about this new recipe?

　G: Well, I think you need to _____ some _____ in it.

　B: You're _____. Thank you.

Everyday English 2 B Listening Activity

(*Phone rings.*)

B: Hello?

G: Hello, Minwoo. _____ is Yena.

B: Hi, Yena. What's _____?

G: I _____ your _____ for my birthday today. Thank you so much.

B: Do you _____ it? How do you _____ about its bright color?

G: I really like it. It can _____ drivers see me _____ in the rain.

B: I'm glad to _____ that.

G: Thank you again. I hope it _____ soon so that I can _____ it.

B: Haha. I _____ so. See you soon!

In Real Life

Jisu: Hello, Mr. Brown. Are you _____ now?

Mr. Brown: Not really.

Jisu: Then, can I talk to you for a _____?

Mr. Brown: Of course. Jisu, what's _____? You look _____.

---

(1) B: 이번 주말에 소풍 가는 것에 대해 어떻게 생각하니?

　G: 난 좋은 생각은 아닌 것 같아. 이번 주말에 비가 올 거야.

　B: 그럼, 콘서트에 가는 건 어때?

　G: 좋아.

(2) M: 어떻게 도와드릴까요?

　G: 제 어머니를 위한 모자를 사고 싶은데요.

　M: 이 빨간색은 어떻게 생각하세요? 매우 인기가 많아요.

　G: 괜찮아 보이네요. 그걸로 살게요.

(3) G: 뭐 하는 중이니?

　B: 새로운 수프를 만들고 있어. 맛볼래?

　G: 좋아. 음… (수프를 맛본다)

　B: 마음에 드니? 이 새 요리법에 대해 어떻게 생각해?

　G: 글쎄, 내 생각엔 소금을 좀 더 넣어야 할 것 같다.

　B: 그러네. 감사해.

(전화벨이 울린다.)

B: 여보세요?

G: 안녕, 민우야. 나 예나야.

B: 안녕, 예나야. 요즘 잘 지내니?

G: 오늘 네가 준 생일 선물 받았어. 너무 고마워.

B: 마음에 드니? 그 선물의 밝은 색은 어떠니?

G: 그거 정말 마음에 들어. 빗속에서도 운전자들이 나를 잘 볼 수 있도록 도와줄 수 있잖아.

B: 그 말을 들으니 기쁘다.

G: 다시 한번 고마워. 내가 이걸 사용해 볼 수 있게 어서 비가 내렸으면 좋겠다.

B: 하하하. 나도 그래. 또 보자!

Jisu: Brown 선생님. 안녕하세요. 지금 바쁘신가요?

Mr. Brown: 아니 별로.

Jisu: 그럼, 잠깐 이야기할 수 있을까요?

Mr. Brown: 물론이지. 지수야, 무슨 일이니? 걱정되어 보이는구나.

Jisu: I'm _____ about my _____. I don't know what I _____ to be in the future.

Mr. Brown: How do you feel about _____ a writer? You like _____, don't you?

Jisu: Well, no. I prefer _____ to _____. But I don't know what kinds of jobs I could do.

Mr. Brown: _____ _____ you come to the _____ _____ tomorrow? Our _____ will talk about their jobs.

Jisu: That will be very _____. Thank you.

Mr. Brown: No _____.

Jisu: 제 미래가 걱정돼요. 미래에 뭘 하고 싶은지 모르겠어요.

Mr. Brown: 작가가 되는 건 어떻게 생각하니? 네가 문학을 좋아하지, 그렇지 않니?

Jisu: 음, 아뇨. 전 문학보다 과학을 더 좋아해요. 그런데 무슨 종류의 일을 할 수 있을지 모르겠어요.

Mr. Brown: 내일 학생 회관으로 오는 건 어떻겠니? 우리 학교 졸업생이 직업에 대해서 이야기할 거야.

Jisu: 그럼 정말 도움이 되겠네요. 감사합니다.

Mr. Brown: 천만에.

Check Your Progress 1

B: Mom, can you _____ to my room?

W: Yes. What are you doing?

B: I'm _____ _____ for a date. It's Jina's _____.

W: Aha! So, you're _____ your clothes _____ _____ times.

B: Yes. Mom, _____ do I _____ in this blue shirt?

W: It _____ _____ _____ you, but are you going to _____ those blue jeans, too?

B: I think so. I _____ jeans to my _____ pants.

W: _____ do you feel _____ _____ a white shirt instead?

B: I think the white one and the jeans _____ better. _____ for your advice.

W: No problem.

B: 엄마, 제 방으로 오실 수 있으세요?
W: 그래. 뭐 하고 있는 중이니?
B: 데이트 가려고 준비 중이에요. 지나의 생일이거든요.
W: 아하! 그래서 옷을 여러 번 입어 보는 중이구나.
B: 네. 엄마, 이 파란색 셔츠는 어때 보여요?
W: 너한테 잘 어울리는구나, 그런데 그 파란색 청바지도 입을 거니?
B: 그러려고요. 다른 바지보다 청바지가 더 좋아요.
W: 대신 흰색 셔츠를 입는 건 어떠니?
B: 흰색 셔츠랑 청바지가 더 잘 어울리는 것 같아요. 조언 감사해요.
W: 천만에.

Check Your Progress 2

B: I got a _____ for the Coolboys concert.

G: You're so _____! When is it?

B: It's next Saturday. I'm _____ of going there _____ my friends.

G: By the way, _____ do you _____ about their new album?

B: I like it. All the songs are so _____, _____ they?

G: Yes, but I prefer their last _____ to the new one.

B: Why?

G: It has more songs of _____ genres.

B: 나 Coolboys 콘서트 티켓을 얻었어.
G: 정말 운이 좋구나! 콘서트는 언제니?
B: 다음 주 토요일이야. 내 친구들이랑 같이 가려고 생각 중이야.
G: 그건 그렇고, 새 앨범에 대해서는 어떻게 생각하니?
B: 난 마음에 들어. 모든 곡들이 정말 신나. 그렇지 않니?
G: 응, 근데 나는 이번 새 앨범보다 지난번 앨범이 더 마음에 들어.
B: 왜?
G: 다른 장르의 곡들이 더 많이 있거든.

※ 다음 우리말에 맞도록 대화를 영어로 쓰시오.

Think Back A

W: _____

B: _____

W: _____

B: _____

B: _____

W: _____

W: Miguel! 함께 신발을 만들자.

B: 할머니, 전 신발을 만들고 싶지 않아요.

W: 그걸 좋아하지 않는 거니? 그럼, 신발 만들기보다 더 좋아하는 건 뭐니?

B: 전 신발 만드는 것보다 음악을 연주하는 게 더 좋아요! 전 음악가가 되고 싶어요.

B: 음악에 대해서 어떻게 생각하세요?

W: 음악은 나쁜 거야! 내 할아버지는 음악 때문에 가족을 떠났단다.

Everyday English 1 Listen and Check

(1) G: _____

B: _____

G: _____

B: _____

(2) B: _____

G: _____

B: _____

G: _____

(1) G: 농구 좋아하니?

B: 응, 좋아해. 하지만 난 농구보다 축구를 더 좋아해.

G: 오, 정말? 축구하는 방법 가르쳐 줄 수 있니?

B: 물론이지.

(2) B: 나는 음악 페스티벌을 기대하고 있어.

G: 나도 그래. 노래하는 거랑 춤추는 거랑 둘 중에 어느 것을 더 좋아하니?

B: 난 노래 부르는 것보다 춤추는 걸 더 좋아해.

G: 난 노래하는 게 좋아. 우리 같이 노래하고 춤추면 정말 재밌겠다.

Everyday English 1 B Listening Activity

W: _____

_____

_____

_____

_____

_____

W: 일을 찾고 계시나요? 그리고 동물을 사랑하시는 분이신가요? 그렇다면, 여기 당신을 위한 최적의 일이 있습니다. 저희는 애완동물 키우는 가족들이 휴가를 갔을 때 애완 동물을 돌봐줄 사람을 찾고 있습니다. 애완동물들을 씻기고 정기적으로 밥을 주고 놀아 주시면 됩니다. 그건 그렇고, 우리는 단기간만 일할 사람보다는 우리와 장기간 일할 수 있는 사람을 선호합니다. 월요일부터 금요일까지, 9시부터 오후 5시까지 일하게 될 겁니다. 애완동물을 돌보는 데 관심이 있으면, 567-1234로 연락 주세요.

Everyday English 2 A Listen and Check

(1) B: _____

G: _____

B: _____

G: _____

(2) M: _____

G: _____

M: _____

G: _____

(3) G: _____

B: _____

G: _____

B: _____

G: _____

B: _____

Everyday English 2 B Listening Activity

(*Phone rings.*)

B: _____

G: _____

B: _____

G: _____

B: _____

G: _____

B: _____

G: _____

B: _____

In Real Life

Jisu: _____

Mr. Brown: _____

Jisu: _____

Mr. Brown: _____

---

(1) B: 이번 주말에 소풍 가는 것에 대해 어떻게 생각하니?

G: 난 좋은 생각은 아닌 것 같아. 이번 주말에 비가 올 거야.

B: 그럼, 콘서트에 가는 건 어때?

G: 좋아.

(2) M: 어떻게 도와드릴까요?

G: 제 어머니를 위한 모자를 사고 싶은데요.

M: 이 빨간색은 어떻게 생각하세요? 매우 인기가 많아요.

G: 괜찮아 보이네요. 그걸로 살게요.

(3) G: 뭐 하는 중이니?

B: 새로운 수프를 만들고 있어. 맛볼래?

G: 좋아. 음… (수프를 맛본다)

B: 마음에 드니? 이 새 요리법에 대해 어떻게 생각해?

G: 글쎄, 내 생각엔 소금을 좀 더 넣어야 할 것 같다.

B: 그러네. 감사해.

(전화벨이 울린다.)

B: 여보세요?

G: 안녕, 민우야. 나 예나야.

B: 안녕, 예나야. 요즘 잘 지내니?

G: 오늘 네가 준 생일 선물 받았어. 너무 고마워.

B: 마음에 드니? 그 선물의 밝은 색은 어떠니?

G: 그거 정말 마음에 들어. 빗속에서도 운전자들이 나를 잘 볼 수 있도록 도와줄 수 있잖아.

B: 그 말을 들으니 기쁘다.

G: 다시 한번 고마워. 내가 이걸 사용해 볼 수 있게 어서 비가 내렸으면 좋겠다.

B: 하하하. 나도 그래. 또 보자!

Jisu: Brown 선생님, 안녕하세요. 지금 바쁘신가요?

Mr. Brown: 아니 별로.

Jisu: 그럼, 잠깐 이야기할 수 있을까요?

Mr. Brown: 물론이지. 지수야, 무슨 일이니? 걱정되어 보이는구나.

Jisu: _____

Mr. Brown: _____

_____

Jisu: _____

_____

Mr. Brown: _____

_____

Jisu: _____

Mr. Brown: _____

Jisu: 제 미래가 걱정돼요. 미래에 뭘 하고 싶은지 모르겠어요.

Mr. Brown: 작가가 되는 건 어떻게 생각하니? 네가 문학을 좋아하지, 그렇지 않니?

Jisu: 음, 아뇨. 전 문학보다 과학을 더 좋아해요. 그런데 무슨 종류의 일을 할 수 있을지 모르겠어요.

Mr. Brown: 내일 학생 회관으로 오는 건 어떻겠니? 우리 학교 졸업생이 직업에 대해서 이야기할 거야.

Jisu: 그럼 정말 도움이 되겠네요. 감사합니다.

Mr. Brown: 천만에.

Check Your Progress 1

B: _____

W: _____

B: _____

W: _____

B: _____

W: _____

B: _____

W: _____

B: _____

W: _____

B: 엄마, 제 방으로 오실 수 있으세요?

W: 그래. 뭐 하고 있는 중이니?

B: 데이트 가려고 준비 중이에요. 지나의 생일이거든요.

W: 아하! 그래서 옷을 여러 번 입어 보는 중이구나.

B: 네. 엄마, 이 파란색 셔츠는 어때 보여요?

W: 너한테 잘 어울리는구나, 그런데 그 파란색 청바지도 입을 거니?

B: 그러려고요. 다른 바지보다 청바지가 더 좋아요.

W: 대신 흰색 셔츠를 입는 건 어떠니?

B: 흰색 셔츠랑 청바지가 더 잘 어울리는 것 같아요. 조언 감사해요.

W: 천만에.

Check Your Progress 2

B: _____

G: _____

B: _____

G: _____

B: _____

G: _____

B: _____

G: _____

B: 나 Coolboys 콘서트 티켓을 얻었어.

G: 정말 운이 좋구나! 콘서트는 언제니?

B: 다음 주 토요일이야. 내 친구들이랑 같이 가려고 생각 중이야.

G: 그건 그렇고, 새 앨범에 대해서는 어떻게 생각하니?

B: 난 마음에 들어. 모든 곡들이 정말 신나. 그렇지 않니?

G: 응, 근데 나는 이번 새 앨범보다 지난번 앨범이 더 마음에 들어.

B: 왜?

G: 다른 장르의 곡들이 더 많이 있거든.

※ 다음 우리말과 일치하도록 빈칸에 알맞은 것을 골라 쓰시오.

1 _____ to _____ _____!
A. Day　　　　B. Careers　　　　C. Welcome

2 _____ _____ our _____ _____!
A. Careers　　B. welcome　　C. Day　　D. to

3 These _____, jobs are _____ to _____ _____.
A. come　　　B. days　　C. by　　D. hard

4 But if you _____ _____ trying your best, you will _____ _____ your career.
A. in　　　B. keep　　C. succeed　　D. on

5 Today, we will _____ back _____ of the _____ of our school, and listen to them talk about their _____.
A. some　　B. jobs　　C. welcome　　D. graduates

6 Are you _____ _____ _____ them?
A. about　　B. excited　　C. meeting

7 _____ _____ I.
A. am　　B. so

8 As you listen to their talks, _____ about _____ you _____ to do in the future.
A. would　　B. think　　C. like　　D. what

9 Please _____ our first _____, Ilkem, the _____ _____.
A. weather　　B. welcome　　C. controller　　D. speaker

10 Hello, _____. _____ _____.
A. I'm　　B. everyone　　C. Ilkem

11 I'm a _____ _____ the _____.
A. studying　　B. scientist　　C. weather

12 Just a _____ years ago, people thought the _____ was _____ to _____.
A. impossible　　B. few　　C. control　　D. weather

13 _____ _____ I.
A. did　　B. so

14 _____ to modern _____, however, my _____ scientists and I can change the weather _____ we want.
A. technology　　B. as　　C. thanks　　D. fellow

15 For _____, we can _____ the rain, _____ a cloud _____ system.
A. using　　B. example　　C. seeding　　D. control

1 직업의 날에 온 것을 환영합니다!

2 우리 직업의 날에 온 것을 환영합니다!

3 요즘은 직업을 얻기가 어렵습니다.

4 하지만 여러분이 계속해서 노력한다면, 여러분의 진로에서 성공할 수 있을 것입니다.

5 오늘, 우리는 우리 학교 졸업생 몇몇을 맞이하고, 그들의 직업에 관해 이야기를 들을 거예요.

6 그들을 만나는 게 신나나요?

7 저도 그렇습니다.

8 그들의 이야기를 들으면서 여러분이 미래에 무엇을 하고 싶은지 생각해 보세요.

9 첫 번째 연설자인 날씨 조절자 Ilkem을 환영합시다.

10 안녕하세요, 여러분. 저는 Ilkem입니다.

11 저는 날씨를 연구하는 과학자입니다.

12 몇 년 전까지만 해도, 사람들은 날씨를 조절하는 것이 불가능하다고 생각했어요.

13 저도 그랬습니다.

14 그러나 현대 기술 덕분에 저의 동료 과학자들과 저는 원하는 대로 날씨를 바꿀 수 있습니다.

15 예를 들어, 우리는 구름 씨 뿌리기 기술을 이용해 강우를 조절할 수 있습니다.

16 We _____ dry ice _____ clouds to _____ them _____.
    A. make   B. spray   C. rain   D. into

17 In China, they made rain in _____ city _____ of Beijing during the opening event of the Olympics and its _____ event as _____.
    A. instead   B. well   C. another   D. closing

18 We can also _____ the side _____ of global warming by _____ the _____.
    A. effects   B. reduce   C. climate   D. controlling

19 We can't _____ the weather _____ _____, but may be _____ to do so soon.
    A. yet   B. control   C. able   D. perfectly

20 Then, we could _____ many kinds of _____ _____ like _____ and storms.
    A. natural   B. prevent   C. floods   D. disasters

21 So you will be _____ to live in a _____ and _____ _____.
    A. safer   B. able   C. environment   D. better

22 _____ _____ you _____ us in making a better environment by _____ the weather?
    A. join   B. controlling   C. don't   D. why

23 Hi, I'm Eva. I'm an _____, and I design _____ _____ _____.
    A. energy   B. architect   C. houses   D. net-zero

24 Many people are _____ about _____ too _____ _____ at home.
    A. using   B. energy   C. worried   D. much

25 _____ _____ my _____.
    A. were   B. parents   C. so

26 _____ I was young, my parents often said, "Eva! _____ many times do I _____ _____ thell you?
    A. how   B. to   C. when   D. have

27 _____ _____ the TV _____ you're not _____ it!"
    A. when   B. off   C. turn   D. watching

28 _____ then, I have wanted to _____ _____ _____.
    A. design   B. houses   C. since   D. energy-saving

29 I studied architecture and _____ _____ _____ to make my dream _____ _____.
    A. come   B. environmental   C. true   D. engineering

30 Now, I design houses that use wind power or _____ _____ _____.
    A. energy   B. sources   C. alternative   D. other

31 The houses _____ _____ _____ _____ they use.
    A. more   B. than   C. make   D. energy

32 You don't _____ to worry about _____ _____ _____.
    A. energy   B. need   C. anymore   D. wasting

33 If you are _____ _____ _____ net-zero energy houses, please come and _____ to me.
    A. talk   B. in   C. interested   D. designing

16 우리는 구름 속에 드라이아이스를 뿌려 구름을 비로 만듭니다.

17 중국에서는 올림픽의 개막식과 폐막식에 북경 대신 다른 도시에 비가 오게끔 했습니다.

18 또한 우리는 기후를 조절함으로써 지구 온난화의 부작용들을 줄일 수 있습니다.

19 아직은 날씨를 완벽하게 조절할 수 없지만, 곧 그렇게 할 수 있을 것입니다.

20 그러면 홍수나 폭풍 같은 다양한 자연재해를 예방할 수 있을 것입니다.

21 그래서 여러분이 좀 더 안전하고 좋은 환경에서 살 수 있을 거예요.

22 여러분도 날씨를 조절하여 더 나은 환경을 만드는 데에 함께 하는 게 어때요?

23 안녕하세요, 저는 Eva입니다. 저는 건축가로, net-zero 에너지 집을 설계합니다.

24 많은 사람들이 집에서 너무 많은 에너지를 사용하는 것에 대해 걱정합니다.

25 저희 부모님도 그랬습니다.

26 제가 어릴 때 부모님께서는 "Eva! 내가 몇 번을 말해야 하니?

27 TV를 보지 않을 때는 꺼!"라고 자주 말씀하셨습니다.

28 그때부터 저는 에너지를 절약하는 집을 설계하고 싶었습니다.

29 저의 꿈을 실현하기 위해 저는 건축과 환경 공학을 공부했습니다.

30 이제 저는 풍력이나 다른 대체 에너지 자원을 사용하는 집들을 설계합니다.

31 그 집들은 사용하는 것보다 더 많은 에너지를 만들어 냅니다.

32 더 이상 에너지를 낭비하는 것을 걱정할 필요가 없습니다.

33 여러분이 net-zero 에너지 집을 설계하는 것에 관심이 있다면, 저에게 와서 얘기하세요.

34 Hello. My name is Jiwon, and I'm _____ _____ _____.

A. planner   B. end-of-life   C. an

35 _____ the number of old people is _____, people are _____ in how to be happy and _____ in their old age.

A. interested   B. as   C. wealthy   D. increasing

36 I help people _____ _____ to live a healthy life _____ _____ to plan for their death.

A. but   B. not   C. also   D. only

37 For _____, I _____ them _____ _____.

A. exercise   B. example   C. regularly   D. help

38 I also give them some tips on how to _____ for _____ and _____ _____ well with their family.

A. along   B. invest   C. get   D. retirement

39 And I _____ teach them _____ _____ make a _____!

A. to   B. even   C. will   D. how

40 This helps their family members _____ a _____ of problems _____ the person _____.

A. after   B. avoid   C. dies   D. lot

41 I _____ _____ _____ _____ I'm doing.

A. of   B. feel   C. what   D. proud

42 Teacher: _____ _____ a _____ _____ to the speakers.

A. hand   B. let's   C. big   D. give

43 I hope today's _____ _____ _____ _____ for you.

A. been   B. talks   C. helpful   D. have

44 I see many students _____ a _____ time _____ something new, _____ worrying about their future.

A. learning   B. while   C. hard   D. having

45 They are _____ _____ they are _____.

A. slow   B. worried   C. learners   D. that

46 _____ _____ I.

A. was   B. so

47 I was _____ _____ _____.

A. a   B. bloomer   C. late

48 I tried to find _____ I was _____ _____, and became a teacher.

A. finally   B. what   C. at   D. good

49 _____, I want to say, "_____ _____ _____, and you can do it."

A. in   B. so   C. yourself   D. believe

---

34 안녕하세요. 제 이름은 지원이고, 저는 임종 설계사입니다.

35 고령 인구가 증가함에 따라 사람들은 어떻게 하면 노년에 행복하고 부유하게 살 수 있는지에 대해 관심을 가집니다.

36 저는 사람들이 건강한 삶을 사는 것을 도울 뿐만 아니라 그들의 죽음을 계획할 수 있게 돕습니다.

37 예를 들어, 저는 그들이 규칙적으로 운동하도록 돕습니다.

38 또한 은퇴 후에 투자를 하는 방법이나 그들의 가족과 잘 어울려 지내는 것에 대한 조언을 합니다.

39 그리고 저는 심지어 그들에게 유언장 쓰는 법을 가르칩니다!

40 이것은 그가 죽고 난 후 가족들이 많은 문제들을 피하는 데에 도움을 줍니다.

41 저는 제가 하는 일이 자랑스럽습니다.

42 선생님: 연설자들에게 큰 박수를 보냅시다.

43 오늘 이야기들이 여러분에게 도움이 되었기를 바랍니다.

44 저는 많은 학생들이 새로운 것을 배우는 데에 어려움을 겪고 그들의 미래에 대해 걱정하는 것을 봅니다.

45 그들은 배우는 속도가 느리다고 걱정합니다.

46 저 또한 그랬습니다.

47 저는 늦게 꽃피우는 사람이었죠.

48 내가 무엇을 잘하는지 찾기 위해 노력했고, 결국은 선생님이 되었습니다.

49 그래서 여러분에게 이렇게 말하고 싶습니다. "여러분 자신을 믿으세요. 그러면 할 수 있습니다."

※ 다음 우리말과 일치하도록 빈칸에 알맞은 것을 골라 쓰시오.

1 Welcome to _____ _____!

2 _____ _____ our Careers Day!

3 These days, jobs are _____ _____ _____ _____.

4 But if you _____ _____ _____ your best, you will _____ _____ your career.

5 Today, we will welcome back some of _____ _____ of our school, and _____ _____ _____ _____ about their jobs.

6 Are you _____ _____ _____ them?

7 _____ _____ _____.

8 As you listen to their talks, think about what you _____ _____ _____ do _____ _____ _____.

9 Please _____ our first speaker, Ilkem, _____ _____ _____.

10 Hello, everyone. _____ _____.

11 I'm a scientist _____ _____ _____.

12 Just _____ _____ _____ ago, people thought the weather was _____ _____ _____.

13 So _____ I.

14 _____ _____ modern technology, _____, my _____ _____ and I can change the weather as we want.

15 For example, we can _____ the rain, _____ a cloud _____ _____.

1	직업의 날에 온 것을 환영합니다!
2	우리 직업의 날에 온 것을 환영합니다!
3	요즘은 직업을 얻기가 어렵습니다.
4	하지만 여러분이 계속해서 노력한다면, 여러분의 진로에서 성공할 수 있을 것입니다.
5	오늘, 우리는 우리 학교 졸업생 몇몇을 맞이하고, 그들의 직업에 관해 이야기를 들을 거예요.
6	그들을 만나는 게 신나나요?
7	저도 그렇습니다.
8	그들의 이야기를 들으면서 여러분이 미래에 무엇을 하고 싶은지 생각해 보세요.
9	첫 번째 연설자인 날씨 조절자 Ilkem을 환영합시다.
10	안녕하세요, 여러분. 저는 Ilkem입니다.
11	저는 날씨를 연구하는 과학자입니다.
12	몇 년 전까지만 해도, 사람들은 날씨를 조절하는 것이 불가능하다고 생각했어요.
13	저도 그랬습니다.
14	그러나 현대 기술 덕분에 저의 동료 과학자들과 저는 원하는 대로 날씨를 바꿀 수 있습니다.
15	예를 들어, 우리는 구름 씨 뿌리기 기술을 이용해 강우를 조절할 수 있습니다.

16 We spray dry ice into clouds to _____ _____ _____ .

17 In China, they made rain in another city _____ _____ Beijing _____ the opening event of the Olympics and its closing event _____ _____ .

18 We can also reduce _____ _____ _____ of global warming _____ _____ the climate.

19 We can't _____ _____ _____ perfectly yet, but may be _____ _____ do so soon.

20 Then, we could prevent many kinds of _____ _____ _____ _____ and _____ .

21 So you will be able to live _____ _____ _____ _____ _____ _____ .

22 _____ _____ _____ _____ us in making a better environment by _____ the weather?

23 Hi, I'm Eva. I'm an _____ , and I design _____ _____ _____ .

24 Many people are worried about _____ _____ _____ _____ at home.

25 So _____ my parents.

26 When I was young, my parents often said, "Eva! How many times _____ _____ _____ _____ _____ you?

27 _____ _____ the TV when you're not watching it!"

28 _____ then, I have wanted to design _____ _____ .

29 I studied architecture and _____ _____ to make my dream _____ _____

30 Now, I design houses that use wind power or other _____ _____ _____ .

31 The houses _____ _____ _____ _____ _____ they use.

32 You don't need to worry about _____ _____ anymore.

33 If you _____ _____ _____ designing net-zero energy houses, please come and talk to me.

16 우리는 구름 속에 드라이아이스를 뿌려 구름을 비로 만듭니다.

17 중국에서는 올림픽의 개막식과 폐막식에 북경 대신 다른 도시에 비가 오게끔 했습니다.

18 또한 우리는 기후를 조절함으로써 지구 온난화의 부작용들을 줄일 수 있습니다.

19 아직은 날씨를 완벽하게 조절할 수 없지만, 곧 그렇게 할 수 있을 것입니다.

20 그러면 홍수나 폭풍 같은 다양한 자연재해를 예방할 수 있을 것입니다.

21 그래서 여러분이 좀 더 안전하고 좋은 환경에서 살 수 있을 거예요.

22 여러분도 날씨를 조절하여 더 나은 환경을 만드는 데에 함께하는 게 어때요?

23 안녕하세요. 저는 Eva입니다. 저는 건축가로, net-zero 에너지 집을 설계합니다.

24 많은 사람들이 집에서 너무 많은 에너지를 사용하는 것에 대해 걱정합니다.

25 저희 부모님도 그랬습니다.

26 제가 어릴 때 부모님께서는 "Eva! 내가 몇 번을 말해야 하니?

27 TV를 보지 않을 때는 꺼!"라고 자주 말씀하셨습니다.

28 그때부터 저는 에너지를 절약하는 집을 설계하고 싶었습니다.

29 저의 꿈을 실현하기 위해 저는 건축과 환경 공학을 공부했습니다.

30 이제 저는 풍력이나 다른 대체 에너지 자원을 사용하는 집들을 설계합니다.

31 그 집들은 사용하는 것보다 더 많은 에너지를 만들어 냅니다.

32 더 이상 에너지를 낭비하는 것을 걱정할 필요가 없습니다.

33 여러분이 net-zero 에너지 집을 설계하는 것에 관심이 있다면, 저에게 와서 얘기하세요.

34 Hello. My name is Jiwon, and I'm an _____ _____.

35 _____ the number of old people _____ _____, people are _____ _____ how to be happy and wealthy in their old age.

36 I help people _____ _____ to live a healthy life _____ _____ to plan for their _____.

37 For _____, I help them _____ _____.

38 I also give them some tips on how to _____ _____ _____ and _____ _____ _____ _____ their family.

39 And I even teach them how to _____ _____!

40 This helps their family members _____ _____ _____ _____ _____ the person _____.

41 I _____ _____ _____ _____ I'm doing.

42 Teacher: Let's _____ _____ _____ _____ _____ the speakers.

43 I hope today's talks have been _____ _____ you.

44 I see many students _____ _____ _____ _____ _____ something new, _____ _____ about their future.

45 They are worried that they are _____ _____.

46 So _____ I.

47 I was _____ _____ _____.

48 I tried to find _____ _____ _____ _____ _____, and finally became a teacher.

49 So, I want to say, "_____ _____, and you can do it."

34 안녕하세요. 제 이름은 지원이고, 저는 임종 설계사입니다.

35 고령 인구가 증가함에 따라 사람들은 어떻게 하면 노년에 행복하고 부유하게 살 수 있는지에 대해 관심을 가집니다.

36 저는 사람들이 건강한 삶을 사는 것을 도울 뿐만 아니라 그들의 죽음을 계획할 수 있게 돕습니다.

37 예를 들어, 저는 그들이 규칙적으로 운동하도록 돕습니다.

38 또한 은퇴 후에 투자를 하는 방법이나 그들의 가족과 잘 어울려 지내는 것에 대한 조언을 합니다.

39 그리고 저는 심지어 그들에게 유언장 쓰는 법을 가르칩니다!

40 이것은 그가 죽고 난 후 가족들이 많은 문제들을 피하는 데에 도움을 줍니다.

41 저는 제가 하는 일이 자랑스럽습니다.

42 선생님: 연설자들에게 큰 박수를 보냅시다.

43 오늘 이야기들이 여러분에게 도움이 되었기를 바랍니다.

44 저는 많은 학생들이 새로운 것을 배우는 데에 어려움을 겪고 그들의 미래에 대해 걱정하는 것을 봅니다.

45 그들은 배우는 속도가 느리다고 걱정합니다.

46 저 또한 그랬습니다.

47 저는 늦게 꽃피우는 사람이었죠.

48 내가 무엇을 잘하는지 찾기 위해 노력했고, 결국은 선생님이 되었습니다.

49 그래서 여러분에게 이렇게 말하고 싶습니다. "여러분 자신을 믿으세요. 그러면 할 수 있습니다."

※ 다음 문장을 우리말로 쓰시오.

1 ▸ Welcome to Careers Day!

➡ _____

2 ▸ Welcome to our Careers Day!

➡ _____

3 ▸ These days, jobs are hard to come by.

➡ _____

4 ▸ But if you keep on trying your best, you will succeed in your career.

➡ _____

5 ▸ Today, we will welcome back some of the graduates of our school, and listen to them talk about their jobs.

➡ _____

6 ▸ Are you excited about meeting them?

➡ _____

7 ▸ So am I.

➡ _____

8 ▸ As you listen to their talks, think about what you would like to do in the future.

➡ _____

9 ▸ Please welcome our first speaker, Ilkem, the weather controller.

➡ _____

10 ▸ Hello, everyone. I'm Ilkem.

➡ _____

11 ▸ I'm a scientist studying the weather.

➡ _____

12 ▸ Just a few years ago, people thought the weather was impossible to control.

➡ _____

13 ▸ So did I.

➡ _____

14 ▸ Thanks to modern technology, however, my fellow scientists and I can change the weather as we want.

➡ _____

15 ▸ For example, we can control the rain, using a cloud seeding system.

➡ _____

16 We spray dry ice into clouds to make them rain.
➡ _____

17 In China, they made rain in another city instead of Beijing during the opening event of the Olympics and its closing event as well.
➡ _____

18 We can also reduce the side effects of global warming by controlling the climate.
➡ _____

19 We can't control the weather perfectly yet, but may be able to do so soon.
➡ _____

20 Then, we could prevent many kinds of natural disasters like floods and storms.
➡ _____

21 So you will be able to live in a better and safer environment.
➡ _____

22 Why don't you join us in making a better environment by controlling the weather?
➡ _____

23 Hi, I'm Eva. I'm an architect, and I design net-zero energy houses.
➡ _____

24 Many people are worried about using too much energy at home.
➡ _____

25 So were my parents.
➡ _____

26 When I was young, my parents often said, "Eva! How many times do I have to tell you?
➡ _____

27 Turn off the TV when you're not watching it!"
➡ _____

28 Since then, I have wanted to design energy-saving houses.
➡ _____

29 I studied architecture and environmental engineering to make my dream come true.
➡ _____

30 Now, I design houses that use wind power or other alternative energy sources.
➡ _____

31 The houses make more energy than they use.
➡ _____

32 You don't need to worry about wasting energy anymore.
➡ _____

33 If you are interested in designing net-zero energy houses, please come and talk to me.
➡ _____

34 Hello. My name is Jiwon, and I'm an end-of-life planner.

➡ _____

35 As the number of old people is increasing, people are interested in how to be happy and wealthy in their old age.

➡ _____

36 I help people not only to live a healthy life but also to plan for their death.

➡ _____

37 For example, I help them exercise regularly.

➡ _____

38 I also give them some tips on how to invest for retirement and get along well with their family.

➡ _____

39 And I even teach them how to make a will!

➡ _____

40 This helps their family members avoid a lot of problems after the person dies.

➡ _____

41 I feel proud of what I'm doing.

➡ _____

42 Teacher: Let's give a big hand to the speakers.

➡ _____

43 I hope today's talks have been helpful for you.

➡ _____

44 I see many students having a hard time learning something new, while worrying about their future.

➡ _____

45 They are worried that they are slow learners.

➡ _____

46 So was I.

➡ _____

47 I was a late bloomer.

➡ _____

48 I tried to find what I was good at, and finally became a teacher.

➡ _____

49 So, I want to say, "Believe in yourself, and you can do it."

➡ _____

※ 다음 괄호 안의 단어들을 우리말에 맞도록 바르게 배열하시오.

1 (to / Welcome / Day! / Careers)
➡ _____

2 (to / welcome / our / Day! / Careers)
➡ _____

3 (days, / these / are / jobs / to / hard / by. / come)
➡ _____

4 (if / but / keep / you / trying / on / best, / your / will / you / in / succeed / career. / your)
➡ _____

5 (we / today, / welcome / will / some / back / the / of / graduates / of / school, / our / and / to / listen / them / about / talk / jobs. / their)
➡ _____
_____

6 (you / are / about / excited / them? / meeting)
➡ _____

7 (I. / am / so)
➡ _____

8 (you / as / to / listen / talks, / their / about / think / you / what / like / would / do / to / the / in / future.)
➡ _____
_____

9 (welcome / please / first / our / speaker, / the / Ilkem, / controller. / weather)
➡ _____

10 (everyone. / hello, / Ilkem. / I'm)
➡ _____

11 (a / I'm / scientist / the / studying / weather.)
➡ _____

12 (a / just / few / ago, / years / thought / people / weather / the / was / to / impossible / control.)
➡ _____
_____

13 (I. / did / so)
➡ _____

14 (to / thanks / technology, / modern / my / however, / fellow / scientists / and / can / I / change / weather / the / we / as / want.)
➡ _____
_____

15 (example, / for / can / we / the / control / rain, / a / using / cloud / system. / seeding)
➡ _____

---

1 직업의 날에 온 것을 환영합니다!

2 우리 직업의 날에 온 것을 환영합니다!

3 요즘은 직업을 얻기가 어렵습니다.

4 하지만 여러분이 계속해서 노력한다면, 여러분의 진로에서 성공할 수 있을 것입니다.

5 오늘, 우리는 우리 학교 졸업생 몇몇을 맞이하고, 그들의 직업에 관해 이야기를 들을 거예요.

6 그들을 만나는 게 신나나요?

7 저도 그렇습니다.

8 그들의 이야기를 들으면서 여러분이 미래에 무엇을 하고 싶은지 생각해 보세요.

9 첫 번째 연설자인 날씨 조절자 Ilkem을 환영합시다.

10 안녕하세요, 여러분. 저는 Ilkem입니다.

11 저는 날씨를 연구하는 과학자입니다.

12 몇 년 전까지만 해도, 사람들은 날씨를 조절하는 것이 불가능하다고 생각했어요.

13 저도 그랬습니다.

14 그러나 현대 기술 덕분에 저의 동료 과학자들과 저는 원하는 대로 날씨를 바꿀 수 있습니다.

15 예를 들어, 우리는 구름 씨 뿌리기 기술을 이용해 강우를 조절할 수 있습니다.

16 (spray / we / ice / dry / clouds / into / make / to / rain. / them)
➡ _____

17 (China, / in / made / they / in / rain / another / instead / city / of / during / Beijing / the / event / opening / of / Olympics / the / and / closing / its / as / event / well.)
➡ _____

18 (can / we / reduce / also / side / the / of / effects / warming / global / by / the / controlling / climate.)
➡ _____

19 (can't / we / the / control / perfectly / weather / but / yet, / be / may / to / able / do / soon. / so)
➡ _____

20 (we / could / then. / prevent / kinds / many / natural / of / like / disasters / floods / storms. / and)
➡ _____

21 (you / so / be / will / to / able / in / live / better / a / and / environment. / safer)
➡ _____

22 (don't / why / join / you / in / us / making / better / a / environment / controlling / by / weather? / the)
➡ _____

23 (I'm / hi, / Eva. // an / I'm / architect, / and / design / I / energy / net-zero / houses.)
➡ _____

24 (people / many / worried / are / using / about / much / too / at / energy / home.)
➡ _____

25 (were / so / parents. / my)
➡ _____

26 (I / when / young, / was / parents / my / said, / often / how / "Eva! / many / do / times / I / to / have / you? / tell)
➡ _____

27 (off / turn / TV / the / you're / when / watching / not / it!")
➡ _____

28 (then, / since / have / I / to / wanted / energy-saving / design / houses.)
➡ _____

29 (studied / I / and / architecture / engineering / environmental / make / to / dream / my / true. / come)
➡ _____

30 (I / now, / houses / design / use / that / power / wind / other / or / alternative / sources. / energy)
➡ _____

31 (houses / the / more / make / than / energy / use. / they)
➡ _____

32 (don't / you / to / need / about / worry / energy / wasting / anymore.)
➡ _____

33 (you / if / interested / are / designing / in / energy / net-zero / houses, / come / please / and / to / talk / me.)
➡ _____
_____

16 우리는 구름 속에 드라이아이스를 뿌려 구름을 비로 만듭니다.

17 중국에서는 올림픽의 개막식과 폐막식에 북경 대신 다른 도시에 비가 오게끔 했습니다.

18 또한 우리는 기후를 조절함으로써 지구 온난화의 부작용들을 줄일 수 있습니다.

19 아직은 날씨를 완벽하게 조절할 수 없지만, 곧 그렇게 할 수 있을 것입니다.

20 그러면 홍수나 폭풍 같은 다양한 자연재해를 예방할 수 있을 것입니다.

21 그래서 여러분이 좀 더 안전하고 좋은 환경에서 살 수 있을 거예요.

22 여러분도 날씨를 조절하여 더 나은 환경을 만드는 데에 함께하는 게 어때요?

23 안녕하세요, 저는 Eva입니다. 저는 건축가로, net-zero 에너지 집을 설계합니다.

24 많은 사람들이 집에서 너무 많은 에너지를 사용하는 것에 대해 걱정합니다.

25 저희 부모님도 그랬습니다.

26 제가 어릴 때 부모님께서는 "Eva! 내가 몇 번을 말해야 하니?

27 TV를 보지 않을 때는 꺼!"라고 자주 말씀하셨습니다.

28 그때부터 저는 에너지를 절약하는 집을 설계하고 싶었습니다.

29 저의 꿈을 실현하기 위해 저는 건축과 환경 공학을 공부했습니다.

30 이제 저는 풍력이나 다른 대체 에너지 자원을 사용하는 집들을 설계합니다.

31 그 집들은 사용하는 것보다 더 많은 에너지를 만들어 냅니다.

32 더 이상 에너지를 낭비하는 것을 걱정할 필요가 없습니다.

33 여러분이 net-zero 에너지 집을 설계하는 것에 관심이 있다면, 저에게 와서 얘기하세요.

34 (hell. // name / my / Jiwon, / is / and / an / I'm / planner. / end-of-life)

➡ _____

35 (the / as / of / number / people / old / increasing, / is / are / people / interested / how / in / be / to / and / happy / in / wealthy / their / age. / old)

➡ _____

36 (help / I / not / people / only / live / to / healthy / a / life / also / but / plan / to / their / for / death.)

➡ _____

37 (example, / for / help / I / exercise / them / regularly.)

➡ _____

38 (also / I / them / give / tips / some / how / on / invest / to / retirement / for / get / and / well / along / their / with / family.)

➡ _____

39 (I / and / teach / even / how / them / make / to / will! / a)

➡ _____

40 (helps / this / family / their / avoid / members / lot / a / problems / of / the / after / dies. / person)

➡ _____

41 (feel / I / of / proud / what / doing. / I'm)

➡ _____

42 (Teacher: / give / let's / big / a / hand / the / to / speakers.)

➡ _____

43 (hope / I / talks / today's / been / have / for / you. / helpful)

➡ _____

44 (see / I / students / many / a / having / time / hard / something / learning / new, / worrying / while / their / about / future.)

➡ _____

45 (are / they / that / worried / are / they / learners. / slow)

➡ _____

46 (was / so / I.)

➡ _____

47 (was / I / a / bloomer. / late)

➡ _____

48 (tried / I / find / to / I / what / good / was / at, / and / became / finally / teacher. / a)

➡ _____

49 (I / so, / to / want / say, / in / "believe / yourself, / you / and / do / can / it.")

➡ _____

34 안녕하세요. 제 이름은 지원이고, 저는 임종 설계사입니다.

35 고령 인구가 증가함에 따라 사람들은 어떻게 하면 노년에 행복하고 부유하게 살 수 있는지에 대해 관심을 가집니다.

36 저는 사람들이 건강한 삶을 사는 것을 도울 뿐만 아니라 그들의 죽음을 계획할 수 있게 돕습니다.

37 예를 들어, 저는 그들이 규칙적으로 운동하도록 돕습니다.

38 또한 은퇴 후에 투자를 하는 방법이나 그들의 가족과 잘 어울려 지내는 것에 대한 조언을 합니다.

39 그리고 저는 심지어 그들에게 유언장 쓰는 법을 가르칩니다!

40 이것은 그가 죽고 난 후 가족들이 많은 문제들을 피하는 데에 도움을 줍니다.

41 저는 제가 하는 일이 자랑스럽습니다.

42 선생님: 연설자들에게 큰 박수를 보냅시다.

43 오늘 이야기들이 여러분에게 도움이 되었기를 바랍니다.

44 저는 많은 학생들이 새로운 것을 배우는 데에 어려움을 겪고 그들의 미래에 대해 걱정하는 것을 봅니다.

45 그들은 배우는 속도가 느리다고 걱정합니다.

46 저 또한 그랬습니다.

47 저는 늦게 꽃피우는 사람이었죠.

48 내가 무엇을 잘하는지 찾기 위해 노력했고, 결국은 선생님이 되었습니다.

49 그래서 여러분에게 이렇게 말하고 싶습니다. "여러분 자신을 믿으세요. 그러면 할 수 있습니다."

※ 다음 우리말을 영어로 쓰시오.

1 직업의 날에 온 것을 환영합니다!

➡ _____

2 우리 직업의 날에 온 것을 환영합니다!

➡ _____

3 요즘은 직업을 얻기가 어렵습니다.

➡ _____

4 하지만 여러분이 계속해서 노력한다면, 여러분의 진로에서 성공할 수 있을 것입니다.

➡ _____

5 오늘, 우리는 우리 학교 졸업생 몇몇을 맞이하고, 그들의 직업에 관해 이야기를 들을 거예요.

➡ _____

6 그들을 만나는 게 신나나요?

➡ _____

7 저도 그렇습니다.

➡ _____

8 그들의 이야기를 들으면서 여러분이 미래에 무엇을 하고 싶은지 생각해 보세요.

➡ _____

9 첫 번째 연설자인 날씨 조절자 Ilkem을 환영합시다.

➡ _____

10 안녕하세요, 여러분. 저는 Ilkem입니다.

➡ _____

11 저는 날씨를 연구하는 과학자입니다.

➡ _____

12 몇 년 전까지만 해도, 사람들은 날씨를 조절하는 것이 불가능하다고 생각했어요.

➡ _____

13 저도 그랬습니다.

➡ _____

14 그러나 현대 기술 덕분에 저의 동료 과학자들과 저는 원하는 대로 날씨를 바꿀 수 있습니다.

➡ _____

15 예를 들어, 우리는 구름 씨 뿌리기 기술을 이용해 강우를 조절할 수 있습니다.

➡ _____

16 우리는 구름 속에 드라이아이스를 뿌려 구름을 비로 만듭니다.

➡ _____

17 중국에서는 올림픽의 개막식과 폐막식에 북경 대신 다른 도시에 비가 오게끔 했습니다.

➡ _____

_____

18 또한 우리는 기후를 조절함으로써 지구 온난화의 부작용들을 줄일 수 있습니다.

➡ _____

19 아직은 날씨를 완벽하게 조절할 수 없지만, 곧 그렇게 할 수 있을 것입니다.

➡ _____

20 그러면 홍수나 폭풍 같은 다양한 자연재해를 예방할 수 있을 것입니다.

➡ _____

21 그래서 여러분이 좀 더 안전하고 좋은 환경에서 살 수 있을 거예요.

➡ _____

22 여러분도 날씨를 조절하여 더 나은 환경을 만드는 데에 함께하는 게 어때요?

➡ _____

23 안녕하세요, 저는 Eva입니다. 저는 건축가로, net-zero 에너지 집을 설계합니다.

➡ _____

24 많은 사람들이 집에서 너무 많은 에너지를 사용하는 것에 대해 걱정합니다.

➡ _____

25 저희 부모님도 그랬습니다.

➡ _____

26 제가 어릴 때 부모님께서는 "Eva! 내가 몇 번을 말해야 하니?

➡ _____

27 TV를 보지 않을 때는 꺼!"라고 자주 말씀하셨습니다.

➡ _____

28 그때부터 저는 에너지를 절약하는 집을 설계하고 싶었습니다.

➡ _____

29 저의 꿈을 실현하기 위해 저는 건축과 환경 공학을 공부했습니다.

➡ _____

30 이제 저는 풍력이나 다른 대체 에너지 자원을 사용하는 집들을 설계합니다.

➡ _____

31 그 집들은 사용하는 것보다 더 많은 에너지를 만들어 냅니다.

➡ _____

32 더 이상 에너지를 낭비하는 것을 걱정할 필요가 없습니다.

➡ _____

33 여러분이 net-zero 에너지 집을 설계하는 것에 관심이 있다면, 저에게 와서 얘기하세요.

➡ _____

34 안녕하세요. 제 이름은 지원이고, 저는 임종 설계사입니다.

➡ _____

35 고령 인구가 증가함에 따라 사람들은 어떻게 하면 노년에 행복하고 부유하게 살 수 있는지에 대해 관심을 가집니다.

➡ _____

➡ _____

36 저는 사람들이 건강한 삶을 사는 것을 도울 뿐만 아니라 그들의 죽음을 계획할 수 있게 돕습니다.

➡ _____

37 예를 들어, 저는 그들이 규칙적으로 운동하도록 돕습니다.

➡ _____

38 또한 은퇴 후에 투자를 하는 방법이나 그들의 가족과 잘 어울려 지내는 것에 대한 조언을 합니다.

➡ _____

39 그리고 저는 심지어 그들에게 유언장 쓰는 법을 가르칩니다!

➡ _____

40 이것은 그가 죽고 난 후 가족들이 많은 문제들을 피하는 데에 도움을 줍니다.

➡ _____

41 저는 제가 하는 일이 자랑스럽습니다.

➡ _____

42 선생님: 연설자들에게 큰 박수를 보냅시다.

➡ _____

43 오늘 이야기들이 여러분에게 도움이 되었기를 바랍니다.

➡ _____

44 저는 많은 학생들이 새로운 것을 배우는 데에 어려움을 겪고 그들의 미래에 대해 걱정하는 것을 봅니다.

➡ _____

45 그들은 배우는 속도가 느리다고 걱정합니다.

➡ _____

46 저 또한 그랬습니다.

➡ _____

47 저는 늦게 꽃피우는 사람이었죠.

➡ _____

48 내가 무엇을 잘하는지 찾기 위해 노력했고, 결국은 선생님이 되었습니다.

➡ _____

49 그래서 여러분에게 이렇게 말하고 싶습니다. "여러분 자신을 믿으세요, 그러면 할 수 있습니다."

➡ _____

※ 다음 우리말과 일치하도록 빈칸에 알맞은 말을 쓰시오.

Everyday English 2 C. Communication Activity

1. A: _____ _____ _____ _____ _____ classical music?

2. B: I don't like it, _____ it's too _____. _____ _____ _____?

3. A: _____ _____ it's very good. I _____ _____ _____ I listen to classical music.

4. B: Then _____ _____ _____ _____ a musician _____ _____ _____?

5. A: That's a _____ _____.

After You Read A

Ilkem

1. I can control the rain, _____ _____ _____ _____ _____ _____.

2. _____ _____ the climate, I _____ _____ _____ _____ of global warming.

Eva

3. I design _____ _____ _____.

4. I make houses that use _____ _____ or _____ _____ _____ _____.

Jiwon

5. I help people _____ _____ _____ _____ a healthy life _____ _____ _____ _____ for their death.

6. This job _____ _____ _____ _____ a lot of problems _____ _____ _____.

Culture & Project Step 1

1. Our group has made a poster _____ _____ _____ _____ _____ _____.

2. _____ _____ _____, we will _____ _____ _____ _____ to space.

3. So, we need someone _____ _____ _____ _____.

4. The space tour guides should know _____ _____ about planets and space _____ _____ they can explain many things _____ _____ _____ _____.

5. _____, they should be healthy and _____ _____ _____ and _____.

1. A: 클래식 음악에 대해서 어떻게 생각하니?
2. B: 난 그것을 좋아하지 않아. 너무 지루하기 때문이야. 너는 어떠니?
3. A: 난 그게 매우 좋다고 생각해. 클래식 음악을 들을 때 차분해지거든.
4. B: 그럼, 미래에 음악가가 되는 건 어떠니?
5. A: 그거 좋은 생각이다.

Ilkem
1. 저는 구름 씨 뿌리기 기술을 이용해 강우를 조절할 수 있습니다.
2. 저는 기후를 조절함으로써 지구 온난화의 부작용들을 줄일 수 있습니다.
Eva
3. 저는 net-zero 에너지 집을 설계합니다.
4. 저는 풍력이나 다른 대체 에너지 자원을 사용하는 집들을 설계합니다.
Jiwon
5. 저는 사람들이 건강한 삶을 사는 것을 도울 뿐만 아니라 그들의 죽음을 계획할 수 있게 돕습니다.
6. 이 직업은 그 사람이 죽고 난 후 가족들이 많은 문제들을 피하는 데에 도움을 줍니다.

1. 우리 모둠은 우주여행 가이드를 찾는 포스터를 만들었다.
2. 미래에, 우리는 우주를 여행할 수 있을 것이다.
3. 그래서 우리는 우주를 우리에게 안내해 줄 누군가가 필요하다.
4. 우주 여행 가이드는 우주에 대하여 여행자들에게 많은 것을 설명할 수 있어야 해서 우주와 행성들에 대해 많이 알아야 한다.
5. 또한, 그들은 건강해야 하고 사람들이 안전하고 편안하게 여행하는 것을 도와야 한다.

※ 다음 우리말을 영어로 쓰시오.

Everyday English 2 C. Communication Activity

1. A: 클래식 음악에 대해서 어떻게 생각하니?
   ➡ _____

2. B: 난 그것을 좋아하지 않아. 너무 지루하기 때문이야. 너는 어떠니?
   ➡ _____

3. A: 난 그게 매우 좋다고 생각해. 클래식 음악을 들을 때 차분해지거든.
   ➡ _____

4. B: 그럼, 미래에 음악가가 되는 건 어떠니?
   ➡ _____

5. A: 그거 좋은 생각이다.
   ➡ _____

After You Read A

Ilkem

1. 저는 구름 씨 뿌리기 기술을 이용해 강우를 조절할 수 있습니다.
   ➡ _____

2. 저는 기후를 조절함으로써 지구 온난화의 부작용들을 줄일 수 있습니다.
   ➡ _____

Eva

3. 저는 net-zero 에너지 집을 설계합니다.
   ➡ _____

4. 저는 풍력이나 다른 대체 에너지 자원을 사용하는 집들을 설계합니다.
   ➡ _____

Jiwon

5. 저는 사람들이 건강한 삶을 사는 것을 도울 뿐만 아니라 그들의 죽음을 계획할 수 있게 돕습니다.
   ➡ _____

6. 이 직업은 그 사람이 죽고 난 후 가족들이 많은 문제들을 피하는 데에 도움을 줍니다.
   ➡ _____

Culture & Project Step 1

1. 우리 모둠은 우주여행 가이드를 찾는 포스터를 만들었다.
   ➡ _____

2. 미래에, 우리는 우주를 여행할 수 있을 것이다.
   ➡ _____

3. 그래서 우리는 우주를 우리에게 안내해 줄 누군가가 필요하다.
   ➡ _____

4. 우주 여행 가이드는 우주에 대하여 여행자들에게 많은 것을 설명할 수 있어야 해서 우주와 행성들에 대해 많이 알아야 한다.
   ➡ _____

   _____

5. 또한, 그들은 건강해야 하고 사람들이 안전하고 편안하게 여행하는 것을 도와야 한다.
   ➡ _____

※ 다음 영어를 우리말로 쓰시오.

01	explain	22	death
02	fault	23	suddenly
03	conflict	24	disabled
04	shine	25	happen
05	master	26	greet
06	adopt	27	proud
07	needs	28	certainly
08	argument	29	judge
09	blame	30	last
10	sudden	31	nobleman
11	support	32	punish
12	leather	33	pity
13	drunk	34	live by
14	punishment	35	now that
15	mess	36	instead of
16	servant	37	bring up
17	regret	38	die of
18	disability	39	with a blank face
19	dwell	40	in advance
20	truth	41	think back
21	convey	42	put simply
		43	walk away from

※ 다음 우리말을 영어로 쓰시오.

01	자랑스러워하는		22	가죽	
02	입양하다		23	처벌	
03	~하는 동안에		24	후회하다	
04	거주하다		25	하인	
05	잘못		26	요구, 욕구	
06	처벌하다		27	주인	
07	귀족		28	갑작스러운	
08	질 좋은, 정교한		29	동정, 연민, 유감	
09	논쟁		30	쌍둥이	
10	인사하다		31	진실, 진리	
11	분명히		32	음식을 차려내다	
12	처벌하다		33	죽음	
13	인류		34	부양하다	
14	탓하다		35	~ 덕분에	
15	싸움, 다툼		36	~로 죽다	
16	장애		37	양육하다	
17	심장마비		38	~하지 못하다, ~을 실패하다	
18	전달하다, 나르다		39	돌이켜 생각하다	
19	판단하다		40	~에게서 멀어지다	
20	지속하다, 계속되다		41	~ 대신에	
21	장애를 가진		42	먼저, 앞서	
			43	알아내다	

※ 다음 영영풀이에 알맞은 단어를 <보기>에서 골라 쓴 후, 우리말 뜻을 쓰시오.

1 _____ : an amount taken off a regular price: _____

2 _____ : to live in a place or in a particular way: _____

3 _____ : to continue to exist: _____

4 _____ : a person who lives next to you or near you: _____

5 _____ : the things you must have for a satisfactory life: _____

6 _____ : a disagreement, or the process of disagreeing: _____

7 _____ : a mistake, especially something for which you are to blame: _____

8 _____ : a person who is hired to do household or personal duties such as cleaning and cooking: _____

9 _____ : to feel sad or sorry about something that you did or did not do: _____

10 _____ : to stop someone or something from being killed, injured, or destroyed: _____

11 _____ : to make something clear or easy to understand by describing or giving information about it: _____

12 _____ : a piece of information that is only known by one person or a few people and should not be told to others: _____

13 _____ : to form, give, or have as an opinion, or to decide about something or someone, especially after thinking carefully: _____

14 _____ : an illness, injury, or condition that makes it difficult for someone to do the things that other people do: _____

15 _____ : to legally take another person's child into your own family and take care of him or her as your own child: _____

16 _____ : to cause someone who has done something wrong or committed a crime to suffer, by hurting them, forcing them to pay money, sending them to prison, etc.: _____

보기			
servant	punish	fault	argument
dwell	secret	discount	last
disability	needs	adopt	explain
regret	neighbor	save	judge

※ 다음 우리말과 일치하도록 빈칸에 알맞은 말을 쓰시오.

Everyday English 1 A Listen and Check

(1) **B:** Who _____ this mess? It was _____ this morning.

   G: It's not my _____. Your dog _____ it.

   B: Oh, my _____! It will _____ a lot of time to _____ it _____.

   G: Let's do it _____. I'll help you.

(2) **G:** Minsu, _____ were you _____ _____ school today?

   B: It was _____ my fault.

   G: What _____?

   B: I got up _____ this morning, so I _____ the bus.

(3) (*Phone rings.*)

   W: Hello, _____ is the shoe shop. _____ may I help you?

   M: I have a _____ _____ the boots that I _____ there yesterday.

   W: What's the _____ _____ them?

   M: They're a bit _____. But it is not my _____. I've _____ worn them.

   W: Sorry _____ that. Please _____ our shop this week.

Everyday English 1 B Listening Activity

G: My dog got _____ this morning. I'm so _____ about him.

B: What did you _____ him yesterday?

G: I _____ him some milk last night.

B: Oh, you _____ _____ _____ a dog milk.

G: I was not sure _____ or not it is _____ for him _____ _____ milk. It was _____ my _____.

B: Don't _____ too much. Did you _____ him _____ the animal _____?

G: Yes, I did. I hope he'll _____ _____ soon.

B: He'll _____ get better _____ your _____ and love.

해석

(1) B: 누가 이렇게 엉망으로 만들었니? 오늘 아침에는 깨끗했는데.
G: 내 잘못이 아니야. 너의 개가 그랬어.
B: 맙소사! 이걸 다 치우려면 시간이 많이 걸리겠다.
G: 같이 해. 내가 도와 줄게.

(2) G: 민수야, 오늘 왜 학교에 늦었니?
B: 다 내 잘못이야.
G: 무슨 일이 있었는데?
B: 오늘 아침에 늦게 일어나서 버스를 놓쳤어.

(3) (전화가 울린다.)
W: 여보세요, 신발 가게입니다. 어떻게 도와드릴까요?
M: 제가 어제께 거기서 산 부츠에 문제가 있는데요.
W: 문제가 무엇입니까?
M: 조금 더러워서요. 근데 제 잘못은 아니에요. 신어 보지도 않았거든요.
W: 죄송합니다. 이번 주에 저희 가게에 들러 주세요.

G: 오늘 아침에 우리집 개가 아팠어. 개가 너무 걱정돼.
B: 어제 개한테 뭘 먹였는데?
G: 어젯밤에 우유를 좀 줬어.
B: 오, 개한테는 우유를 먹이면 안 돼.
G: 난 개가 우유를 먹으면 안전한지 아닌지 확신하지 못 했거든. 다 내 잘못이야.
B: 너무 걱정하지 마. 수의사에게 데려 갔었니?
G: 응, 데려갔었어. 개가 빨리 나아지길 바랄 뿐이야.
B: 네 보살핌과 사랑으로 분명히 회복할 거야.

(1) B: Did you hear that Minsu is in the _____?

G: Oh, I didn't know that. _____ we _____ to visit him?

B: No, he doesn't want _____ to visit him. He is just _____ about _____ _____.

G: Then should I make a _____ _____ my notes for him?

B: That's a good _____.

(2) B: Jina, you look _____. What's the _____?

G: My partner _____ hear _____. I don't know _____ _____ _____ with her.

B: Have you _____ communicating _____ her by writing?

G: Yes, I have. But the problem is that we do not _____ have a pencil.

B: Then, you are _____ to learn how to use _____ language.

Everyday English 2 B Listening Activity

B: Jina, what are you _____ to do this winter vacation?

G: I'm _____ _____ _____ some _____ work for people with _____. Would you like to _____ me?

B: Oh, that's a good idea. But I'm a bit _____ about it.

G: What _____ you feel like that?

B: I'm not sure _____ I am _____ _____ help them. Could you give me some _____?

G: You're _____ _____ _____ their needs.

B: What do you _____ by their _____?

G: You should help them _____ when they _____ you to do so.

In Real Life

Inho: Lina, you look so _____. What's the _____?

Lina: Oh, Inho. I had an _____ with Ryan.

Inho: Was it your _____?

Lina: No, it wasn't my fault! There was just a _____ between us.

Inho: In that _____, you're _____ _____ up with him as soon as _____.

---

(1) B: 민수가 병원에 입원했다는 소식 들었니?

G: 오, 난 몰랐어. 우리 민수에게 병문안 가야 하지 않을까?

B: 아니, 민수가 병문안 오는 걸 원치 않아. 민수는 그저 수업을 놓치는 게 걱정스러운가봐.

G: 그럼, 내가 그를 위해 내 노트를 복사해 줄까?

B: 좋은 생각이야.

(2) B: 지나야, 혼란스러워 보인다. 무슨 일이니?

G: 내 파트너가 아무것도 들을 수가 없어. 그녀와 어떻게 의사소통해야 할지 모르겠어.

B: 글을 써서 의사소통하려고 시도해 봤니?

G: 응, 해 봤어. 근데 문제는 우리가 연필을 항상 갖고 있는 건 아니라는 거야.

B: 그럼, 너는 수화를 사용하는 법을 배워야 해.

B: Jina야, 이번 겨울 방학에 무엇을 할 계획이니?

G: 난 장애가 있는 사람들을 위해 자원봉사를 할 생각을 하고 있어. 너도 같이 할래?

B: 오, 그거 좋은 생각이다. 그런데 난 좀 걱정이 돼.

G: 왜 그렇게 느끼니?

B: 내가 그 사람들을 도울 준비가 되어 있는지 확신하지 못하겠어. 네가 조언 좀 해 줄래?

G: 넌 그 사람들의 요구를 존중해야 돼.

B: 그 사람들의 요구라는 게 무슨 의미니?

G: 그들이 너에게 그렇게 해 달라고 요청할 때에만 도움을 줘야 해.

Inho: Lina야, 너 너무 우울해 보인다. 무슨 일 있니?

Lina: 오, 인호야. 나 Ryan과 말다툼을 했어.

Inho: 네 잘못이었니?

Lina: 아니, 내 잘못이 아니었어! 단지 우리 사이에 오해가 있었거든.

Inho: 그런 경우라면, 최대한 빨리 Ryan과 화해를 해야 돼.

Lina: Well, Ryan got so _____ that he wouldn't talk with me.

Inho: But who _____? He might _____ it now, just like you.

Lina: Do you think _____?

Inho: Yes, everyone wants to _____ good _____.

Lina: Thanks for your _____. I hope I can _____ _____ _____ him soon.

Lina: 글쎄, 그 애는 화가 너무 나서 나랑 이야기하려고 하지 않을 거야.

Inho: 그렇지만, 누가 알겠어? 그 애도 지금 너처럼 후회하고 있을지.

Lina: 그렇게 생각하니?

Inho: 응, 모두들 좋은 우정을 유지하고 싶어하거든.

Lina: 네 조언 고마워. 나도 곧 그 애랑 화해하기를 바라.

Check Your Progress 2

W: Thank you for _____ "Play World." Are you _____ _____ to this month's play? This month's play is *Hamlet* There are two _____ points about this play. First, it is a 21st _____ version of Shakespeare's *Hamlet*. It has _____ the _____ and the dead language of the 16th century that most of today's _____ might feel uncomfortable with. _____, the famous actor, Park Mujin, _____ in this play. His _____ shows a _____ _____ of the main character, Hamlet. Please _____ in mind that you will need to _____ your ticket online. It won't be your _____ if you _____ this play. But you'll certainly _____ _____ it.

W: "연극 세상"을 시청해 주셔서 감사합니다. 이 달의 연극을 기대하고 계신가요? 이 달의 연극은 "햄릿"입니다. 이 연극에는 두 가지 흥미로운 점이 있습니다. 첫째, 셰익스피어가 쓴 햄릿의 21세기 버전이라는 점입니다. 오늘날의 관객들 대부분이 불편하다고 느끼실 16세기 의상과 사장된 고어를 변화시켰습니다. 둘째, 유명한 배우인 박무진이 이 연극에 출연합니다. 그의 연기는 주연인 햄릿에 대한 깊은 이해를 반영합니다. 티켓은 인터넷으로 예매하셔야 한다는 점을 숙지해 주시기 바랍니다. 이 연극을 놓치게 되더라도 여러분의 책임은 아닐 겁니다. 그러나 연극을 놓치게 된다면 분명 후회하게 되실 겁니다.

Check Your Progress 3

(*Phone rings.*)

W: Hello. This is the Culture Theater. _____ may I help you?

B: I'd like to book four _____ for *Sleeping Beauty* this Friday.

W: Okay, let me _____. The _____ are at 6 p.m., and 8 p.m. Which one do you _____?

B: 6 p.m. please.

W: Oh, I'm sorry but we only have two seats _____ for that time.

B: _____ mind. It's all my fault for calling so late. What about 8 p.m.?

W: There are _____ seats at 8 p.m. That will be 60 dollars in _____.

B: Can I get a student _____? We are all students.

W: Sure, it's 30% _____.

B: What _____ I do to _____ the _____?

W: You're _____ _____ _____ your student ID card.

(전화가 울린다)

W: 여보세요. 컬처 극장입니다. 무엇을 도와드릴까요?

B: 이번 주 금요일에 하는 '잠자는 미녀'네 좌석을 예매하고 싶은데요.

W: 네, 확인해 보겠습니다. 공연은 저녁 6시와 8시에 있습니다. 어느 걸 선호하십니까?

B: 6시 걸로 해주세요.

W: 오, 죄송하지만, 그 시간은 두 석만 남아 있습니다.

B: 괜찮습니다. 제가 늦게 전화한 것이 잘못인 걸요. 8시는 어떤가요?

W: 저녁 8시 좌석은 충분히 있습니다. 총 60달러입니다.

B: 학생 할인을 받을 수 있을까요? 저희 모두 학생이라서요.

W: 그럼요. 30프로 할인이 됩니다.

B: 할인을 받으려면 뭘 해야 하나요?

W: 학생증을 가져 오셔야 합니다.

※ 다음 우리말에 맞도록 대화를 영어로 쓰시오.

Everyday English 1 A Listen and Check

(1) B: _____

 G: _____

 B: _____

 G: _____

(2) G: _____

 B: _____

 G: _____

 B: _____

(3) (*Phone rings.*)

 W: _____

 M: _____

 W: _____

 M: _____

 W: _____

(1) B: 누가 이렇게 엉망으로 만들었니? 오늘 아침에는 깨끗했는데.
 G: 내 잘못이 아니야. 너의 개가 그랬어.
 B: 맙소사! 이걸 다 치우려면 시간이 많이 걸리겠다.
 G: 같이 해. 내가 도와 줄게.

(2) G: 민수야, 오늘 왜 학교에 늦었니?
 B: 다 내 잘못이야.
 G: 무슨 일이 있었는데?
 B: 오늘 아침에 늦게 일어나서 버스를 놓쳤어.

(3) (전화가 울린다.)
 W: 여보세요, 신발 가게입니다. 어떻게 도와드릴까요?
 M: 제가 어저께 거기서 산 부츠에 문제가 있는데요.
 W: 문제가 무엇입니까?
 M: 조금 더러워서요. 근데 제 잘못은 아니에요. 신어 보지도 않았거든요.
 W: 죄송합니다. 이번 주에 저희 가게에 들러 주세요.

Everyday English 1 B Listening Activity

 G: _____

 B: _____

 G: _____

 B: _____

 G: _____

 B: _____

 G: _____

 B: _____

 G: 오늘 아침에 우리집 개가 아팠어. 개가 너무 걱정돼.
 B: 어제 개한테 뭘 먹였는데?
 G: 어젯밤에 우유를 좀 줬어.
 B: 오, 개한테는 우유를 먹이면 안 돼.
 G: 난 개가 우유를 먹으면 안전한지 아닌지 확신하지 못 했거든. 다 내 잘못이야.
 B: 너무 걱정하지 마. 수의사에게 데려갔었니?
 G: 응, 데려갔었어. 개가 빨리 나아지길 바랄 뿐이야.
 B: 네 보살핌과 사랑으로 분명히 회복할 거야.

Everyday English 2 A Listen and Check

(1) B: _____

　　G: _____

　　B: _____

　　_____

　　G: _____

　　B: _____

(2) B: _____

　　G: _____

　　_____

　　B: _____

　　G: _____

　　B: _____

Everyday English 2 B Listening Activity

B: _____

G: _____

　_____

B: _____

G: _____

B: _____

G: _____

B: _____

G: _____

In Real Life

Inho: _____

Lina: _____

Inho: _____

Lina: _____

Inho: _____

(1) B: 민수가 병원에 입원했다는 소식 들었니?
　　G: 오, 난 몰랐어. 우리 민수에게 병문안 가야 하지 않을까?
　　B: 아니, 민수가 병문안 오는 걸 원치 않아. 민수는 그저 수업을 놓치는 게 걱정스러운가봐.
　　G: 그럼, 내가 그를 위해 내 노트를 복사해 줄까?
　　B: 좋은 생각이야.

(2) B: 지나야, 혼란스러워 보인다. 무슨 일이니?
　　G: 내 파트너가 아무것도 들을 수가 없어. 그녀와 어떻게 의사소통해야 할지 모르겠어.
　　B: 글을 써서 의사소통하려고 시도해 봤니?
　　G: 응, 해 봤어. 근데 문제는 우리가 연필을 항상 갖고 있는 건 아니라는 거야.
　　B: 그럼, 너는 수화를 사용하는 법을 배워야 해.

B: Jina야, 이번 겨울 방학에 무엇을 할 계획이니?
G: 난 장애가 있는 사람들을 위해 자원봉사를 할 생각을 하고 있어. 너도 같이 할래?
B: 오, 그거 좋은 생각이다. 그런데 난 좀 걱정이 돼.
G: 왜 그렇게 느끼니?
B: 내가 그 사람들을 도울 준비가 되어 있는지 확신하지 못하겠어. 네가 조언 좀 해 줄래?
G: 넌 그 사람들의 요구를 존중해야 돼.
B: 그 사람들의 요구라는 게 무슨 의미니?
G: 그들이 너에게 그렇게 해 달라고 요청할 때에만 도움을 줘야 해.

Inho: Lina야, 너 너무 우울해 보인다. 무슨 일 있니?
Lina: 오, 인호야. 나 Ryan과 말다툼을 했어.
Inho: 네 잘못이었니?
Lina: 아니, 내 잘못이 아니었어! 단지 우리 사이에 오해가 있었거든.
Inho: 그런 경우라면, 최대한 빨리 Ryan과 화해를 해야 돼.

Lina: _____

Inho: _____

Lina: _____

Inho: _____

Lina: _____

Lina: 글쎄, 그 애는 화가 너무 나서 나랑 이야기하려고 하지 않을 거야.

Inho: 그렇지만, 누가 알겠어? 그 애도 지금 너처럼 후회하고 있을지.

Lina: 그렇게 생각하니?

Inho: 응, 모두들 좋은 우정을 유지하고 싶어하거든.

Lina: 네 조언 고마워. 나도 곧 그 애랑 화해하기를 바라.

Check Your Progress 2

W: _____

_____

_____

_____

_____

_____

_____

_____

W: "연극 세상"을 시청해 주셔서 감사합니다. 이 달의 연극을 기대하고 계신가요? 이 달의 연극은 "햄릿"입니다. 이 연극에는 두 가지 흥미로운 점이 있습니다. 첫째, 셰익스피어가 쓴 햄릿의 21세기 버전이라는 점입니다. 오늘날의 관객들 대부분이 불편하다고 느끼실 16세기 의상과 사장된 고어를 변화시켰습니다. 둘째, 유명한 배우인 박무진이 이 연극에 출연합니다. 그의 연기는 주연인 햄릿에 대한 깊은 이해를 반영합니다. 티켓은 인터넷으로 예매하셔야 한다는 점을 숙지해 주시기 바랍니다. 이 연극을 놓치게 되더라도 여러분의 책임은 아닐 겁니다. 그러나 연극을 놓치게 된다면 분명 후회하게 되실 겁니다.

Check Your Progress 3

(Phone rings.)

W: _____

B: _____

W: _____

_____

B: _____

W: _____

B: _____

W: _____

B: _____

W: _____

B: _____

W: _____

(전화가 울린다)

W: 여보세요. 컬처 극장입니다. 무엇을 도와드릴까요?

B: 이번 주 금요일에 하는 '잠자는 미녀' 네 좌석을 예매하고 싶은데요.

W: 네, 확인해 보겠습니다. 공연은 저녁 6시와 8시에 있습니다. 어느 걸 선호하십니까?

B: 6시 걸로 해주세요.

W: 오, 죄송하지만, 그 시간은 두 석만 남아 있습니다.

B: 괜찮습니다. 제가 늦게 전화한 것이 잘못인 걸요. 8시는 어떤가요?

W: 저녁 8시 좌석은 충분히 있습니다. 총 60달러입니다.

B: 학생 할인을 받을 수 있을까요? 저희 모두 학생이라서요.

W: 그럼요. 30프로 할인이 됩니다.

B: 할인을 받으려면 뭘 해야 하나요?

W: 학생증을 가져 오셔야 합니다.

※ 다음 우리말과 일치하도록 빈칸에 알맞은 것을 골라 쓰시오.

1 Three _____ _____
  A. Smiles   B. Mysterious

  Scene #1.

2 *It's winter. A poor shoe maker, Simon, _____ to buy a warm coat. _____ his way _____ home, he finds a man, Michael, _____ in the street without any clothes.*
  A. back   B. fails   C. lying   D. on

3 Simon: I'm not sure _____ he is dead _____ not. But I don't think I can save him because I'm _____ and have little money. (*walking away from Michael at first, but coming back again*) Poor man. Are you okay? Why are you _____ here?
  A. drunk   B. lying   C. or   D. whether

4 Michael: I can't tell you everything. _____ _____, I am _____ _____.
  A. simply   B. punished   C. put   D. being

5 Simon: But it's _____ _____. _____ go home _____.
  A. let's   B. cold   C. together   D. outside

  Scene #2.

6 *Simon comes home and _____ Matrena, his wife. She finds he _____ _____ _____.*
  A. has   B. greets   C. nothing   D. brought

7 Matrena: (_____ *and angry*) Simon, you were _____ _____ buy a coat for our family. But there's _____. And who is this man?
  A. to   B. nothing   C. surprised   D. supposed

8 Simon: I did not have _____ money to buy the coat. I'm sorry. And I know _____ about this man. But it wasn't my _____. I had to _____ him home. I mean just look at him. Don't you think he needs help?
  A. nothing   B. enough   C. bring   D. fault

9 Matrena: (_____ _____ *Michael* _____ _____) Okay, Simon.
  A. with   B. looking   C. pity   D. at

10 (*Michael* _____ _____ the _____ _____.)
  A. first   B. smiles   C. time   D. for

11 _____ *a week, Michael does no* _____ *to* _____ _____.
  A. support   B. work   C. for   D. himself

12 Simon: (*looking at Michael*) Michael, I'm afraid you've _____ doing nothing _____ you came here. It's time you started to _____ a _____ for yourself. If you work for me, I will give you food. Would you like to work with me?
  A. earn   B. been   C. living   D. since

13 Michael: (_____ a _____ _____) Yes, I _____.
  A. face   B. with   C. would   D. blank

1 세 가지의 신비로운 미소
  장면 1.
2 겨울이다. 가난한 구두장이 Simon은 따뜻한 코트를 사는 데 실패한다. 그는 집에 돌아오는 길에 옷을 입지 않고 길거리에 누워 있는 Michael이라는 한 남자를 발견한다.
3 Simon: 저 남자가 죽은 건지 아닌 건지 모르겠군. 하지만 나는 취해 있고, 돈도 거의 없어서 저 남자를 구할 수 없을 것 같아. (처음엔 Michael에게서 발걸음을 돌리지만, 다시 돌아오며) 불쌍한 사람이군. 괜찮으세요? 왜 여기 누워 있는 거죠?
4 Michael: 당신에게 말 못할 사정이 있어요. 간단히 말하자면, 저는 벌을 받고 있어요.
5 Simon: 하지만 밖은 추워요. 같이 집으로 갑시다.
  장면 2.
6 Simon은 집으로 와서 그의 아내인 Matrena와 인사한다. 그녀는 그가 아무것도 가져오지 않은 것을 알게 된다.
7 Matrena: (놀라서 화내며) Simon, 당신은 우리 가족을 위해 코트를 사 오기로 했잖아요. 하지만 아무것도 없네요. 그리고 이 남자는 누구예요?
8 Simon: 코트를 살 정도로 충분한 돈이 없었어요. 미안해요. 그리고 이 남자에 관해서는 아무것도 모르지만, 내 잘못은 아니에요. 나는 이 남자를 집에 데려와야만 했어요. 이 남자를 보세요. 도움이 필요해 보이지 않나요?
9 Matrena: (Michael을 불쌍하게 바라보며) 그래요, Simon.
10 (Michael은 처음으로 미소를 짓는다.)
11 1주일간, Michael은 스스로 자신의 생계를 유지하기 위해 아무 일도 하지 않는다.
12 Simon: (Michael을 바라보며) Michael, 당신이 이곳에 와서 계속 빈둥거리고 있어 걱정되네요. 당신 자신을 위해 생계를 꾸려야 할 때에요. 저를 위해서 일해 준다면, 제가 당신에게 음식을 제공할게요. 저랑 같이 일하시겠어요?
13 Michael: (무표정한 얼굴로) 네, 그렇게 할게요.

Scene #3.

14 *A year later, Simon has become _____, _____ to Michael's great _____ in making shoes. One day, a nobleman comes to _____ his boots.*

    A. order   B. thanks   C. skills   D. famous

15 Nobleman: I'd like to order fine _____ boots that have to _____ for a year. I'm not _____ _____ you can make them. Can you do that?

    A. sure   B. leather   C. whether   D. last

16 *(Michael watches the man _____ and _____ for the _____ .)*

    A. second   B. carefully   C. time   D. smiles

17 Simon: Yes, sir. _____ _____ .

    A. worry   B. don't

18 *(The _____ _____ the _____ .)*

    A. shop   B. nobleman   C. leaves

19 Simon: Michael, please _____ some _____ boots.

    A. leather   B. make   C. thick

20 _____ : _____ .

    A. okay   B. Michael

21 *(_____ , Michael makes _____ slippers _____ _____ boots.)*

    A. instead   B. however   C. of   D. soft

22 Simon: *(finding the slippers)* Michael! I told you there _____ be no _____ . _____ do you _____ you are doing?

    A. mistakes   B. think   C. should   D. what

23 Servant: *(running into the shop)* Please _____ boots and start making soft slippers for a dead body _____ . My master has died of a heart _____ .

    A. instead   B. stop   C. attack   D. making

24 Simon: *(_____ _____ Michael _____ _____)* How did you know?

    A. in   B. looking   C. surprise   D. at

25 _____ : _____ …

    A. well   B. Michael

Scene #4.

26 *A _____ years _____ , a woman _____ visits the shoe shop _____ twin girls.*

    A. with   B. few   C. customer   D. later

27 Customer: I'm here _____ _____ some _____ shoes for these _____ girls.

    A. twin   B. buy   C. leather   D. to

28 Simon: *(_____ that one of the girls has a _____)* I'm sorry about your daughter's foot. May I ask you if she was _____ _____ a disability?

    A. disability   B. with   C. seeing   D. born

장면 3.

14 1년 후, Simon은 Michael의 훌륭한 구두 제작 솜씨 덕분에 유명해졌다. 어느 날, 한 귀족이 부츠를 주문하러 가게에 온다.

15 귀족: 나는 1년을 신어도 끄떡 없는 튼튼한 가죽 부츠를 주문하고 싶습니다. 당신이 그 부츠를 만들 수 있을지 모르겠네요. 할 수 있겠습니까?

16 (Michael은 귀족을 유심히 살펴보고는 두 번째로 미소 짓는다.)

17 Simon: 네, 나리. 걱정하지 마세요.

18 (귀족은 가게를 떠난다.)

19 Simon: Michael, 두꺼운 가죽 부츠를 만들어 주세요.

20 Michael: 네.

21 (하지만, Michael은 부츠 대신 부드러운 슬리퍼를 만든다.)

22 Simon: (슬리퍼를 발견하며) Michael! 제가 실수하지 말라고 했잖아요. 지금 뭐 하고 있는 겁니까?

23 하인: (가게로 뛰어들며) 부츠는 그만 만들고 대신 죽은 사람에게 신길 부드러운 슬리퍼를 만들어 주세요. 나리가 심장마비로 돌아가셨습니다.

24 Simon: (놀라서 Michael을 바라보며) 당신은 어떻게 알았습니까?

25 Michael: 글쎄요…

장면 4.

26 몇 년 후, 한 여인이 쌍둥이 소녀들과 함께 신발 가게에 방문한다.

27 손님: 이 쌍둥이 소녀들에게 신길 가죽 신발을 사러 왔습니다.

28 Simon: (장애를 가진 한 소녀를 보며) 따님 한쪽 발이 안타깝네요. 실례지만, 태어날 때부터 장애가 있었는지 여쭤 봐도 될까요?

29 Customer: Oh, I'm not her _____ mother. Her mother hurt this girl's leg while she was _____ _____ to her. Their parents are both dead now. I felt sorry for them. I loved these twins so much that I decided to _____ them.

A. giving   B. adopt   C. real   D. birth

30 (*Michael* _____ *the* _____ _____.)

A. for   B. smiles   C. time   D. third

Scene #5.

31 (_____, a _____ _____ _____ *from Michael.*)

A. light   B. suddenly   C. shines   D. mysterious

32 Simon: What's this _____ _____ _____ you?

A. shining   B. light   C. from

33 Michael: It's _____ _____ I _____ here.

A. time   B. about   C. left

34 Simon: What do you _____? And _____ did you _____?

A. why   B. smile   C. mean   D. just

35 Michael: Let me explain. I am an angel. I was sent here as a _____, and I was _____ to learn three _____. Every time I learned one of them, I smiled. Now that I have learned all three of them, I am _____ to go back.

A. punishment   B. ready   C. supposed   D. truths

36 Simon: I see. What _____ _____ you _____?

A. learned   B. truths   C. have

Scene #6.

37 *Michael* _____ _____ _____ *each time that he smiled. Simon and Matrena listen* _____ *to him.*

A. carefully   B. back   C. to   D. thinks

38 Michael: First, I learned that love _____ in human beings when Matrena _____ me. This was the answer to the first _____: Learn what dwells in human beings. I smiled because I learned the truth. But I still had two more to _____ out.

A. pitied   B. figure   C. dwells   D. lesson

39 Simon: _____ _____ _____ ?

A. they   B. were   C. what

40 Michael: The second was, "Learn _____ is not given to people." When the nobleman ordered that his boots were to _____ for a year, I knew he would die soon. Then I _____ people know little about their own _____ needs.

A. realized   B. last   C. what   D. future

41 Simon: _____ was the _____ _____ ?

A. truth   B. what   C. last

42 Michael: It was from the story of the woman and the twin girls. After the _____ of their mother, the woman _____ them _____ with her love. Then, I learned people live by having true love for each other. That was the third lesson: What people live _____.

A. by   B. death   C. up   D. brought

---

29 손님: 오, 저는 이 아이의 생모가 아니에요. 생모가 아이를 낳던 중에 아이가 다리를 다치게 됐어요. 그들의 부모님은 이미 돌아가셨습니다. 나는 이 쌍둥이가 너무 불쌍했어요. 이 아이들을 너무 사랑해서 입양하기로 결정했습니다.

30 (Michael은 세 번째로 미소를 짓는다.)

장면 5.

31 (갑자기 Michael에게서 신비한 빛이 빛난다.)

32 Simon: 당신에게서 나오는 이 빛은 도대체 뭔가요?

33 Michael: 이제 제가 떠날 때가 왔군요.

34 Simon: 무슨 말씀이시죠? 그리고 당신은 왜 미소를 지었던 건가요?

35 Michael: 설명해 드릴게요. 저는 천사입니다. 저는 벌을 받아 여기로 보내졌고, 세 가지 진리를 깨달아야 했습니다. 제가 진리를 하나씩 깨달을 때마다 미소를 지었던 것입니다. 저는 세 가지 진리를 모두 깨달았기 때문에 돌아갈 준비를 마쳤습니다.

36 Simon: 그렇군요. 당신이 깨달은 진리는 무엇이었나요?

장면 6.

37 Michael은 그가 미소 지었을 때를 회상한다. Simon과 Matrena는 그의 말을 주의 깊게 듣는다.

38 Michael: 첫째, Matrena가 저를 가여워했을 때 인간 내면에 사랑이 존재한다는 것을 저는 깨달았습니다. 이는 '인간 내면에 무엇이 존재하는가'라는 첫 번째 교훈에 관한 답이었던 것입니다. 저는 그 진실을 깨달았기 때문에 미소를 지었습니다. 하지만 저는 아직도 두 가지를 더 알아내야만 했어요.

39 Simon: 그것들은 뭐였나요?

40 Michael: 두 번째는 "인간에게 주어지지 않은 것은 무엇인가"였습니다. 그 귀족이 1년을 신어도 끄떡없는 부츠를 주문했을 때, 저는 그가 곧 죽을 것을 알고 있었습니다. 사람은 자신의 미래에 필요한 것을 알지 못한다는 사실을 그때 저는 깨달았습니다.

41 Simon: 마지막 진리는 무엇이었나요?

42 Michael: 쌍둥이 소녀와 여인의 이야기를 듣고 깨달았습니다. 쌍둥이의 생모가 사망한 후, 그 여인은 그들을 사랑으로 키웠습니다. 그때, 저는 사람은 서로를 향한 참된 사랑으로 산다는 점을 알게 됐습니다. 그것이 '사람은 무엇으로 사는가'에 관한 세 번째 교훈이었습니다.

※ 다음 우리말과 일치하도록 빈칸에 알맞은 것을 골라 쓰시오.

1   Three _____ Smiles

    Scene #1.

2   *It's winter. A poor shoe maker, Simon, _____ _____ _____ a warm coat. _____ his _____ _____ home, he finds a man, Michael, _____ in the street without any clothes.*

3   Simon: I'm not sure _____ he is dead _____ _____ . But I don't think I can save him because I'm _____ and have little money. (*walking away from Michael at first, but coming back again*) Poor man. Are you _____ ? _____ are you _____ here?

4   Michael: I can't tell you everything. _____ _____ , I am _____ _____ .

5   Simon: But it's cold _____ . Let's go home together.

    Scene #2.

6   *Simon comes home and _____ Matrena, his wife. She finds he _____ _____ _____ .*

7   Matrena: (*surprised and angry*) Simon, you _____ _____ _____ buy a coat for our family. But there's _____ . And who is this man?

8   Simon: I did not have _____ _____ _____ _____ the coat. I'm sorry. And I know nothing about this man. But it wasn't my _____ . I had to bring him home. I mean just look at him. _____ _____ _____ he needs _____ ?

9   Matrena: (*looking at Michael _____ _____ *) Okay, Simon.

10   (*Michael smiles _____ _____ _____ _____ .*)

11   *For a week, Michael does no work to _____ _____ .*

12   Simon: (*looking at Michael*) Michael, I'm afraid you've been doing nothing since you came here. _____ _____ _____ _____ to earn a living for yourself. If you work for me, I will give you food. Would you like _____ _____ with me?

13   Michael: (*with a _____ face*) Yes, I would.

---

1 세 가지의 신비로운 미소
    장면 1.

2 겨울이다. 가난한 구두장이 Simon은 따뜻한 코트를 사는 데 실패한다. 그는 집에 돌아오는 길에 옷도 입지 않고 길거리에 누워 있는 Michael이라는 한 남자를 발견한다.

3 Simon: 저 남자가 죽은 건지 아닌 건지 모르겠군. 하지만 나는 취해 있고, 돈도 거의 없어서 저 남자를 구할 수 없을 것 같아. (처음엔 Michael에게서 발걸음을 돌리지만, 다시 돌아오며) 불쌍한 사람이군. 괜찮으세요? 왜 여기 누워 있는 거요?

4 Michael: 당신에게 말 못할 사정이 있어요. 간단히 말하자면, 저는 벌을 받고 있어요.

5 Simon: 하지만 밖은 추워요. 같이 집으로 갑시다.
    장면 2.

6 Simon은 집으로 와서 그의 아내인 Matrena와 인사한다. 그녀는 그가 아무것도 가져오지 않은 것을 알게 된다.

7 Matrena: (놀라서 화내며) Simon, 당신은 우리 가족을 위해 코트를 사 오기로 했잖아요. 하지만 아무것도 없네요. 그리고 이 남자는 누구예요?

8 Simon: 코트를 살 정도로 충분한 돈이 없었어요. 미안해요. 그리고 이 남자에 관해서는 아무것도 모르지만, 내 잘못은 아니에요. 나는 이 남자를 집에 데려와야만 했어요. 이 남자를 보세요. 도움이 필요해 보이지 않나요?

9 Matrena: (Michael을 불쌍하게 바라보며) 그래요, Simon.

10 (Michael은 처음으로 미소를 짓는다.)

11 1주일간, Michael은 스스로 자신의 생계를 유지하기 위해 아무 일도 하지 않는다.

12 Simon: (Michael을 바라보며) Michael, 당신이 이곳에 와서 계속 빈둥거리고 있어 걱정되네요. 당신 자신을 위해 생계를 꾸려야 할 때예요. 저를 위해서 일해 준다면, 제가 당신에게 음식을 제공할게요. 저랑 같이 일하시겠어요?

13 Michael: (무표정한 얼굴로) 네, 그렇게 할게요.

Scene #3.

14 *A year later, Simon has become famous, _____ _____ Michael's great _____ in making shoes. One day, a nobleman comes to _____ his boots.*

15 Nobleman: I'd like to order _____ _____ boots _____ _____ _____ _____ for a year. _____ _____ _____ _____ you can make them. Can you do that?

16 (*Michael watches the man _____ and smiles _____ _____ _____ _____ .*)

17 Simon: Yes, sir. _____ _____ .

18 (*The nobleman _____ the shop.*)

19 Simon: Michael, please make some thick _____ _____ .

20 Michael: Okay.

21 (*However, Michael makes soft slippers _____ _____ boots.*)

22 Simon: (*finding the slippers*) Michael! I told you _____ _____ _____ no _____ . _____ do you think you are doing?

23 Servant: (*running into the shop*) Please _____ _____ boots and start making soft slippers for a dead body _____ . My master has _____ _____ a _____ _____ .

24 Simon: (*looking at Michael _____ _____ *) How did you know?

25 Michael: Well ...

Scene #4.

26 *A few years _____ , a woman _____ visits the shoe shop with twin girls.*

27 Customer: I'm here _____ _____ some leather shoes for these twin girls.

28 Simon: (_____ *that one of the girls has a disability*) I'm sorry _____ your daughter's foot. May I ask you _____ she was born _____ _____ _____ ?

장면 3.

14 1년 후, Simon은 Michael의 훌륭한 구두 제작 솜씨 덕분에 유명해졌다. 어느 날, 한 귀족이 부츠를 주문하러 가게에 온다.

15 귀족: 나는 1년을 신어도 끄떡없는 튼튼한 가죽 부츠를 주문하고 싶습니다. 당신이 그 부츠를 만들 수 있을지 모르겠네요. 할 수 있겠습니까?

16 (Michael은 귀족을 유심히 살펴보고는 두 번째로 미소 짓는다.)

17 Simon: 네, 나리. 걱정하지 마세요.

18 (귀족은 가게를 떠난다.)

19 Simon: Michael, 두꺼운 가죽 부츠를 만들어 주세요.

20 Michael: 네.

21 (하지만, Michael은 부츠 대신 부드러운 슬리퍼를 만든다.)

22 Simon: (슬리퍼를 발견하며) Michael! 제가 실수하지 말라고 했잖아요. 지금 뭐 하고 있는 겁니까?

23 하인: (가게로 뛰어들며) 부츠는 그만 만들고 대신 죽은 사람에게 신길 부드러운 슬리퍼를 만들어 주세요. 나리가 심장마비로 돌아가셨습니다.

24 Simon: (놀라서 Michael을 바라보며) 당신은 어떻게 알았습니까?

25 Michael: 글쎄요…

장면 4.

26 몇 년 후, 한 여인이 쌍둥이 소녀들과 함께 신발 가게에 방문한다.

27 손님: 이 쌍둥이 소녀들에게 신길 가죽 신발을 사러 왔습니다.

28 Simon: (장애를 가진 한 소녀를 보며) 따님 한쪽 발이 안타깝네요. 실례지만, 태어날 때부터 장애가 있었는지 여쭤 봐도 될까요?

29 Customer: Oh, I'm not her _____ mother. Her mother hurt this girl's leg while she was _____ _____ _____ her. Their parents are both dead now. I felt sorry for them. I loved these twins _____ _____ _____ I decided to adopt them.

30 (*Michael smiles for the third time.*)

Scene #5.

31 (*Suddenly, a mysterious light _____ _____ Michael.*)

32 Simon: What's this light _____ from you?

33 Michael: It's _____ time I _____ here.

34 Simon: What do you mean? And _____ did you _____ _____?

35 Michael: Let me explain. I am an angel. I _____ _____ here _____ a _____, and I _____ _____ _____ learn three truths. _____ _____ I learned one of them, I smiled. _____ _____ I have learned all three of them, I _____ _____ _____ go back.

36 Simon: I see. What truths _____ _____ _____?

Scene #6.

37 *Michael _____ _____ _____ each time that he smiled. Simon and Matrena listen carefully to him.*

38 Michael: First, I learned that love _____ _____ human beings when Matrena _____ me. This was the answer to the first lesson: Learn _____ dwells in human beings. I smiled because I learned the truth. But I still had two more _____ _____ _____.

39 Simon: What were they?

40 Michael: The second was, "Learn _____ is not given to people." When the nobleman ordered that his boots _____ _____ _____ for a year, I knew he would die soon. Then I _____ people _____ _____ _____ their own _____ _____.

41 Simon: What was the _____ _____?

42 Michael: It was from the story of the woman and the twin girls. After the death of their mother, the woman _____ _____ _____ with her love. Then, I learned people live _____ _____ _____ _____ _____ each other. That was the third lesson: _____ _____ _____ _____.

29 손님: 오, 저는 이 아이의 생모가 아니에요. 생모가 아이를 낳던 중에 아이가 다리를 다치게 됐어요. 그들의 부모님은 이미 돌아가셨습니다. 나는 이 쌍둥이가 너무 불쌍했어요. 이 아이들을 너무 사랑해서 입양하기로 결정했습니다.

30 (Michael은 세 번째로 미소를 짓는다.)

장면 5.

31 (갑자기 Michael에게서 신비한 빛이 빛난다.)

32 Simon: 당신에게서 나오는 이 빛은 도대체 뭔가요?

33 Michael: 이제 제가 떠날 때가 왔군요.

34 Simon: 무슨 말씀이시죠? 그리고 당신은 왜 미소를 지었던 건가요?

35 Michael: 설명해 드릴게요. 저는 천사입니다. 저는 벌을 받아 여기로 보내졌고, 세 가지 진리를 깨달아야 했습니다. 제가 진리를 하나씩 깨달을 때마다 미소를 지었던 것입니다. 저는 세 가지 진리를 모두 깨달았기 때문에 돌아갈 준비를 마쳤습니다.

36 Simon: 그렇군요. 당신이 깨달은 진리는 무엇이었나요?

장면 6.

37 Michael은 그가 미소 지었을 때를 회상한다. Simon과 Matrena는 그의 말을 주의 깊게 듣는다.

38 Michael: 첫째, Matrena가 저를 가여워했을 때 인간 내면에 사랑이 존재한다는 것을 저는 깨달았습니다. 이는 '인간 내면에 무엇이 존재하는가'라는 첫 번째 교훈에 관한 답이었던 것입니다. 저는 그 진실을 깨달았기 때문에 미소를 지었습니다. 하지만 저는 아직도 두 가지를 더 알아내야만 했어요.

39 Simon: 그것들은 뭐였나요?

40 Michael: 두 번째는 "인간에게 주어지지 않은 것은 무엇인가"였습니다. 그 귀족이 1년을 신어도 끄떡없는 부츠를 주문했을 때, 저는 그가 곧 죽을 것을 알고 있었습니다. 사람은 자신의 미래에 필요한 것을 알지 못한다는 사실을 그때 저는 깨달았습니다.

41 Simon: 마지막 진리는 무엇이었나요?

42 Michael: 쌍둥이 소녀와 여인의 이야기를 듣고 깨달았습니다. 쌍둥이의 생모가 사망한 후, 그 여인은 그들을 사랑으로 키웠습니다. 그때, 저는 사람은 서로를 향한 참된 사랑으로 산다는 점을 알게 됐습니다. 그것이 '사람은 무엇으로 사는가'에 관한 세 번째 교훈이었습니다.

Step3

※ 다음 문장을 우리말로 쓰시오.

1 Three Mysterious Smiles
➡ _____

Scene #1.: 장면 1.

2 It's winter. A poor shoe maker, Simon, fails to buy a warm coat. On his way back home, he finds a man, Michael, lying in the street without any clothes.
➡ _____

3 Simon: I'm not sure whether he is dead or not. But I don't think I can save him because I'm drunk and have little money. (walking away from Michael at first, but coming back again) Poor man. Are you okay? Why are you lying here?
➡ _____

4 Michael: I can't tell you everything. Put simply, I am being punished.
➡ _____

5 Simon: But it's cold outside. Let's go home together.
➡ _____

Scene #2.: 장면 2.

6 Simon comes home and greets Matrena, his wife. She finds he has brought nothing.
➡ _____

7 Matrena: (surprised and angry) Simon, you were supposed to buy a coat for our family. But there's nothing. And who is this man?
➡ _____

8 Simon: I did not have enough money to buy the coat. I'm sorry. And I know nothing about this man. But it wasn't my fault. I had to bring him home. I mean just look at him. Don't you think he needs help?
➡ _____

9 Matrena: (looking at Michael with pity) Okay, Simon.
➡ _____

10 (Michael smiles for the first time.)
➡ _____

11 For a week, Michael does no work to support himself.
➡ _____

12 Simon: (looking at Michael) Michael, I'm afraid you've been doing nothing since you came here. It's time you started to earn a living for yourself. If you work for me, I will give you food. Would you like to work with me?
➡ _____

13 Michael: (with a blank face) Yes, I would.
➡ _____

Scene #3.: 장면 3.

14 A year later, Simon has become famous, thanks to Michael's great skills in making shoes. One day, a nobleman comes to order his boots.

➡ _____

15 Nobleman: I'd like to order fine leather boots that have to last for a year. I'm not sure whether you can make them. Can you do that?

➡ _____

16 (Michael watches the man carefully and smiles for the second time.)

➡ _____

17 Simon: Yes, sir. Don't worry.

➡ _____

18 (The nobleman leaves the shop.)

➡ _____

19 Simon: Michael, please make some thick leather boots.

➡ _____

20 Michael: Okay.

➡ _____

21 (However, Michael makes soft slippers instead of boots.)

➡ _____

22 Simon: (finding the slippers) Michael! I told you there should be no mistakes. What do you think you are doing?

➡ _____

23 Servant: (running into the shop) Please stop making boots and start making soft slippers for a dead body instead. My master has died of a heart attack.

➡ _____

24 Simon: (looking at Michael in surprise) How did you know?

➡ _____

25 Michael: Well ...

➡ _____

Scene #4.: 장면 4.

26 A few years later, a woman customer visits the shoe shop with twin girls.

➡ _____

27 Customer: I'm here to buy some leather shoes for these twin girls.

➡ _____

28 Simon: (seeing that one of the girls has a disability) I'm sorry about your daughter's foot. May I ask you if she was born with a disability?

➡ _____

29 Customer: Oh, I'm not her real mother. Her mother hurt this girl's leg while she was giving birth to her. Their parents are both dead now. I felt sorry for them. I loved these twins so much that I decided to adopt them.

➡ _____

30 (Michael smiles for the third time.)

➡ _____

Scene #5.: 장면 5.

31 (Suddenly, a mysterious light shines from Michael.)
➡ _____

32 Simon: What's this light shining from you?
➡ _____

33 Michael: It's about time I left here.
➡ _____

34 Simon: What do you mean? And why did you just smile?
➡ _____

35 Michael: Let me explain. I am an angel. I was sent here as a punishment, and I was supposed to learn three truths. Every time I learned one of them, I smiled. Now that I have learned all three of them, I am ready to go back.
➡ _____
_____
_____

36 Simon: I see. What truths have you learned?
➡ _____

Scene #6.: 장면 6.

37 Michael thinks back to each time that he smiled. Simon and Matrena listen carefully to him.
➡ _____

38 Michael: First, I learned that love dwells in human beings when Matrena pitied me. This was the answer to the first lesson: Learn what dwells in human beings. I smiled because I learned the truth. But I still had two more to figure out.the answer to the first lesson: Learn what dwells in human beings. I smiled because I learned the truth. But I still had two more to figure out.
➡ _____
_____
_____

39 Simon: What were they?
➡ _____

40 Michael: The second was, "Learn what is not given to people." When the nobleman ordered that his boots were to last for a year, I knew he would die soon. Then I realized people know little about their own future needs.
➡ _____
_____
_____

41 Simon: What was the last truth?
➡ _____

42 Michael: It was from the story of the woman and the twin girls. After the death of their mother, the woman brought them up with her love. Then, I learned people live by having true love for each other. That was the third lesson: What people live by.
➡ _____
_____
_____

※ 다음 괄호 안의 단어들을 우리말에 맞도록 바르게 배열하시오.

1 (Mysterious / Three / Smiles)
➡ _____

Scene #1.

2 (winter. / it's // poor / a / maker, / shoe / Simon, / to / fails / a / buy / coat. / warm // his / on / way / home, / back / finds / he / man, / a / Michael, / in / lying / street / the / without / street / clothes. / any)
➡ _____
_____

3 (Simon: / not / I'm / whether / sure / is / he / not. / or / dead // I / but / think / don't / I / save / can / because / him / drunk / I'm / and / little / have / money. // away / (walking / from / at / Michael / first, / coming / but / again) / back // man. / poor // you / are / okay? // are / why / lying / you / here?)
➡ _____
_____
_____

4 (Michael: / can't / I / you / tell / everything. // simply, / put / am / I / punished. / being)
➡ _____

5 (Simon: / it's / but / outside. / cold // go / let's / together. / home)
➡ _____

Scene #2.

6 (comes / Simon / home / greets / and / Matrena, / wife. / his // finds / she / has / he / nothing. / brought)
➡ _____

7 (Matrena: / angry) / and / (surprised / Simon, / were / you / supposed / buy / to / coat / a / our / for / family. // there's / but / nothing. // who / and / this / is / man?)
➡ _____

8 (Simon: / did / I / have / not / enough / to / money / the / buy / coat. // sorry. / I'm // and / know / I / about / nothing / man. / this // it / but / wasn't / falult. / my // had / I / to / him / bring / home. // mean / I / look / just / at / him. // you / don't / he / think / help? / needs)
➡ _____
_____

9 (Matrena: / at / (looking / with / Michael / pity) // Simon. / okay)
➡ _____

10 (smiles / (Michael / the / for / time.) / first)
➡ _____

1 세 가지의 신비로운 미소
장면 1.

2 겨울이다. 가난한 구두장이 Simon은 따뜻한 코트를 사는 데 실패한다. 그는 집에 돌아오는 길에 옷도 입지 않고 길거리에 누워 있는 Michael이라는 한 남자를 발견한다.

3 Simon: 저 남자가 죽은 건지 아닌 건지 모르겠군. 하지만 나는 취해 있고, 돈도 거의 없어서 저 남자를 구할 수 없을 것 같아. (처음엔 Michael에게서 발걸음을 돌리지만, 다시 돌아오며) 불쌍한 사람이군. 괜찮으세요? 왜 여기 누워 있는 거요?

4 Michael: 당신에게 말 못할 사정이 있어요. 간단히 말하자면, 저는 벌을 받고 있어요.

5 Simon: 하지만 밖은 추워요. 같이 집으로 갑시다.
장면 2.

6 Simon은 집으로 와서 그의 아내인 Matrena와 인사한다. 그녀는 그가 아무것도 가져오지 않은 것을 알게 된다.

7 Matrena: (놀라서 화내며) Simon, 당신은 우리 가족을 위해 코트를 사 오기로 했잖아요. 하지만 아무것도 없네요. 그리고 이 남자는 누구예요?

8 Simon: 코트를 살 정도로 충분한 돈이 없었어요. 미안해요. 그리고 이 남자에 관해서는 아무것도 모르지만, 내 잘못은 아니에요. 나는 이 남자를 집에 데려와야만 했어요. 이 남자를 보세요. 도움이 필요해 보이지 않나요?

9 Matrena: (Michael을 불쌍하게 바라보며) 그래요, Simon.

10 (Michael은 처음으로 미소를 짓는다.)

11 (a / for / week, / does / Michael / no / to / work / himself. / support)

➡ _____

12 (Simon: / at / (looking / Michael) / I'm / Michael, / you've / afraid / doing / been / since / nothing / came / you / here. // time / it's / started / you / earn / to / living / a / yourself. / for // you / if / for / work / me, / will / I / you / give / food. // you / would / to / like / with / work / me?)

➡ _____

➡ _____

➡ _____

13 (Michael: / a / (with / face) / blank / yes, / would. / I)

➡ _____

Scene #3.

14 (later, / a / year / has / Simon / become / famous, / to / thanks / great / Michael's / skills / making / in / shoes. // day, / one / nobleman / a / to / comes / his / order / boots.)

➡ _____

➡ _____

15 (Nobleman: / like / I'd / order / to / leather / fine / that / boots / to / have / for / last / year. / a // not / I'm / whether / sure / can / you / them. / make / you / can / that? / do)

➡ _____

➡ _____

16 (watches / (Michael / man / the / carefully / smiles / and / the / for / time. / second)

➡ _____

17 (Simon: / sir. / yes, // worry. / don't)

➡ _____

18 (nobelman / (the / the / leveas / shop.))

➡ _____

19 (Simon: / Michael, make / please / thick / some / boots. / leather)

➡ _____

20 (Okay. / Michael:)

➡ _____

21 (Michael / (however, / soft / makes / instead / slippers / boots.) / of)

➡ _____

22 (Simon: / the / (finding / slippers) // Michael! / told / I / there / you / should / no / be / mistakes. // do / what / think / you / are / you / doing?)

➡ _____

➡ _____

11 1주일간, Michael은 스스로 자신의 생계를 유지하기 위해 아무 일도 하지 않는다.

12 Simon: (Michael을 바라보며) Michael, 당신이 이곳에 와서 계속 빈둥거리고 있어 걱정되네요. 당신 자신을 위해 생계를 꾸려야 할 때에요. 저를 위해서 일해 준다면, 제가 당신에게 음식을 제공할게요. 저랑 같이 일하시겠어요?

13 Michael: (무표정한 얼굴로) 네, 그렇게 할게요.

장면 3.

14 1년 후, Simon은 Michael의 훌륭한 구두 제작 솜씨 덕분에 유명해졌다. 어느 날, 한 귀족이 부츠를 주문하러 가게에 온다.

15 귀족: 나는 1년을 신어도 끄떡 없는 튼튼한 가죽 부츠를 주문하고 싶습니다. 당신이 그 부츠를 만들 수 있을지 모르겠네요. 할 수 있겠습니까?

16 (Michael은 귀족을 유심히 살펴보고는 두 번째로 미소 짓는다.)

17 Simon: 네, 나리. 걱정하지 마세요.

18 (귀족은 가게를 떠난다.)

19 Simon: Michael, 두꺼운 가죽 부츠를 만들어 주세요.

20 Michael: 네.

21 (하지만, Michael은 부츠 대신 부드러운 슬리퍼를 만든다.)

22 Simon: (슬리퍼를 발견하며) Michael! 제가 실수하지 말라고 했잖아요. 지금 뭐 하고 있는 겁니까?

23 (Servant: / into / (running / shop) / the // stop / please / making / and / boots / start / soft / making / for / slippers / a / body / dead / instead. // master / my / died / has / of / heart / a / attack.)
➡ _____
_____
_____

24 (Simon: / at / (looking / Michael / surprise) / in // did / how / know? / you)
➡ _____

25 (Well / Michael: / ....)
➡ _____

Scene #4.

26 (few / a / later, / years / woman / a / visits / customer / shoe / the / with / shop / girls. / twin)
➡ _____

27 (Customer: / here / I'm / buy / to / leather / some / for / shoes / these / girls. / twin)
➡ _____

28 (Simon: / that / (seeing / of / one / girls / the / a / has / disability) // sorry / I'm / your / about / foot. / daughter's // I / may / you / ask / she / if / born / was / a / with / disability?)
➡ _____
_____

29 (Customer: / I'm / oh, / her / not / mother. / real // mother / her / this / hurt / leg / girl's / she / while / giving / was / to / birth / her. / parents / their / both / are / now. / dead // felt / I / them. / for // loved / I / twins / these / much / so / that / decided / I / adopt / to / them.)
➡ _____
_____
_____

30 (smiles / (Michael / the / for / time.) / third)
➡ _____

Scene #5.

31 (a / suddenly, / mysterious / shines / light / Michael.) / from)
➡ _____

32 (Simon: / this / what's / shining / light / you? / from)
➡ _____

33 (Michael: / about / it's / time / left / I / here.)
➡ _____

34 (Simon: / do / what / mean? / you // why / and / you / did / smile? / just)
➡ _____

35 (Michael: / me / let / explain. // am / I / angel. / an // was / I / here / sent / a / as / punishment, / and / was / I / to / supposed / learn / truths. / three // time / every / learned / I / of / one / them, / smiled. / I // that / now / have / I / learned / three / all / them, / of / am / I / to / ready / back. / go)
➡ _____
_____
_____
_____

---

23 하인: (가게로 뛰어들며) 부츠는 그만 만들고 대신 죽은 사람에게 신길 부드러운 슬리퍼를 만들어 주세요. 나리가 심장마비로 돌아가셨습니다.

24 Simon: (놀라서 Michael을 바라보며) 당신은 어떻게 알았습니까?

25 Michael: 글쎄요…

장면 4.

26 몇 년 후, 한 여인이 쌍둥이 소녀들과 함께 신발 가게에 방문한다.

27 손님: 이 쌍둥이 소녀들에게 신길 가죽 신발을 사러 왔습니다.

28 Simon: (장애를 가진 한 소녀를 보며) 따님 한쪽 발이 안타깝네요. 실례지만, 태어날 때부터 장애가 있었는지 여쭤 봐도 될까요?

29 손님: 오, 저는 이 아이의 생모가 아니에요. 생모가 아이를 낳던 중에 아이가 다리를 다치게 됐어요. 그들의 부모님은 이미 돌아가셨습니다. 나는 이 쌍둥이가 너무 불쌍했어요. 이 아이들을 너무 사랑해서 입양하기로 결정했습니다.

30 (Michael은 세 번째로 미소를 짓는다.)

장면 5.

31 (갑자기 Michael에게서 신비한 빛이 빛난다.)

32 Simon: 당신에게서 나오는 이 빛은 도대체 뭔가요?

33 Michael: 이제 제가 떠날 때가 왔군요.

34 Simon: 무슨 말씀이시죠? 그리고 당신은 왜 미소를 지었던 건가요?

35 Michael: 설명해 드릴게요. 저는 천사입니다. 저는 벌을 받아 여기로 보내졌고, 세 가지 진리를 깨달아야 했습니다. 제가 진리를 하나씩 깨달을 때마다 미소를 지었던 것입니다. 저는 세 가지 진리를 모두 깨달았기 때문에 돌아갈 준비를 마쳤습니다.

36 (Simon: / see. / I // truths / what / you / have / learned?)

➡ _____

Scene #6.

37 (thinks / Michael / to / back / time / each / he / that / smiled. // and / Simon / Matrena / carefully / listen / him. / to)

➡ _____

_____

38 (Michael: / I / first, / learned / love / that / in / dwells / beings / human / Matrena / when / me. / pitied. // was / this / answer / the / the / to / lesson: / first // what / learn / dwells / human / in / begins. // smiled / I / I / because / the / learned / truth. // I / but / had / still / more / two / figure / to / out.)

➡ _____

_____

_____

39 (Simon: / were / what / they?)

➡ _____

40 (Michael: / second / the / was, / what / "learn / not / is / to / given / people." // the / when / ordered / nobleman / that / boots / his / to / were / for / last / year, / a / knew / I / would / he / soon. / die // I / realized / then / know / people / little / about / own / their / needs. / future)

➡ _____

_____

_____

41 (Simon: / was / what / last / the / truth?)

➡ _____

42 (Michael: / was / it / the / from / story / the / of / woman / and / twin / the / girls. // the / after / of / death / mother, / their / the / brought / woman / up / them / her / with / love. // I / then, / people / learned / live / having / by / love / true / other. / for / each // was / that / third / the / lesson: / people / what / by. / live)

➡ _____

_____

_____

36 Simon: 그렇군요. 당신이 깨달은 진리는 무엇이었나요?

장면 6.

37 Michael은 그가 미소 지었을 때를 회상한다. Simon과 Matrena는 그의 말을 주의 깊게 듣는다.

38 Michael: 첫째, Matrena가 저를 가여워했을 때 인간 내면에 사랑이 존재한다는 것을 저는 깨달았습니다. 이는 '인간 내면에 무엇이 존재하는가'라는 첫 번째 교훈에 관한 답이었던 것입니다. 저는 그 진실을 깨달았기 때문에 미소를 지었습니다. 하지만 저는 아직도 두 가지를 더 알아내야만 했어요.

39 Simon: 그것들은 뭐였나요?

40 Michael: 두 번째는 "인간에게 주어지지 않은 것은 무엇인가"였습니다. 그 귀족이 1년을 신어도 끄떡없는 부츠를 주문했을 때, 저는 그가 곧 죽을 것을 알고 있었습니다. 사람은 자신의 미래에 필요한 것을 알지 못한다는 사실을 그때 저는 깨달았습니다.

41 Simon: 마지막 진리는 무엇이었나요?

42 Michael: 쌍둥이 소녀와 여인의 이야기를 듣고 깨달았습니다. 쌍둥이의 생모가 사망한 후, 그 여인은 그들을 사랑으로 키웠습니다. 그때, 저는 사람은 서로를 향한 참된 사랑으로 산다는 점을 알게 됐습니다. 그것이 '사람은 무엇으로 사는가'에 관한 세 번째 교훈이었습니다.

※ 다음 우리말을 영어로 쓰시오.

1 세 가지의 신비로운 미소

➡ _____

Scene #1.: 장면 1.

2 겨울이다. 가난한 구두장이 Simon은 따뜻한 코트를 사는 데 실패한다. 그는 집에 돌아오는 길에 옷도 입지 않고 길거리에 누워 있는 Michael이라는 한 남자를 발견한다.

➡ _____

3 Simon: 저 남자가 죽은 건지 아닌 건지 모르겠군. 하지만 나는 취해 있고, 돈도 거의 없어서 저 남자를 구할 수 없을 것 같아. (처음엔 Michael에게서 발걸음을 돌리지만, 다시 돌아오며) 불쌍한 사람이군. 괜찮으세요? 왜 여기 누워 있는 거요?

➡ _____

_____

4 Michael: 당신에게 말 못할 사정이 있어요. 간단히 말하자면, 저는 벌을 받고 있어요.

➡ _____

5 Simon: 하지만 밖은 추워요. 같이 집으로 갑시다.

➡ _____

Scene #2.: 장면 2.

6 Simon은 집으로 와서 그의 아내인 Matrena와 인사한다. 그녀는 그가 아무것도 가져오지 않은 것을 알게 된다.

➡ _____

7 Matrena: (놀라서 화내며) Simon, 당신은 우리 가족을 위해 코트를 사 오기로 했잖아요. 하지만 아무것도 없네요. 그리고 이 남자는 누구예요?

➡ _____

8 Simon: 코트를 살 정도로 충분한 돈이 없었어요. 미안해요. 그리고 이 남자에 관해서는 아무것도 모르지만, 내 잘못은 아니에요. 나는 이 남자를 집에 데려와야만 했어요. 이 남자를 보세요. 도움이 필요해 보이지 않나요?

➡ _____

9 Matrena: (Michael을 불쌍하게 바라보며) 그래요, Simon.

➡ _____

10 (Michael은 처음으로 미소를 짓는다.)

➡ _____

11 1주일간, Michael은 스스로 자신의 생계를 유지하기 위해 아무 일도 하지 않는다.

➡ _____

12 Simon: (Michael을 바라보며) Michael, 당신이 이곳에 와서 계속 빈둥거리고 있어 걱정되네요. 당신 자신을 위해 생계를 꾸려야 할 때에요. 저를 위해서 일해 준다면, 제가 당신에게 음식을 제공할게요. 저랑 같이 일하시겠어요?

➡ _____

_____

13 Michael: (무표정한 얼굴로) 네, 그렇게 할게요.

➡ _____

Scene #3.: 장면 3.

14 1년 후, Simon은 Michael의 훌륭한 구두 제작 솜씨 덕분에 유명해졌다. 어느 날, 한 귀족이 부츠를 주문하러 가게에 온다.

➡ _____

15 귀족: 나는 1년을 신어도 끄떡없는 튼튼한 가죽 부츠를 주문하고 싶습니다. 당신이 그 부츠를 만들 수 있을지 모르겠네요. 할 수 있겠습니까?

➡ _____
_____

16 (Michael은 귀족을 유심히 살펴보고는 두 번째로 미소 짓는다.)

➡ _____

17 Simon: 네, 나리. 걱정하지 마세요.

➡ _____

18 (귀족은 가게를 떠난다.)

➡ _____

19 Simon: Michael, 두꺼운 가죽 부츠를 만들어 주세요.

➡ _____

20 Michael: 네.

➡ _____

21 (하지만, Michael은 부츠 대신 부드러운 슬리퍼를 만든다.)

➡ _____

22 Simon: (슬리퍼를 발견하며) Michael! 제가 실수하지 말라고 했잖아요. 지금 뭐 하고 있는 겁니까?

➡ _____

23 하인: (가게로 뛰어들며) 부츠는 그만 만들고 대신 죽은 사람에게 신길 부드러운 슬리퍼를 만들어 주세요. 나리가 심장마비로 돌아가셨습니다.

➡ _____

24 Simon: (놀라서 Michael을 바라보며) 당신은 어떻게 알았습니까?

➡ _____

25 Michael: 글쎄요…

➡ _____

Scene #4.: 장면 4.

26 몇 년 후, 한 여인이 쌍둥이 소녀들과 함께 신발 가게에 방문한다.

➡ _____

27 손님: 이 쌍둥이 소녀들에게 신길 가죽 신발을 사러 왔습니다.

➡ _____

28 Simon: (장애를 가진 한 소녀를 보며) 따님 한쪽 발이 안타깝네요. 실례지만, 태어날 때부터 장애가 있었는지 여쭤 봐도 될까요?

➡ _____

29 손님: 오, 저는 이 아이의 생모가 아니에요. 생모가 아이를 낳던 중에 아이가 다리를 다치게 됐어요. 그들의 부모님은 이미 돌아가셨습니다. 나는 이 쌍둥이가 너무 불쌍했어요. 이 아이들을 너무 사랑해서 입양하기로 결정했습니다.

➡ _____
_____
_____

30 (Michael은 세 번째로 미소를 짓는다.)

➡ _____

Scene #5.: 장면 5.

31 ▶ (갑자기 Michael에게서 신비한 빛이 빛난다.)

➡ _____

32 ▶ Simon: 당신에게서 나오는 이 빛은 도대체 뭔가요?

➡ _____

33 ▶ Michael: 이제 제가 떠날 때가 왔군요.

➡ _____

34 ▶ Simon: 무슨 말씀이시죠? 그리고 당신은 왜 미소를 지었던 건가요?

➡ _____

35 ▶ Michael: 설명해 드릴게요. 저는 천사입니다. 저는 벌을 받아 여기로 보내졌고, 세 가지 진리를 깨달아야 했습니다. 제가 진리를 하나씩 깨달을 때마다 미소를 지었던 것입니다. 저는 세 가지 진리를 모두 깨달았기 때문에 돌아갈 준비를 마쳤습니다.

➡ _____

_____

_____

36 ▶ Simon: 그렇군요. 당신이 깨달은 진리는 무엇이었나요?

➡ _____

Scene #6.: 장면 6.

37 ▶ Michael은 그가 미소 지었을 때를 회상한다. Simon과 Matrena는 그의 말을 주의 깊게 듣는다.

➡ _____

38 ▶ Michael: 첫째, Matrena가 저를 가여워했을 때 인간 내면에 사랑이 존재한다는 것을 저는 깨달았습니다. 이는 '인간 내면에 무엇이 존재하는가'라는 첫 번째 교훈에 관한 답이었던 것입니다. 저는 그 진실을 깨달았기 때문에 미소를 지었습니다. 하지만 저는 아직도 두 가지를 더 알아내야만 했어요.

➡ _____

_____

_____

_____

39 ▶ Simon: 그것들은 뭐였나요?

➡ _____

40 ▶ Michael: 두 번째는 "인간에게 주어지지 않은 것은 무엇인가"였습니다. 그 귀족이 1년을 신어도 끄떡없는 부츠를 주문했을 때, 저는 그가 곧 죽을 것을 알고 있었습니다. 사람은 자신의 미래에 필요한 것을 알지 못한다는 사실을 그때 저는 깨달았습니다.

➡ _____

_____

_____

41 ▶ Simon: 마지막 진리는 무엇이었나요?

➡ _____

42 ▶ Michael: 쌍둥이 소녀와 여인의 이야기를 듣고 깨달았습니다. 쌍둥이의 생모가 사망한 후, 그 여인은 그들을 사랑으로 키웠습니다. 그때, 저는 사람은 서로를 향한 참된 사랑으로 산다는 점을 알게 됐습니다. 그것이 '사람은 무엇으로 사는가'에 관한 세 번째 교훈이었습니다.

➡ _____

_____

_____

※ 다음 우리말과 일치하도록 빈칸에 알맞은 말을 쓰시오.

After You Read A

1. I did not have _____ _____ _____ _____ the coat. I'm sorry.
2. And I _____ _____ _____ this man.
3. But it wasn't my _____. I _____ _____ _____ him home.
4. I mean just _____ _____ him! _____ you think he _____ _____?
5. He looked _____ _____ _____ I _____ _____ _____ him some help.

After You Read B

1. Michael _____ _____ _____ learn three _____ _____ _____ _____.
2. When Matrena _____ Michael _____ _____ her home, he learns that love _____ _____ _____ _____ _____.
3. The nobleman _____ _____ _____ boots that _____ _____ _____ for a year.
4. _____ _____ of the nobleman said, "Please _____ _____ boots and _____ _____ _____ _____ for a dead body _____. My master has _____ _____ _____ _____ _____ _____."
5. The woman _____ the twin girls, _____ _____ _____ _____ _____.

Check Your Progress 1

1. B: Jina, _____ you _____ _____ your English homework?
2. G: No, I _____.
3. B: Why? You're _____ _____ _____ today.
4. G: It was _____ _____ _____. I _____ my homework. But just before I _____ _____ _____ _____ _____ it, the computer _____ _____.
5. B: _____ _____ _____! If I _____ you, I _____ _____ the teacher _____ _____ _____ _____ _____ _____.
6. G: Yeah, I _____. But I think I'd _____ _____ it again _____ _____ _____ _____ _____.
7. B: Can I _____ _____ _____ _____ _____ with that?
8. G: _____ _____ _____ _____ you! I'll _____ you _____ I _____ _____ _____.

1. 나는 코트를 살 정도로 충분한 돈이 없었어요. 미안해요.
2. 그리고 이 남자에 관해서는 아무것도 몰라요.
3. 하지만 내 잘못은 아니에요. 나는 이 남자를 집에 데려와야만 했어요.
4. 내 말은, 이 남자를 보세요! 도움이 필요해 보이지 않나요?
5. 그가 너무 불쌍해 보여서 그에게 도움을 주지 않을 수 없었다.

1. Michael은 벌로 세 가지 진리를 깨달아야 했다.
2. Matrena가 Michael을 그녀의 집에 머물게 허락할 때, 그는 인간 내면에 사랑이 존재한다는 것을 깨닫는다.
3. 귀족은 1년을 신어도 끄떡없는 튼튼한 가죽 부츠를 주문한다.
4. 귀족의 하인이 말했다, "부츠는 그만 만들고 대신 죽은 사람에게 신길 부드러운 슬리퍼를 만들어 주세요. 나리가 심장마비로 돌아가셨습니다."
5. 그 여인은 쌍둥이 소녀들을 입양했는데, 그들 중 한 명이 장애가 있었다.

1. B: Jina야, 너 영어 숙제 제출했니?
2. G: 아니, 안 냈어.
3. B: 왜? 오늘까지 내야 하잖아.
4. G: 다 내 잘못이야. 숙제는 다 했어. 하지만 내가 그걸 저장하기 바로 전에 컴퓨터가 고장나 버렸어.
5. B: 불쌍해라! 내가 너라면, 선생님께 왜 숙제를 제출 못했는지 말씀 드릴 거야.
6. G: 응, 나도 그렇게 생각해. 그렇지만 최대한 빨리 다시 하는 게 더 낫다는 생각이 들어.
7. B: 내가 좀 도와줄까?
8. G: 정말 친절하구나! 도움이 필요하면 널 전화할게.

※ 다음 우리말을 영어로 쓰시오.

After You Read A

1. 나는 코트를 살 정도로 충분한 돈이 없었어요. 미안해요.
➡ _____

2. 그리고 이 남자에 관해서는 아무것도 몰라요.
➡ _____

3. 하지만 내 잘못은 아니에요. 나는 이 남자를 집에 데려와야만 했어요.
➡ _____

4. 내 말은, 이 남자를 보세요! 도움이 필요해 보이지 않나요?
➡ _____

5. 그가 너무 불쌍해 보여서 그에게 도움을 주지 않을 수 없었다.
➡ _____

After You Read B

1. Michael은 벌로 세 가지 진리를 깨달아야 했다.
➡ _____

2. Matrena가 Michael을 그녀의 집에 머물게 허락할 때, 그는 인간 내면에 사랑이 존재한다는 것을 깨닫는다.
➡ _____

3. 귀족은 1년을 신어도 끄떡없는 튼튼한 가죽 부츠를 주문한다.
➡ _____

4. 귀족의 하인이 말했다. "부츠는 그만 만들고 대신 죽은 사람에게 신길 부드러운 슬리퍼를 만들어 주세요. 나리가 심장마비로 돌아가셨습니다."
➡ _____

5. 그 여인은 쌍둥이 소녀들을 입양했는데, 그들 중 한 명은 장애가 있었다.
➡ _____

Check Your Progress 1

1. B: Jina야, 너 영어 숙제 제출했니?
➡ _____

2. G: 아니, 안 냈어.
➡ _____

3. B: 왜? 오늘까지 내야 하잖아.
➡ _____

4. G: 다 내 잘못이야. 숙제는 다 했어. 하지만 내가 그걸 저장하기 바로 전에 컴퓨터가 고장나 버렸어.
➡ _____

5. B: 불쌍해라! 내가 너라면, 선생님께 왜 숙제를 제출 못했는지 말씀 드릴 거야.
➡ _____

6. G: 응, 나도 그렇게 생각해. 그렇지만 최대한 빨리 다시 하는 게 더 낫다는 생각이 들어.
➡ _____

7. B: 내가 좀 도와줄까?
➡ _____

8. G: 정말 친절하구나! 도움이 필요하면 널 전화할게.
➡ _____

MEMO

MEMO

영어 기출 문제집

적중100

2학기

정답 및 해설

금성 | 최인철

중 **3**

적중100

영어 기출 문제집

영어 기출 문제집

적중100

2학기

정답 및 해설

금성 | 최인철

중 3

적중100

Careers Day

01 occupation   02 ④

03 (1) Solar panels can only operate in sunlight.

  (2) The rain prevented them from eating outdoors.

  (3) He regularly babysits our children for us.

04 ①

05 (1) welcome to   (2) since then   (3) instead of

06 ②

01 helpful(도움이 되는)과 useful(유용한)은 동의어 관계에 있는 단어들이다. 따라서 career(경력, 직업)와 동의어 관계에 있는 단어는 occupation(직업, 업무)이다.

02 ④에서 쓰인 minute는 형용사로 '극미한, 작은'이라는 뜻으로 사용되었다.

03 (1) operate 작동하다, 가동시키다 (2) prevent 방지하다, 막다 (3) regularly 정기적으로, 규칙적으로

04 '어떤 상황의 예상치 못한 결과'라는 뜻의 영영풀이가 가리키는 것은 side effect(부작용)이다.

05 (1) be welcome to 자유롭게 ~해도 좋다 (2) since then 그 이후로 (3) instead of ~ 대신에

06 turn off ~를 끄다 / put off 미루다, 연기하다 / believe in ~를 믿다 / put in ~에 넣다, 꽂다

01 decrease   02 had a hard time

03 (1) moment   (2) counselor   (3) purpose

04 (1) The money has been invested for a certain period.

  (2) The critic made helpful comments on my work.

  (3) We avoided a pack of journalists waiting outside.

05 (1) The most important thing in interviews is to stay calm.

  (2) A late bloomer, she wrote her great novel when she was 52.

  (3) He found the whole thing very boring.

01 boring(지루한, 재미없는)과 exciting(흥미진진한)은 반의어 관계에 있는 단어들이다. 따라서 increase(증가하다, 증가시키다)와 반의어 관계에 있는 단어는 decrease(줄이다, 감소시키다)이다.

02 have a hard time ~ing ~하는 데 어려움을 겪다

03 (1) moment 잠시, 순간, 때 (2) counselor 상담 전문가 (3) purpose 목적

04 (1) invest 투자하다 (2) helpful 도움이 되는, 유용한 (3) avoid 피하다, 방지하다

05 (1) calm 침착한 (2) bloomer 재능을 발휘하는 사람 (3) boring 지루한

1 I like playing music better[more] than making shoes!

2 ③

01 'B보다 A를 더 선호한다'라고 대답할 때는 'I like A better[more] than B.'라는 표현을 쓸 수 있다.

02 빈칸에 들어갈 말로 적절한 것은 의견을 나타낼 때 쓸 수 있는 표현들이다. ③ I want는 문맥상 적절하지 않다.

1 F   2 T   3 T   4 T

Think Back A

together / don't, doing, than / better, musician / about / because

Everyday English 1 Listen and Check

(1) basketball / teach, play

(2) forward, prefer, to / would, if

Everyday English 1 B Listening Activity

looking, here, someone, care, while, vacation, regularly, By the way, long time, taking

시험대비 기본평가   p.18

01 But I prefer soccer to basketball.

02 G wants to learn how to play soccer from B.

03 ③

04 They are going to a concert this weekend.

01 'B보다 A를 더 선호한다.'라고 대답할 때는 'I prefer A to B.'라고 표현할 수 있다.

02 위 대화에서 G가 B에게 축구하는 법을 가르쳐 줄 수 있겠냐고("Can you teach me how to play soccer?") 물었다.

03 B가 이번 주말에 소풍을 가는 것이 어떠냐고 묻자, 상대방은 이번 주말에 비가 올 것이기 때문에 좋은 생각이 아니라고 말한다(B). 이어서 B가 그러면 콘서트에 가는 것은 어떠냐고 묻자(C), 상대방이 좋은 생각이라고 말하는 (A) 순서로 이어지는 것이 가장 적절하다.

04 위 두 화자가 이번 주말에 할 일은 소풍이 아니라 콘서트에 가는 것이다.

시험대비 실력평가   p.19~20

01 ⑤   02 ②   03 ①   04 ③

05 B's present   06 ④

07 I prefer history to math   08 ④   09 ⑤

10 ⑤

11 A feels calm when he/she listens to classical music.

01 ⓔ는 are interested in의 목적어이므로 동명사 taking이 되어야 한다.

02 앞서 화자는 애완동물을 돌보면서 해야 할 일을 말했고 빈칸 뒤에서는 일하는 시간이나 날짜 등 취업 조건에 대해서 이야기한다. 따라서 화제를 전환하는 ② By the way(그건 그렇고, 그런데)가 들어가는 것이 가장 적절하다.

03 위 대화 초반에 'here is the best job for you'라고 말한 것에서 알 수 있듯이 ① '애완동물 돌보미를 구하는 것'이 위 글의 목적이다.

04 (A) 과거형 received가 들어가야 한다. (B) 동사 help의 목적보어로는 동사원형이 들어가야 한다. (C) 미래에 오는 일에 대해 기원하는 내용이므로 rains가 들어가야 한다.

05 대명사 it이 가리키는 것은 문맥상 B가 G에게 준 선물이다.

06 예나는 앞서 민우가 준 선물에 대해 'I really like it.'라고 말했다.

07 'B보다 A를 더 선호한다'라고 대답할 때는 'I prefer A to B.'라고 쓸 수 있다.

08 A는 코미디 영화를 액션 영화보다 더 좋아한다고 말했다.("I prefer comedy movies to action movies.")

09 B의 대답인 'I prefer pears than strawberries.'에서 than을 to로 고쳐야 한다.

10 (A)는 상대방의 의견을 묻는 표현으로, 'How do you feel about ~?'과 'What do you think about?', 'What do you think of ~?' 등과 같은 표현을 쓸 수 있다.

11 A는 클래식 음악을 들으면 차분해진다고 말했다.("I feel calm when I listen to classical music.")

서술형 시험대비   p.21

01 What do you think about[of] becoming a writer?

02 I prefer science to literature.

03 literature

04 How do you feel about eating fast food?

05 you're trying your clothes on several times

06 B prefers blue jeans to his other pants.

07 B is going to wear a white shirt and the blue jeans.

01 'How do you feel about ~?'은 상대방의 의견을 묻는 표현으로, 'What do you think about[of] ~?'으로 대체할 수 있다.

02 선호를 나타내는 표현으로는 'B보다 A를 더 선호한다'라고 말하는 'I prefer A to B.' 등이 있다.

03 '문자로 쓰인 예술 작품으로, 특히 높고 지속되는 예술적 가치를 지닌 것'이라는 뜻을 가진 영영풀이가 가리키는 것은

literature(문학)이다.

04 'How do you feel about ~?'은 상대방의 의견을 묻는 표현으로, '~에 대해 어떻게 생각하니?'라고 해석한다.

05 try ~ on ~을 입어 보다 / several times 여러 번

06 B는 자신이 다른 바지보다도 청바지를 더 좋아한다고 말했다.

07 B는 엄마의 조언대로 하얀 셔츠에 청바지를 입는 것이 훨씬 잘 어울린다고 말했다.

Grammar

핵심 Check
p.22~23

1 (1) to understand (2) for (3) use

2 (1) The students in my school are exercising hard for their health. So am I.

(2) My younger sister got sick while studying math. So did her classmates.

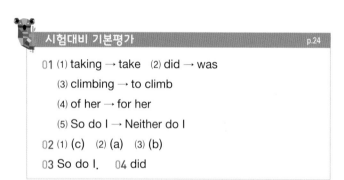

시험대비 기본평가
p.24

01 (1) taking → take (2) did → was
  (3) climbing → to climb
  (4) of her → for her
  (5) So do I → Neither do I

02 (1) (c) (2) (a) (3) (b)

03 So do I. 04 did

01 (1) '난이 형용사+to부정사'이므로 taking을 take로 바꾸는 것이 적절하다. (2) 긍정문 문장의 동의를 표현할 때 'So'를 이용하여 표현할 수 있다. 이 때 주어와 동사의 위치는 도치가 되며 앞 문장에서 be동사가 쓰인 문장의 동의를 할 때는 시제와 주어의 수를 일치시켜 사용하므로 did를 was로 바꾸는 것이 적절하다. (3) '난이 형용사+to부정사'로 to부정사의 의미상의 주어는 'for+목적격'을 쓰므로 climbing을 'to climb'으로 쓴다. (4) '난이 형용사+to부정사'로 to부정사의 의미상의 주어는 'for+목적격'을 쓴다. (5) 부정문 문장의 동의를 말할 때 'Neither'를 이용하여 표현할 수 있다.

02 (1), (2)는 긍정문의 동의를 표현할 때 'So'를 이용하여 표현하고 이때 주어와 동사의 위치는 도치된다. (1)은 일반동사가 쓰인 문장에 대한 동의로 시제를 일치시켜 do를 써서 표현하는 것이 적절하다. (2)는 be동사가 쓰인 문장에 대한 동의로 'So' 다

음에 'was'가 오는 것이 적절하다. (3)은 부정문 문장의 동의를 표현할 때 'Neither를 사용하며 앞 문장에서 동사에 조동사 'have'가 있으므로 동의를 표현할 때 'have'를 활용하는 것이 적절하다,

03 긍정문 문장의 동의를 표현할 때 'So'를 이용하여 표현할 수 있고 주어와 동사의 위치는 도치가 된다. 앞 문장에서 일반동사가 쓰였으므로 대동사 'do'를 활용하여 쓴다.

04 긍정문 문장의 동의를 표현할 때 'So'를 이용하여 표현할 수 있고 주어와 동사의 위치는 도치가 된다. 앞 문장에서 일반동사가 쓰인 문장을 동의할 때는 대동사 'do'를 활용하고 시제와 주어의 수를 일치시켜 사용한다.

시험대비 실력평가
p.25~27

01 is → does 02 ⑤ 03 ① 04 ②

05 Neither do I. 06 ④

07 Neither am I. 08 ② 09 ①

10 ② 11 ④ 12 ①

13 (1) tough (2) to (3) cut

14 (1) do (2) does 15 ② 16 ①

17 ③, ⑤ 18 ④ 19 ⑤ 20 ②

01 앞 문장의 동사가 일반동사인 경우, 주어의 수와 시제에 따라 'do'를 활용한다. 주어가 she이고 현재이므로 does를 쓰는 것이 적절하다.

02 앞 문장의 동사가 일반동사인 경우, 주어의 수와 시제에 따라 'do'를 활용한다. 주어가 I이고 과거이므로 did로 쓰는 것이 적절하다.

03 긍정문 문장의 동의를 표현할 때 'So'를 이용하여 표현할 수 있고 주어와 동사의 위치는 도치가 된다. 앞 문장에서 조동사가 'can'이 쓰인 문장을 동의할 때는 그대로 'can'을 활용하여 쓰는 것이 적절하다. ⑤번은 부정문이므로 'Neither could I.'가 적절하다.

04 ②번을 제외한 나머지에는 did가 들어가야 한다. ②번은 was가 들어가야 한다.

05 부정문에 동의를 표현할 때 'Neither'를 사용하며 문장에 조동사 'doesn't'가 있으므로 'do'를 활용하는 것이 적절하다,

06 '난이 형용사+to부정사'로 for를 to로 바꿔 쓰는 것이 적절하다.

07 부정문의 문장에 동의를 표현할 때 'Neither를 사용하며 주어진 문장은 be동사가 쓰인 문장이므로 동의하는 문장의 주어 I에 맞춰 am이 오는 것이 적절하다.

08 그 책이 너무 어려워서 나는 그것을 이해할 수 없었다. '난이 형용사+to부정사' 어순으로 쓰고 to부정사의 의미상의 주어는 'for+목적격'을 쓰는 것이 적절하다.

09 긍정문 문장에 동의를 표현할 때 'So'를 이용하여 표현하고 이 때 주어와 동사의 위치는 도치된다. be동사가 쓰인 문장에 대한 동의로 'So' 다음에 be동사가 오는데 시제와 주어의 수를 일치시켜야 하므로 'am'이 오는 것이 적절하다.

10 '난이 형용사+to부정사'로 to부정사의 의미상의 주어는 'for+목적격'을 쓰므로 of me를 for me로 쓰는 것이 적절하다.

11 • 나 목 말라. • 내 부모님은 내가 그 시험에 통과할 수 있을지 없을지 확신을 못했어.

12 긍정문 문장에 동의를 표현할 때 'So'를 이용하여 표현할 수 있고 주어와 동사의 위치는 도치가 된다. 일반동사가 쓰인 문장에 동의할 때는 대동사 'do'를 활용하고 시제와 주어의 수를 일치시켜야 한다.

13 어법에 맞게 배열하면, (1) It is tough to study late at night. (2) It is impossible to please her. (3) The masking tape is easy to cut.이다.

14 긍정문 문장에 동의를 표현할 때 'So'를 이용하여 표현하고 이 때 주어와 동사의 위치는 도치된다. (1)은 일반동사가 쓰인 문장에 대한 동의로 시제를 일치시켜 do를 써서 표현하는 것이 적절하다. (2)는 빈칸에 들어갈 단어의 주어와 수를 일치시켜 does가 오는 것이 적절하다.

15 '난이 형용사+to부정사'로 to read가 오는 것이 적절하다.

16 A: 나는 내 할머니에게 편지를 썼어. B: 내 친구도 그녀의 할머니에게 편지를 썼어.

17 A: 내 남동생은 치과에 갈 때마다 울어. B: ___도 그래. 긍정문 문장에 동의를 표현할 때 'So'를 이용하여 표현하고 이때 주어와 동사의 위치는 도치된다. 동사가 일반동사인 경우, 주어의 수와 시제에 따라 do, does 또는 did를 활용한다. 빈칸 앞에 does가 왔으므로 주어는 3인칭 단수여야 한다.

18 ④의 it은 인칭대명사이다.

19 부사적 용법의 to see가 오는 것이 적절하다.

20 부정문 문장에 동의를 표현할 때 'Neither'를 사용하며 앞에 조동사 'can'이 있으므로 'can'을 활용하는 것이 적절하다.

🦉 서술형 시험대비
p.28~29

01 (1) This beef is tough to chew.
(2) Fire scenes were really painful to shoot on hot summer days.
(3) The river flow is impossible to control.
(4) This manual is easy to understand.
(5) A motorcycle is dangerous to ride.
(6) Physics was difficult to understand.
(7) His playing is pleasant to listen to.

02 (1) It is tough to chew this beef.
(2) It was really painful to shoot fire scenes on hot summer days.
(3) It is impossible to control the river flow.
(4) It is easy to understand this manual.
(5) It is dangerous to ride a motorcycle.
(6) It was difficult to understand physics.
(7) It is pleasant to listen to his playing.

03 (1) is very comfortable to
(2) So did he

04 (1) If she is happy, so am I.
(2) She likes a cat, and so does he.
(3) I will not tell about the problem, and neither will she.

05 (1) It is pleasant to listen to music.
Music is pleasant to listen to.
(2) It is not difficult for us to pass the exam.
(3) It was difficult to understand the local dialect.
The local dialect was difficult to understand.

06 It is hard to persuade

07 (1) Neither will I. (2) So did I.
(3) Neither can I. (4) So will I.

08 His English is difficult for us to understand.

09 (1) so did you. (2) so could he.
(3) so does he. (4) so did Paul.

10 It is dangerous for him to swim in this river.

---

01 '주어+be동사+난이 형용사+to부정사' 어순이다.

02 'It+be동사+난이 형용사+to부정사'에서 to부정사의 목적어를 문장의 주어로 해서 '주어+be동사+난이 형용사+to부정사'로 바꿔 쓸 수 있다.

03 (1) '주어+be동사+난이 형용사+to부정사' (2) 긍정문 문장의 동의를 표현할 때 'So'를 이용하여 표현하고 이때 주어와 동사의 위치는 도치된다. 동사가 일반동사이므로, 주어와 시제에 따라 did를 쓰는 것이 적절하다.

04 (1) 그녀가 행복하다면 나도 그래. So를 이용하고 is가 쓰였으므로 주어와 시제를 일치시켜 am으로 쓰는 것이 적절하다. (2) 그녀는 고양이를 좋아하고 그도 고양이를 좋아한다. So를 이용하고 일반동사가 쓰였으므로 주어와 시제를 일치시켜 does로 쓰는 것이 적절하다. (3) 나는 그 문제에 대해 말하지 않을 것이고 그녀 역시 그렇다. Neither를 이용하고 will이 쓰였으므로 will로 쓰는 것이 적절하다.

05 'It+be동사+난이 형용사+to부정사'에서 to부정사의 목적어를 문장의 주어로 해서 '주어+be동사+난이 형용사+to부정사'로 바꿔 쓸 수 있다.

06 John을 설득하는 것은 어렵다. 'It+be동사+난이 형용사+to부정사'에서 to부정사의 목적어를 문장의 주어로 해서 '주어+be동사+난이 형용사+to부정사'로 바꿔 쓸 수 있다.

07 긍정문 문장의 동의를 표현할 때 'So'를 이용하여 표현하고 부정문 문장의 동의를 표현할 때는 'Neither'를 이용하여 표현한다. 이때 주어와 동사의 위치는 도치된다. (1) 조동사 will이 쓰인 부정문을 동의하는 것으로 'Neither will I.'가 적절하다. (2) 일반동사의 과거형이 쓰인 문장에 대한동의로 시제와 주어를 일치시켜 did를 써서 표현하는 것이 적절하다. (3) 조동사 can이 쓰인 부정문을 동의하는 것으로 'Neither can I.'가 적절하다. (4) 조동사 will이 쓰인 긍정문을 동의하는 것으로 'So will I.'가 적절하다.

08 그의 영어를 우리가 이해하는 것은 어렵다. 'It+be동사+난이 형용사+to부정사'에서 to부정사의 목적어를 문장의 주어로 해서 '주어+be동사+난이 형용사+to부정사'로 바꿔 쓸 수 있다.

09 긍정문 문장의 동의를 표현할 때 'So'를 이용하여 표현하고 이때 주어와 동사의 위치는 도치된다. (1), (4)는 일반동사가 쓰인 문장에 대한 동의로 시제 일치를 시켜 did를 써서 표현하는 것이 적절하다. (2) 조동사의 과거형이 쓰인 문장에 대한 동의를 표현할 때 그대로 조동사의 과거형을 쓴다. (3) 일반동사가 쓰인 문장에 대한 동의로 시제와 주어의 수를 일치시켜 does를 쓰는 것이 적절하다.

10 이 강은 그가 수영하기에는 위험해. 'It+be동사+난이 형용사+to부정사'에서 to부정사의 목적어를 문장의 주어로 해서 '주어+be동사+난이 형용사+to부정사'로 바꿔 쓸 수 있다.

[교과서]
Reading

확인문제					p.30
1 T	2 F	3 T	4 F	5 T	6 F

확인문제					p.31
1 T	2 F	3 T	4 F	5 T	6 F

확인문제					p.32
1 T	2 F	3 T	4 F	5 T	6 F

01 Careers Day
02 Welcome to
03 to come by
04 keep on trying
05 the graduates, listen to them talk
06 excited about
07 So am I
08 would like to
09 the weather controller
10 I'm Ilkem
11 studying the weather
12 impossible to control
13 did   14 Thanks to
15 using   16 make them rain
17 instead of, during
18 the side effects
19 control the weather
20 natural disasters like
21 in a better and safer environment
22 Why don't you join
23 net-zero energy houses
24 using too much energy
25 were
26 do I have to tell
27 Turn off
28 energy-saving houses
29 come true
30 alternative energy sources
31 make more energy
32 wasting energy
33 are interested in
34 end-of-life planner
35 As, is increasing
36 not only, but also
37 exercise regularly
38 invest for retirement, get along well with
39 make a will
40 avoid a lot of problems
41 feel proud of
42 give a big hand to
43 helpful for
44 having a hard time learning
45 slow learners
46 was
47 a late bloomer
48 what I was good at
49 Believe in yourself

1 Welcome to Careers Day!

2 Welcome to our Careers Day!

3 These days, jobs are hard to come by.

4 But if you keep on trying your best, you will succeed in your career.

5 Today, we will welcome back some of the graduates of our school, and listen to them talk about their jobs.

6 Are you excited about meeting them?

7 So am I.

8 As you listen to their talks, think about what you would like to do in the future.

9 Please welcome our first speaker, Ilkem, the weather controller.

10 Hello, everyone. I'm Ilkem.

11 I'm a scientist studying the weather.

12 Just a few years ago, people thought the weather was impossible to control.

13 So did I.

14 Thanks to modern technology, however, my fellow scientists and I can change the weather as we want.

15 For example, we can control the rain, using a cloud seeding system.

16 We spray dry ice into clouds to make them rain.

17 In China, they made rain in another city instead of Beijing during the opening event of the Olympics and its closing event as well.

18 We can also reduce the side effects of global warming by controlling the climate.

19 We can't control the weather perfectly yet, but may be able to do so soon.

20 Then, we could prevent many kinds of natural disasters like floods and storms.

21 So you will be able to live in a better and safer environment.

22 Why don't you join us in making a better environment by controlling the weather?

23 Hi, I'm Eva. I'm an architect, and I design net-zero energy houses.

24 Many people are worried about using too much energy at home.

25 So were my parents.

26 When I was young, my parents often said, "Eva! How many times do I have to tell you?

27 Turn off the TV when you're not watching it!"

28 Since then, I have wanted to design energy-saving houses,too?

29 I studied architecture and environmental engineering to make my dream come true.

30 Now, I design houses that use wind power or other alternative energy sources.

31 The houses make more energy than they use.

32 You don't need to worry about wasting energy anymore.

33 If you are interested in designing net-zero energy houses, please come and talk to me.

34 Hello. My name is Jiwon, and I'm an end-of-life planner.

35 As the number of old people is increasing, people are interested in how to be happy and wealthy in their old age.

36 I help people not only to live a healthy life but also to plan for their death.

37 For example, I help them exercise regularly.

38 I also give them some tips on how to invest for retirement and get along well with their family.

39 And I even teach them how to make a will!

40 This helps their family members avoid a lot of problems after the person dies.

41 I feel proud of what I'm doing.

42 Teacher: Let's give a big hand to the speakers.

43 I hope today's talks have been helpful for you.

44 I see many students having a hard time learning something new, while worrying about their future.

45 They are worried that they are slow learners.

46 So was I.

47 I was a late bloomer.

48 I tried to find what I was good at, and finally became a teacher.

49 So, I want to say, "Believe in yourself, and you can do it."

01 ③

02 some of the graduates of our school   03 ④

04 ③   05 ⑤   06 ②   07 ②

08 exercising → (to) exercise   09 ③

10 Neither → So   11 ①, ②, ④

12 We can also reduce the side effects of global warming by controlling the climate.

13 ③   14 ④   15 to talk → talk

16 ②, ⑤   17 too, also   18 ③   19 ④

01 ⓐ succeed in: ~에 성공하다, ⓑ be excited about: ~에 대해 흥분하다

02 '우리 학교 졸업생 몇몇'을 가리킨다.

03 직업의 날의 초대 손님들은 '다양한 분야의 전문가들'이 아니라 '학교 졸업생 중 몇몇'이다.

04 앞에 나오는 내용과 상반되는 내용이 뒤에 이어지므로 however가 가장 적절하다. ① 게다가, 더욱이, ④ 비슷하게, 유사하게, ⑤ 다시 말해서

05 ⓑ와 ⑤: ~하는 대로, 자기가 남에게 바라는 대로 남에게 해주어라. ① [때] ~하고 있을 때, ② [양보] ~이지만, ~이건만, ③ [비례] ~함에 따라, ~할수록, ④ [원인·이유] ~이므로, ~이기 때문에

06 이 글은 '날씨를 연구하는 과학자들이 강우를 조절하는 것과 같이 원하는 대로 날씨를 바꿀 수 있고, 기후를 조절함으로써 지구 온난화의 부작용들을 줄일 수 있는 등, 날씨를 조절하여 우리를 좀 더 안전하고 좋은 환경에서 살게 해줄 수 있다'는 내용의 글이므로, 제목으로는 ②번 '날씨를 조절하는 것의 몇 가지 좋은 점들'이 적절하다.

07 (B)는 주어진 글의 마지막 문장의 내용을 자세히 설명하는 것이므로 제일 먼저 오고 (C)의 The houses가 (A)의 마지막 문장에 나오는 houses를 가리키므로 (A) 다음에 (C)가 와야 한다. 그러므로 (B)-(A)-(C)의 순서가 적절하다.

08 help의 목적격보어에 현재분사를 쓸 수 없고 원형부정사나 to부정사를 써야 하기 때문에, (to) exercise로 고치는 것이 적절하다.

09 ⓑ와 ③: 유언장(명사), ① 의지(명사), ② 무엇을 해 달라는 부탁을 할 때 씀(조동사), ④ 일반적인 진리를 나타낼 때 씀(조동사), ⑤ ~일[할] 것이다(미래의 일에 대해 말하거나 예측할 때 씀)(조동사)

10 Neither는 상대방의 '부정문'에 대해 '나도 역시 ~하지 않다'라며 동의하거나 동사구를 반복할 때 사용하는 것이므로, Neither를 So로 고치는 것이 적절하다.

11 ⓑ와 ①, ②, ④: 현재분사, ③, ⑤: 동명사

12 the side effects of global warming: 지구 온난화의 부작용들, by ~ing: ~함으로써

13 '구름 씨 뿌리기 기술을 이용해 강우를 조절하는 데 시간이 얼마 걸리는지'는 대답할 수 없다. ① He is a scientist studying the weather. ② Yes. ④ To make rain in another city instead of Beijing during the opening event of the Olympics and its closing event as well. ⑤ We could prevent many kinds of natural disasters like floods and storms.

14 주어진 문장의 them에 주목한다. ④번 앞 문장의 'some of the graduates of our school'을 받고 있으므로 ④번이 적절하다.

15 지각동사 listen to의 목적격보어이므로 to talk를 talk로 고치는 것이 적절하다. 아직 이야기를 시작하지 않은 시점이므로, 진행을 강조할 때 사용하는 현재분사 'talking'으로 고치는 것은 적절하지 않다.

16 ⓐ와 ②, ⑤: 부사적 용법, ①, ④: 명사적 용법, ③: 형용사적 용법

17 'So am I.'는 앞 문장에 대해 동의하거나 동사구를 반복할 때 부사 'so'를 사용하여 표현한 구문이므로, 'too'나 'also'를 사용하여 고치는 것이 적절하다.

18 이 글은 '더 이상 에너지를 낭비하는 것을 걱정할 필요가 없는 풍력이나 다른 대체 에너지 자원을 사용하는 집들을 설계하여 에너지를 절약하는 것'에 관한 글이므로, 주제로는 ③번 '에너지를 절약할 수 있는 집을 설계하기'가 적절하다. ④ 태양열 발전의 효율성

19 'net-zero 에너지 집들이 얼마나 많은 대체 에너지 자원을 사용하는지'는 알 수 없다. ① She is an architect who designs net-zero energy houses. ② She has wanted to design energy-saving houses. ③ She studied architecture and environmental engineering. ⑤ Yes.

20 come true = become a reality: 실현되다

21 (A)와 ①, ④: 계속 용법, ②, ⑤: 경험 용법, ③: 완료 용법

22 그들은 풍력이나 다른 '대체 에너지 자원'을 사용하는 집들이고, 사용하는 것보다 '더 많은 에너지'를 만들어 내기 때문에 더 이상 에너지를 낭비하는 것을 걱정할 필요가 없는 집이다.

23 내가 무엇을 '잘하는지' 찾기 위해 노력했다고 해야 하므로 'for'를 'at'으로 고치는 것이 적절하다. be good at: ~을 잘하다, be good for: ~에 좋다

24 주어진 문장의 So에 주목한다. ②번 앞 문장에 대해 동의하거나 동사구를 반복하기 위해 So를 사용한 것이므로 ②번이 적절하다.

25 앞의 내용의 예가 나오고 있으므로 For example이 가장 적절하다. ① 그러므로, ③ 사실은, ④ 즉[말하자면], ⑤ 뿐만 아니라, 더욱이

26 '의문사+to부정사'는 '의문사+주어+should[can]+동사원형'으로 바꿔 쓸 수 있다.

01 Careers Day

02 it is

03 So am I.

04 (A) their jobs   (B) what they would like to do

05 I thought the weather was impossible to control, too. 또는 I also thought the weather was impossible to control.

06 such as

07 (A) a cloud seeding system   (B) dry ice

08 were

09 the houses

10 use less energy

11 (1) difficulty 또는 trouble   (2) a problem

12 late

---

01 Careers Day: 직업의 날, 학교 졸업생이나 지역사회의 인사들을 학교로 모셔 와서 그들의 직업에 대해 토론하도록 함으로써 학생들이 여러 직업들에 대해 배울 수 있는 행사이다.

02 'It' 가주어, 'to' 이하 진주어 문장에서 전치사의 목적어 자리에 있던 'jobs'를 주어 자리로 이동시킨 구문이므로, 도로 'It' 가주어, 'to' 이하 진주어 문장으로 고치는 것이 적절하다.

03 이 문장이 내포하는 의미는 'I am excited about meeting them, too.'이기 때문에 be 동사를 사용하여 'So am I.'라고 하는 것이 적절하다.

04 오늘, 학교 졸업생 몇몇이 '그들의 직업'에 관해 이야기를 할 것이다. 학생들은 그들의 이야기를 들으면서 미래에 '무엇을 하고 싶은지' 생각할 수 있다.

05 '저도 역시 날씨를 조절하는 것이 불가능하다고 생각했어요.'라는 뜻이다.

06 like = such as: ~와 같은

07 날씨를 연구하는 과학자들은 '구름 씨 뿌리기 기술'을 이용해 강우를 조절할 수 있는데, 그 과정 도중에 그들은 구름 속에 '드라이아이스'를 뿌려 구름을 바로 만든다.

08 앞 문장 'Many people are worried about ~'에 이어지는 문장으로 '우리 부모님도 그랬었다(걱정했었다).'라는 의미가 되려면 be 동사의 과거형을 사용하여 'So were my parents.'라고 쓰는 것이 적절하다.

09 '그 집들'을 가리킨다.

10 net-zero 에너지 집들은 풍력이나 다른 대체 에너지 자원을 사용하여, 만들어 내는 것보다 '더 적은 에너지를 사용하기' 때문에 에너지를 절약할 수 있다.

11 have a hard time ~ing = have difficulty 또는 trouble ~ing = have a problem ~ing: ~하는 데 어려움을 겪다

12 a late bloomer: 늦게 꽃피우는 사람, 만성형(晚成型)의 사람, 인생에서 비교적 늦은 시기에 어떤 분야에서 숙달되거나 성공을 성취하는 사람, proficiency: 숙달, 능숙

01 irregularly   02 ③   03 ③

04 The number of tourists decreases in October all over the world.

05 ⑤   06 ③, ⑤   07 ②

08 how do you feel about their new album?   09 ④

10 I think taking a trip around the world is good.

11 (A) which   (B) to take   (C) having

12 How do you feel about visiting our store to see one?

13 ②   14 ④   15 ③   16 ①

17 It is difficult for me to study French.

18 Neither did I.   19 she   20 ⑤

21 is dangerous to handle some robots

22 trying   23 do → am   24 ③   25 ⑤

26 (A) didn't   (B) another city   27 ②, ③

28 ②   29 ④   30 ③

---

01 reduce(줄이다, 낮추다)와 increase(증가하다, 커지다)는 반의어 관계에 있는 단어들이다. 따라서 regularly(정기적으로, 규칙적으로)와 반의어 관계에 있는 단어는 irregularly(비정기적으로)이다.

02 ③에서 쓰인 graduate는 '졸업하다'라는 동사적 의미로 사용되었다.

03 주어진 문장에서 season은 '계절, 때'라는 뜻으로 사용되었다. ③에서는 '양념을 하다'라는 뜻으로 사용되었다.

04 the number of ~의 수

05 '사람과 동식물이 사는 곳의 공기, 물, 땅'이라는 뜻의 영영 풀이가 가리키는 것은 ⑤environment(환경)이다.

06 prefer는 better나 than과 함께 쓰일 수 없다.

07 주어진 문장은 '그건 다음 주 토요일이야.'라는 뜻으로 콘서트가 언제냐고 묻고 난 다음인 ②에 들어가는 것이 가장 적절하다.

08 상대방의 의견을 묻는 표현으로는 'How do you feel about ~?'을 쓸 수 있다.

09 G는 최신 앨범보다 지난 앨범을 더 좋아한다고 말했다. ("but I prefer their last album to the new one.")

10 의견을 나타내는 표현으로는 'I think ~.'가 있다. / take a trip 여행을 하다

11 (A) 관계대명사가 꾸며주는 것이 a smart camera이므로 which가 적절하다. (B) 진주어 (C) without ~ing ~하지 않고

12 'How do you feel about ~?'는 상대방의 의견을 묻는 표현으

로 '~하는 것에 대해 어떻게 생각하시나요?'라고 해석한다.

13 위 글의 마지막 문장에서 알 수 있듯이, 새로 나온 카메라 광고를 위한 글이다.

14 A: 치아가 아프지만 나는 치과에 가는 것을 싫어해. B: 내 여동생도 그래. 일반동사가 쓰인 앞 문장에 대한 동의로 시제와 주어의 수를 일치시켜 does가 오는 것이 적절하다.

15 ③의 It은 인칭대명사이다. ① 권투 경기를 보는 것은 흥미롭다. ② 그가 대도시에서 혼자 사는 것은 불가능하다. ③ 그것은 큰 사이즈의 T셔츠이다. ④ 영화배우를 만나는 것은 굉장하다. ⑤ 낚시하러 가는 것은 지루하다.

16 긍정문 문장의 동의를 표현할 때 'So'를 이용하여 표현하고 이때 주어와 동사의 위치는 도치된다. (1) 일반동사가 쓰인 앞 문장에 대한 동의로 시제를 일치시켜 did를 써서 표현하는 것이 적절하다. (2) 현재완료형이 쓰인 앞 문장에 대한 동의를 표현할 때 조동사의 현재완료형의 has를 쓰는 것이 적절하다. (3) 과거완료형이 쓰인 앞 문장에 대한 동의로 had를 쓰는 것이 적절하다.

17 'It+be동사+난이 형용사+for+의미상의 주어+to부정사'

18 어렸을 때 나는 노래 부르는 것을 좋아하지 않았다. 부정문 문장에 동의를 표현할 때는 'Neither'를 이용한다. 이때 주어와 동사의 위치는 도치된다. 일반동사를 부정하는 과거형이 쓰였으므로 'Neither did I.'로 쓰는 것이 적절하다.

19 so에 의해 주어와 동사가 도치된 것으로 빈칸은 주어 자리이기 때문에 she가 오는 것이 적절하다.

20 'It(가주어)+be동사+난이 형용사+to부정사(진주어)'로 to부정사의 의미상의 주어는 'for+목적격'이므로 she는 빈칸에 들어갈 수 없다.

21 일부 로봇을 다루는 것은 위험하다. 'It+be동사+난이 형용사+to부정사'에서 to부정사의 목적어를 문장의 주어로 해서 '주어+be동사+난이 형용사+to부정사'로 바꿔 쓸 수 있다.

22 keep on ~ing: 계속 ~하다(집요하게 반복되는 동작·상태의 계속)

23 이 문장이 내포하는 의미는 'I am excited about meeting them, too.'이기 때문에 do를 be동사 am으로 고치는 것이 적절하다.

24 이 글은 '직업의 날에 학교 졸업생 몇몇을 맞이하여 그들의 직업에 관해 이야기를 들으면서, 학생들이 미래에 무엇을 하고 싶은지 생각해 보라'고 말하는 글이므로, 제목으로는 ③번 '졸업생들이 직업에 대해 말하는 것을 들어보자'가 적절하다. ① School Open Day: 학교 공개의 날

25 앞의 내용의 예가 나오고 있으므로 For example이 가장 적절하다. ① 즉[말하자면], ③ ~임에 비하여[반하여], ④ 게다가

26 구름 씨 뿌리기 기술을 이용해 북경 대신 '다른 도시'에 비가 오게끔 함으로써, 올림픽의 개막식과 폐막식에 북경에는 비가 '내리지 않았다.'

27 ⓐ와 ①, ④, ⑤: 동명사, ②, ③: 현재분사

28 ②번 다음 문장의 The houses에 주목한다. 주어진 문장의 houses를 받고 있으므로 ②번이 적절하다.

29 위 글은 '일기'이다. ② (신문·잡지의) 글, 기사, ③ 수필, ⑤ (책·연극·영화 등에 대한) 논평[비평], 감상문

30 net-zero 에너지 집 건축가는 에너지를 '절약하는' 집을 설계한다.

단원별 예상문제
p.52~55

01 ①
02 (1) succeed iny   (2) get along well with
  (3) feel proud of
03 How do you feel about this new recipe?
04 the soup   05 ⑤
06 G is looking for a hat.   07 ④
08 B is getting ready for Jina's birthday.
09 She suggests B to wear a white shirt.
10 ④   11 ①
12 It is impossible for me to be there before eight.
13 ②   14 ③   15 ④
16 doing → to do   17 clouds   18 ②
19 ①   20 ②   21 ④   22 ③
23 ⑤   24 ④

01 '두 개 혹은 더 많은 것 사이에서 선택을 제공하는'이라는 뜻의 영영풀이가 가리키는 단어는 ① alternative(대체 가능한)이다.

02 (1) succeed in ~에 성공하다 (2) get along well with ~와 잘 지내다 (3) feel proud of ~에 긍지를 느끼다

03 'How do you feel about ~?'는 상대방의 의견을 묻는 표현으로 '~하는 것에 대해 어떻게 생각하시나요?'라고 해석한다.

04 대명사 it이 가리키는 것은 문맥상 새로운 요리법으로 만든 수프다.

05 대화 후반에 G가 B에게 수프에 소금을 좀 더 넣으라고 말했으므로 B의 다음 행동은 ⑤ '수프에 소금 넣기'다.

06 G는 엄마를 위한 모자를 사고 싶다고("I'd like to buy a hat for my mother.") 말했다.

07 G는 엄마에게 드릴 모자를 사기 위해 상점에 갔고 M은 모자를 추천해 주고 있으므로 ④ '점원-고객'의 관계가 가장 적절하다.

08 B가 대화 초반에 Jina의 생일이라고 말했다.

09 B의 엄마는 B에게 하얀 셔츠를 입으라고 말했다.("How do you feel about wearing a white shirt instead?")

10 B는 청바지를 다른 바지들보다 선호한다고 말했다.("I prefer jeans to my other pants.")

11 'I prefer ~.' 또는 'I like 목적어 better.'와 같은 표현은 선호를 나타내는 표현이다.

12 8시 전에 내가 거기에 도착하는 것은 불가능하다. 그곳에 8시 전에 도착하는 것이 불가능한 것이지 내가 불가능한 것이 아니다.

13 A: 그녀는 어제 '어벤져스'를 봤어. 긍정 문장의 동의를 표현할 때는 'So'를 이용하여 표현한다. 이때 주어와 동사의 위치는 도치된다. A에서 일반동사의 과거가 쓰였으므로 B에는 'So did we.'가 오는 것이 적절하다.

14 부정문 문장의 동의를 표현할 때는 'Neither'를 이용하여 표현한다. 이때 주어와 동사의 위치는 도치된다. 앞에서 조동사 won't가 쓰였으므로 B에는 'Neither will Jack.'이 오는 것이 적절하다.

15 ⓑ와 ④: graduate: 《美》 (각종 학교의) 졸업생; 《英》 (대학/학과) 졸업생, ①, ⑤: 졸업하다, ② 날이 차츰 밝아 온다. 서서히 (~으로) 변화하다, 차츰 (~이) 되다, ③ (~에게) 학위를 수여하다, <학생을> 졸업시키다

16 would like 뒤에 동명사는 쓸 수 없고 to부정사만 쓸 수 있으므로 to do로 고치는 것이 적절하다. would like to 동사원형: ~하고 싶다

17 '구름'을 가리킨다.

18 Why don't you 동사원형? = How about ~ing? = Why not 동사원형? = What about ~ing? = What do you say to ~ing?: ~하는 게 어때?

19 이 글은 '날씨를 연구하는 과학자들이 강우를 조절하는 것과 같이 원하는 대로 날씨를 바꿀 수 있고, 기후를 조절함으로써 지구 온난화의 부작용들을 줄일 수 있는 등, 날씨를 조절하여 우리를 좀 더 안전하고 좋은 환경에서 살게 해줄 수 있다'는 내용의 글이므로, 주제로는 ①번 '날씨를 조절함으로써 우리가 가질 수 있는 이익들'이 적절하다.

20 선행사를 포함한 관계대명사 'what'을 쓰는 것이 적절하다.

21 주어진 문장의 This에 주목한다. ④번 앞 문장의 내용을 받고 있으므로 ④번이 적절하다.

22 '사람들이 아플 때 임종 설계사가 그들을 병원에 데리고 간다.'는 내용은 없다.

23 앞 문장에 대해 동의하거나 동사구를 반복할 때 부사 'so'를 사용하여 표현할 수 있다.

24 '글쓴이가 언제 꿈을 성취할 수 있을 것인지'는 대답할 수 없다. ① The writer wants to be a train operator on the Trans-Siberian-Railroad. ② Because the writer thinks trains are fun to operate. ③ Yes. At the age of 13, the writer went to Busan by train which the writer's uncle operated. The writer's uncle was proud of helping people travel comfortably. So were his colleagues. ⑤ The writer will study hard, exercise regularly and will read a lot of books about trains.

서술형 실전문제
p.56~57

01 (C) – (A) – (B)

02 than → to

03 B is going to go to the concert next Saturday.

04 B thinks (that) all the songs are so exciting.

05 (1) You are not mad, and neither is he.

  (2) She hates black nail color, and so do I.

  (3) My father doesn't like pizza, and neither does my mother.

  (4) His Airpot is gorgeous. So is yours, Jihye.

  (5) If you don't care about this class, then neither do I.

  (6) She was relieved to hear that, and so was he.

06 (1) It is not easy to hate someone.

  (2) It is difficult to find a true love.

    A true love is difficult to find.

  (3) It is hard to observe a lunar eclipse.

    A lunar eclipse is hard to observe.

07 it was impossible to control the weather

08 Why don't you join us in making a better environment by controlling the weather?

09 (A) change the weather

  (B) controlling the climate

10 are → is

11 I help people to plan for their death as well as to live a healthy life.

12 I even teach them how to make a will!

01 B가 음악 페스티벌에 가는 것을 기대한다고 말하자 상대방이 (C)에서 자신도 그렇다고 말하면서 춤추는 것과 노래하는 것 중에 어느 것을 선호하냐고 묻는다. 이에 B는 (A)에서 노래하는 것보다 춤추는 것을 좋아한다고 말했고 이에 상대방은 (B)에서 노래하는 것을 좋아한다고 말하면서 같이 춤추고 노래하면 재밌겠다고 말하는 순서로 가는 것이 가장 자연스럽다.

02 prefer는 to와 함께 쓰인다. prefer A to B B보다 A를 선호하다

03 B는 콘서트에 가는데, 그것은 다음 주 토요일에 열린다고 말했다.

04 B는 새 앨범의 모든 노래가 다 신난다고("All the songs are so exciting") 언급했다.

05 (1) 너는 미치지 않았어. 그리고 그도 그래. (2) 그녀는 검정색 손톱 색깔을 싫어하고 나 역시 그래. (3) 나의 아빠는 피자를 싫어해. 나의 엄마도 싫어해. (4) 그의 에어팟은 멋져. 너의 것도 멋져, 지혜야. (5) 만약 네가 이 수업에 신경 안 쓴다면 나도 신경 안 써. (6) 그녀는 그것을 듣고 나서 안도했고, 그도 그랬어.

06 'It+be동사+난이 형용사+to부정사'에서 to부정사의 목적어를 문장의 주어로 해서 '주어+be동사+난이 형용사+to부정사'로 바꿔 쓸 수 있다.

07 'it' 가주어, 'to' 이하 진주어 문장에서 to부정사의 목적어 자리에 있던 'the weather'를 주어 자리로 이동시킨 구문이므로, 'it' 가주어, 'to' 이하 진주어 문장으로 고치는 것이 적절하다.

08 Why don't you 동사원형?: ~하는 게 어때?

09 현대 기술 덕분에 날씨를 연구하는 과학자들은 원하는 대로 '날씨를 바꿀 수 있고', '기후를 조절함으로써' 지구 온난화의 부작용들을 줄일 수 있다.

10 'the number'가 주어이기 때문에, 'are'를 'is'로 고치는 것이 적절하다.

11 not only A but also B = B as well as A: A뿐만 아니라 B도

12 '심지어 사람들에게 유언장 쓰는 법을 가르친다!'는 앞 문장의 내용을 가리킨다.

창의사고력 서술형 문제
p.58

|모범답안|

01 a smart camera, very strong, use my fingers, percent off

02 (A) a train operator   (B) trains are fun to operate
(C) my uncle operated
(D) helping people travel comfortably
(E) study hard and exercise regularly
(F) read a lot of books about trains

01 어제 나는 길을 걸어가고 있었는데, 그때 가게 앞에서 전단지를 보았다. 그 전단지 내용은, 새로운 STARS 카메라가 출시되었으며, 이것은 최고의 순간을 잡아주는 스마트 카메라라고 한다. 그건 매우 작지만 튼튼하다고 하고, 더불어 그걸로 좋은 사진을 쉽게 찍을 수 있다고 한다. 손을 사용할 필요도 없이, 이 카메라에 대고 말함으로써 사진을 찍을 수 있다. 더군다나, 지금 30퍼센트 세일이라고 한다. 난 정말 그 카메라가 갖고 싶다.

단원별 모의고사
p.59~63

01 ⑤   **02** ②

03 have kept on

04 (A) while   (B) who

05 ③   **06** feed   **07** ①

08 It's because G wants to use the present.

09 (B) – (A) – (C)   **10** ③

11 How do you feel about becoming a writer?

12 ③   **13** ⑤   **14** ②, ③

15 ②

16 (A) it was impossible to control the weather 또는 the weather was impossible to control
(B) so are architects

17 (1) It is hard to estimate how many children suffer from dyslexia.
(2) It is hard to endure such pain.
(3) It is hard to find a job.
(4) It is hard to make a comparison between him and his brother.
(5) It is hard to suit everybody.
(6) It is hard to start a new job sometimes.

18 ①   **19** ②

20 (A) reduce   (B) natural disasters

21 alternative

22 My parents were worried about using too much energy at home, too. 또는 My parents were also worried about using too much energy at home.

23 ⑤   **24** Let's give a big hand

25 If you

---

01 '보통 늙어서 일을 그만 두고 떠나는 행위'라는 뜻의 영영풀이가 가리키는 것은 ⑤ retirement(은퇴, 퇴직)이다.

02 음식과 관련된 여러 가지 문화적 관습들이 있다. 예를 들어, 미역국은 한국에서 임산부들이 빠른 회복을 할 수 있도록 도와준다고 믿어진다. / for example 예를 들어

03 keep on ~ing 계속해서 ~하다

04 (A) while ~하는 동안에 (B) 관계대명사가 꾸며주는 대상이 those (people)이므로 who가 들어가야 한다.

05 ③ '어떤 애완동물을 화자가 언급하는가'라는 질문에 대한 대답은 위 글에서 언급되지 않았다.

06 '사람이나 집단 또는 동물에게 먹을 것을 주다'라는 영영풀이가 가리키는 단어는 feed(먹이를 주다)이다.

07 상대방의 의견을 묻는 표현으로는 'How do you feel about ~?'과 'What do you think about ~?', 'What about ~?', 'What do you think of ~?' 등과 같은 표현이 있다. 이 표현

들 모두 '~에 대해서 어떻게 생각하니/느끼니?'라고 해석한다.

08 위 대화 G의 말에서 알 수 있듯이, 그 선물을 써보고 싶어서(I hope it rains soon so that I can use it.)이다.

09 A가 클래식 음악에 대해 어떻게 생각하냐고 묻자 상대방이 (B)에서 지루해서 별로 좋아하지 않는다고 말하며 A는 어떠냐고 되묻는다. 이어서 A는 (A)에서 매우 좋아하며, 클래식 음악을 들을 때 차분해진다고 말하자 상대방이 (C)에서 미래에 음악가가 되는 것이 어떻겠냐고 묻는 순서가 마지막 대답인 '좋은 생각이야'와 이어지면서 문맥상 가장 자연스럽다.

10 '제 미래에 대해서 걱정이 돼서요.'라는 문장은, Brown 선생님이 지수에게 근심 있어 보인다고 말한 뒤인 ③에 위치하는 것이 가장 자연스럽다.

11 '~에 대해서 어떻게 생각하니/느끼니?'라고 상대방의 의견을 묻는 표현으로는 'How do you feel about ~?' 등이 있다.

12 지수는 문학보다 과학을 더 좋아한다고("I prefer science to literature.") 말했다.

13 그는 뉴스를 이해하기 어려웠다. ① to부정사의 의미상의 주어가 빠졌으므로 옳지 못하다. ②, ③ 어색한 문장이다. ④ it을 삭제해야 한다. understand에 대한 목적어는 the news이다.

14 'It+be동사+난이 형용사+to부정사'에서 to부정사의 목적어를 문장의 주어로 해서 '주어+be동사+난이 형용사+to부정사'로 바꿔 쓸 수 있다.

15 일단 바이러스를 제거하면 인터넷에 다시 연결되어도 안전하다. It+be동사+난이 형용사+to부정사

16 (A) 'It+be동사+난이 형용사+to부정사'에서 to부정사의 목적어를 문장의 주어로 해서 '주어+be동사+난이 형용사+to부정사'로 바꿔 쓸 수 있다. (B) 긍정문 문장의 동의를 표현할 때 'so'를 이용하여 표현하고 이때 주어와 동사의 위치는 도치된다. 앞 문장에서 be동사가 쓰였으므로 시제와 주어의 수를 일치시켜 'so are architects'로 쓰는 것이 적절하다.

17 It+be동사+hard(난이 형용사)+to부정사

18 ⓐ와 ①, ②, ④, ⑤: 부사적 용법, ③: 명사적 용법

19 주어진 문장의 For example에 주목한다. ②번 앞 문장의 예를 설명하고 있으므로 ②번이 적절하다.

20 기후를 조절함으로써, 우리는 지구 온난화의 부작용들을 '줄일 수 있고' 홍수나 폭풍 같은 다양한 '자연재해'를 예방할 수 있다. 그 결과, 우리는 더 나은 환경을 만들 수 있다.

21 alternative: 대체 가능한, 이미 가지고 있는 것과 다른, 대신 행해지거나 사용될 수 있는

22 '우리 부모님도 역시 집에서 너무 많은 에너지를 사용하는 것에

대해 걱정했었다.'라는 뜻이다.

23 net-zero 에너지 집들은 '사용하는' 것보다 더 많은 에너지를 '만들어 낸다.'

24 give a big hand: 큰 박수를 보내다

25 '명령문, and' 구문은 'If you'를 사용하여 바꿔 쓸 수 있다. 이 경우, '접속사 and'를 생략하는 것이 적절하다.

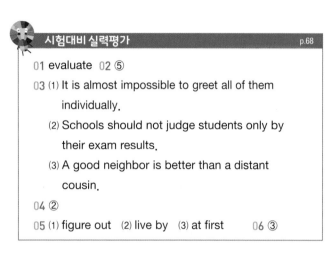

What People Live By

Lesson 8

시험대비 실력평가   p.68

01 evaluate   02 ⑤

03 (1) It is almost impossible to greet all of them individually.
  (2) Schools should not judge students only by their exam results.
  (3) A good neighbor is better than a distant cousin.

04 ②

05 (1) figure out   (2) live by   (3) at first   06 ③

01 certainly(분명히)와 definitely(명확히, 분명히)는 유사한 뜻을 가진 단어들이다. 따라서 judge(판단하다)와 유의어 관계에 있는 단어는 evaluate(평가하다, 감정하다)이다.

02 ⑤ last는 '지난, 바로 이전의'라는 뜻으로 사용되었다.

03 (1) greet 인사하다 (2) judge 판단하다 (3) neighbor 이웃

04 '합법적으로 다른 사람의 아이를 본인의 가족으로 데려와 친자식처럼 보살피다'라는 뜻을 가진 영영풀이가 가리키는 것은 ② adopt(입양하다)이다.

05 (1) figure out 알아내다 (2) live by ~에 따라 살다 (3) at first 처음에는

06 in surprise 놀라서 / hand in 제출하다 / think back 돌이켜 생각하다 / hold back 저지하다, 비밀로 하다

서술형 시험대비   p.69

01 lose   02 walk away from

03 (1) volunteers   (2) Servants   (3) leather

04 (1) She loves to win an argument.
  (2) John often comes into conflict with his boss.
  (3) He died of a heart attack during an operation.

05 (1) The punishment was very fair.
  (2) I suppose you haven't met many noblemen.
  (3) Human beings need food, clothing and shelter.

01 conflict(싸움, 다툼)와 agreement(일치, 조화, 동의)는 반의어 관계에 있는 단어들이다. 따라서 gain(무게를 늘리다, 얻다)와 반의어 관계에 있는 단어는 lose(잃다, 상실하다)이다.

02 walk away from ~에게서 멀어지다

03 (1) volunteer 자원봉사자; 자원하다 (2) servant 하인 (3) leather 가죽

04 (1) argument 논쟁 (2) conflict 싸움, 다툼 (3) heart attack 심장마비

05 (1) punishment 처벌 (2) nobleman 귀족 (3) human beings 인류

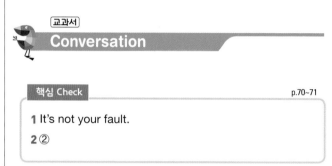

교과서 Conversation

핵심 Check   p.70~71

1 It's not your fault.

2 ②

02 ② don't have to는 '~하지 않아도 된다'라는 뜻으로 다른 표현들처럼 의무를 나타내는 표현이 아니다.

교과서 대화문 익히기

Check(√) True or False   p.72

1 T   2 F   3 T   4 F

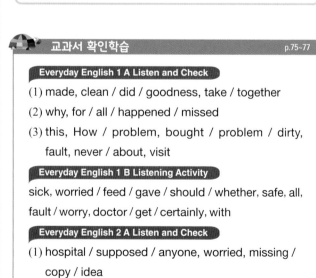

교과서 확인학습   p.75~77

Everyday English 1 A Listen and Check

(1) made, clean / did / goodness, take / together
(2) why, for / all / happened / missed
(3) this, How / problem, bought / problem / dirty, fault, never / about, visit

Everyday English 1 B Listening Activity

sick, worried / feed / gave / should / whether, safe, all, fault / worry, doctor / get / certainly, with

Everyday English 2 A Listen and Check

(1) hospital / supposed / anyone, worried, missing / copy / idea
(2) confused / cannot, anything, communicate / tried / always / supposed, sign

Everyday English 2 B Listening Activity

planning / volunteer, disabilities, join / worried / makes / whether, advice / respect / mean, needs /

only, ask

시험대비 기본평가 p.78

01 (C) - (B) - (A)

02 ③

03 Then should I make a copy of my notes for him?

04 ①

---

01 B는 누가 어질러 놓았냐고 묻자 상대방이 (C)에서 자신이 잘못이 아니라 B의 개가 그랬다고 말한다. 이어서 (B)에서 어질러 놓은 것을 치우려면 시간이 많이 들겠다고 하자 (A)에서 상대방이 도와준다고 말하는 순서로 이어지는 것이 문맥상 가장 적절하다.

02 과거의 잘못이므로 was로 써야 한다.

03 의무를 나타내는 표현으로는 조동사 should/ought to/have to/must 등이 있다. 위 대화에서는 '~하는 게 좋겠다'라는 의미로 개인적인 충고나 조언 등에 쓰이는 should를 쓰는 것이 가장 적절하다. / make a copy 복사하다, 복사본을 만들다

04 ① 민수가 왜 병원에 입원했는지는 위 대화에서 언급되어 있지 않다.

시험대비 실력평가 p.79~80

01 ⓑ to him → him　　02 ①　　03 ⑤

04 ④　　05 ②　　06 disability

07 who → that[which]　　08 ①

09 the boots that M bought there yesterday　10 ②

11 G is going to learn how to use sign language.

---

01 give는 간접목적어(~에게)와 직접목적어(~을/를) 등 목적어를 두 개 취할 수 있는데, 이때 'give+간접목적어+직접목적어' 또는 'give+직접목적어+to 간접목적어'의 어순으로 쓸 수 있다.

따라서 ⓑto him을 him으로 고쳐야 한다.

02 대화 초반 G의 말에서 개가 너무 걱정된다고("I'm so worried about him.") 언급되어 있다.

03 ⑤ 개한테 무엇이 안전하고 안전하지 않은지에 대해서는 언급되지 않았다.

04 (A) 현재진행형 문장이 쓰여서 가까운 미래를 나타낸다. (B) 앞에 전치사 of가 사용되었으므로 동명사 ~ing이 적절하다. (C) 앞에서 B가 걱정된다고 현재 시제로 말했으므로 '왜 그렇게 느끼니?'라고 현재 시제로 물어보는 것이 적절하다.

05 'be supposed to ~'는 '~해야 한다', '~하기로 되어 있다'는 뜻으로 의무를 나타내는 표현이다. ② don't need to는 '~할 필요가 없다'는 뜻이다.

06 '어떤 사람이 다른 사람들이 하는 일들을 못하게 하는 조건이나 질병, 부상'이라는 영영풀이가 가리키는 것은 disabilitiy(장애)를 가리킨다.

07 M의 말에서 관계대명사 who가 수식하는 것이 the boots라는 사물이므로 관계대명사 that이나 which로 고쳐 써야 한다.

08 위 대화의 내용으로 미루어 볼 때, W와 M의 관계는 신발 가게의 점원과 손님 간의 관계로 보는 것이 가장 적절하다.

09 '그것들'과 관련된 문제가 뭐냐고 물어봤으므로, 이 상황에서 '그것들'은 'M이 어제 그 가게에서 산 부츠'를 가리킨다.

10 위 대화에서 B는 G에게 파트너와의 의사소통을 하기 위해 수화를 배워야 한다고 충고했다. 따라서 빈칸 (A)에 들어가기에 적절한 표현은 의무를 나타내는 표현이다.

11 B는 G에게 수화를 배우라고 충고한다.

서술형 시험대비 p.81

01 Inho advised Lina to make up with Ryan as soon as possible.

02 Lina와 말다툼한 것

03 You're supposed to run for an hour every day.

04 It's because B wanted to book tickets.

05 B is going to watch the performance at 8 p.m.

06 B has to bring his/her student ID card.

---

01 'Inho는 Lina에게 Ryan과 가능한 한 빨리 화해하라고 말했다.

02 대명사 it이 가리키는 것은 Ryan이 후회할지도 모르는 일을 의미한다. 문맥상 Lina와 다툰 일을 의미한다.

03 'be supposed to ~'는 ~하기로 되어 있다', '~해야 한다'라는 의미이며, 약속이나 규칙 등 예정된 일에 대해 묻고 답할 수 있다.

04 대화 초반 B의 말("I'd like to book four seats for *Sleeping*

Beauty this Friday.")에서 극장에 전화한 이유를 알 수 있다.

05 6시와 8시 공연이 있었지만 8시 공연에서만 충분한 좌석이 있었으므로 8시 공연을 보기로 했다.

06 학생 할인을 받기 위해서는 학생증을 가져와야 한다고 W의 말 ("You're supposed to bring your student ID card.")에 언급되어 있다.

감정을 나타낼 때 쓴다. 밑줄 친 우리말을 8 단어로 영작하라고 했으므로 you should take our puppy for a walk로 쓰는 것이 적절하다.

04 두 문장 모두 빈칸에 '~인지 아닌지'라는 의미가 들어가는 것이 적절하므로 if 또는 whether가 들어가는 것이 적절하다.

교과서
Grammar

핵심 Check   p.82~83

1 (1) whether (2) Whether

2 (1) ○ (2) ○

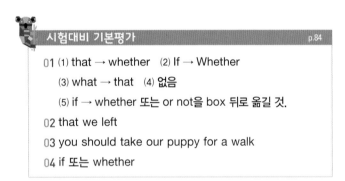

시험대비 기본평가   p.84

01 (1) that → whether (2) If → Whether
   (3) what → that (4) 없음
   (5) if → whether 또는 or not을 box 뒤로 옮길 것.
02 that we left
03 you should take our puppy for a walk
04 if 또는 whether

01 (1) '~인지 아닌지'를 표현할 때 whether를 쓰므로 that을 whether로 고치는 것이 적절하다. (2) If로 주어를 이끌 수 없으므로 If를 Whether로 고쳐야 한다. (3) 'It's time that 가정법' 표현은 현재 일어나지 않은 일에 관한 화자의 불만족이나 재촉 등의 주관적인 감정을 나타낸다. 이미 네가 숙제를 끝냈어야 할 시간인데 그렇지 못하다는 아쉬움을 표현하는 문장이므로 what을 that으로 고치는 것이 적절하다. (4) 'It's time that+주어+should+동사원형'은 'It's time that+주어+가정법'의 또 다른 표현이다. 'It's time that ~'에 이어 'we should work'가 나왔으므로 어색한 곳이 없다. (5) or not이 if 바로 다음에 나왔으므로 or not을 삭제하거나 if를 whether로 고치는 것이 적절하다. 또는 or not을 box 뒤로 옮겨야 한다.

02 'It's high time (that)+가정법 과거'는 현재 일어나지 않은 일에 대한 화자의 불만족이나 재촉 등의 주관적인 감정을 나타낸다. 그러므로 빈칸에 '(that) we left'가 오는 것이 적절하다.

03 '~해야 할 때이다.'라는 의미는 'It's time that 가정법 과거'로 쓰고 현재 일어나지 않은 일에 대한 화자의 불만이나 재촉 등의

시험대비 실력평가   p.85~87

01 it's time (that) I cut down on the junk food (that) I
   eat.   02 ③   03 ④   04 ④
05 ①, ④   06 Isn't it about
07 high 또는 about, repaired 08 ④   09 ②, ③
10 ①, ④   11 ①, ⑤
12 (1) whether (2) comes (3) to   13 ④
14 ④   15 ②, ④   16 whether[if], or not
17 It's about time you were free from that.
18 ②, ⑤

01 엄마: 소미야, 점점 뚱뚱해지고 있구나. 소미: 맞아요. 제 생각엔 제가 먹는 정크 푸드를 줄여야 할 때라고 생각해요. '~할 때이다'를 표현할 때 'It's (about) time (that)+주어+과거형 동사'로 쓰므로 괄호 안의 단어를 이용하여 It's time (that) I cut down on the junk food (that) I eat로 쓰는 것이 적절하다.

02 내가 당신을 믿고 안 믿고는 이제 상관없다. '~인지 아닌지'로 해석되며 주절에 'or not'과 함께 쓰일 수 있는 접속사는 whether이다.

03 ④ 그녀가 차를 가졌었는지는 나에게 중요하지 않다. '~인지 아닌지'의 의미를 나타내며 명사절을 이끌 수 있는 접속사는 if와 whether가 있다. 'if'는 목적어로만 쓰이기 때문에 If를 Whether로 고치는 것이 적절하다. ① 그가 회의에 참석할지 그에게 물었다. ② 그가 오든 안 오든 나는 관심 없다. ③ 그는 자기가 날 수 있는지 보려고 애를 썼다. ⑤ 그녀는 웃어야 할지 울어야 할지 몰랐다.

04 우리가 고국으로 돌아가야 할 때이다. 'It is (high) time that we should 동사원형'은 'It is (high) time that 주어 과거형 동사'로 바꿔 쓸 수 있으므로 have returned를 returned로 쓰는 것이 적절하다.

05 • 이 버스가 CN 타워에 가는지 아니? • 이번 인터뷰에 Jack이 통과했는지 궁금하다. • 다음 회의가 토론토에서 개최될지 모른다. 세 문장 모두 '~인지 아닌지'의 내용을 이끌 수 있는 명사절 접속사는 if와 whether이므로 ①, ④를 고르는 것이 적절하다.

06 'It is about time that ~'에서 주어와 동사를 도치시켜 의문문으로 만든다. 주어진 우리말에 따라 빈칸에는 'Isn't it about'이 들

어가는 것이 적절하다.

07 내 차가 어제 고장 나서 자동차 서비스 센터에 들렀다. → 내 차를 수리할 때이다.

08 ④ 그의 축구팀이 경기에서 이길지 질지는 중요하지 않다. '~인지 아닌지'를 표현할 때 whether와 if를 쓸 수 있다. If가 이끄는 주어에 or not이 왔고, 주어를 이끌 수 있는 접속사는 whether이므로 If를 Whether로 고치는 것이 적절하다. ① 그녀가 나를 좋아하는지 모르겠다. ② 온라인 쇼핑이 오프라인보다 더 싼지 모르겠다. ③ 그가 아픈지 아닌지 모른다. ⑤ 우리가 제시간에 영화관에 도착할지 모르겠다.

09 그는 은행에 돈이 전혀 없어. 이제 저축을 해야 할 때가 됐어. '~할 때이다.'는 'It's about time+주어+과거 동사', 'It's about time that+주어+should+동사원형 ~'이므로 ②번과 ③번을 고르는 것이 적절하다.

10 그가 내일 올지 안 올지 궁금하다. wonder의 목적어를 이끄는 접속사가 올 자리이고 '~인지 아닌지'의 의미가 들어가야 하므로 ①, ④를 고르는 것이 적절하다.

11 ① 우리나라가 교육에 투자해야 할 때라고 생각해. ⑤ 우리나라가 좋은 해결책을 제시해야 할 때라고 생각해. A: 코비드-19 때문에 우리는 상황이 별로 좋지 않다. 특히 교육 분야에서 그래. 이에 대한 답변으로 교육 분야의 발전이나 투자를 해야 할 때라는 의미가 들어가야 하므로 ①번과 ⑤번을 고르는 것이 적절하다. ② 교육 분야에 투자할 때가 아니라고 생각한다. ③ 이 사람들이 이러한 행동에 대해 벌금을 물어야 할 때라고 생각한다. ④ 우리는 다음 단계를 준비하지 않아도 된다고 생각한다.

12 어법에 맞게 배열하면, (1) You have got to go to school, whether you like it or not. (2) If she comes tomorrow, I will be happy. (3) They thought deeply whether to continue the talk.

13 • 그녀가 화났니? - 그녀가 화난건지 아닌지 모르겠어. • 가죽 부츠 만드는 수업 들어 볼래? - 내가 좋은 가죽 부츠를 만들 수 있을지 확실치 않아.

14 '그가 원하든 원하지 않든'의 내용이 들어가야 하므로 ④를 고르는 것이 적절하다. whether는 '~이든 아니든'의 뜻으로 부사절을 이끌 수 있다.

15 '~인지 아닌지'의 의미가 들어가야 하므로 ②, ④를 고르는 것이 적절하다.

16 우리는 어떤 여성이 결혼 했는지 안 했는지 모를 때 Mrs나 Miss 대신 Ms를 사용한다. '~인지 아닌지'라는 의미가 들어가야 하므로 whether[if], or not을 쓰는 것이 적절하다.

17 It's about time 주어+과거 동사는 '~할 때이다.'의 의미로 현재 상황에 대한 불만 또는 주관적 감정을 표현한다.

18 'It's about time that 주어+should+동사원형' 구문은 당위성의 내용이 포함되어 있다. '내 연구실은 코비드-19 백신을 만들었다.'라는 내용 뒤에 '우리의 성공을 알릴 때가 됐다.' 또는 '많은 회사들이 내 연구실에 투자할 때가 됐다.'라는 내용이 오는 것이 자연스러우므로 ②, ⑤를 고르는 것이 적절하다.

서술형 시험대비

p.88~89

01 (1) It's high time my father showed up.
It's high time my father should show up.
(2) It's high time we stopped.
It's high time we should stop.
(3) I think it's high time I went back home.
I think it's high time I should go back home.
(4) It's high time we updated our software.
It's high time we should update our software.
(5) It's high time we started taking global warming seriously.
It's high time we should start taking global warming seriously.
(6) It's high time you learned to face the facts.
It's high time you should learn to face the facts.
(7) It's high time the weather started cooling off.
It's high time the weather should start cooling off.
(8) It's high time we took serious steps.
It's high time we should take serious steps.

02 (1) We don't know whether she is married or not.
(2) It depends on whether or not she has money.
(3) I doubt whether it'll work or not.
(4) I wasn't sure whether you would like it or not.
(5) We talked about whether we should go or not.

03 if

04 (1) Does the house have a garden?
(2) Will they go camping this weekend?

05 high schools taught their students about banking and finance

06 It's high time (that) you threw away those old shoes.

07 either → whether

08 should leave 또는 left

09 (1) we asked for a raise
(2) we should settle the matter
(3) the exam were[was] easy

01 It's high time+주어+과거 동사 = It's high time+주어 +should+동사원형: ~할 때이다

02 'whether or not ~'이나 'whether A or not'으로 '~인지 아닌지' 를 나타내고 'or not'을 활용하라고 했으므로 'or not'을 whether 다음이나 문장의 끝에 쓴다. whether절이 각 동사나 전치사 등의 목적어가 되도록 영작한다.

03 • 그리고 이 반지를 원한다면, 그 잃어버린 불쌍한 수달을 찾는 것을 도와주세요. • 네가 무엇이 필요하든 나에게 바로 전화해 줘. 알았지? • 이 이야기가 익숙하게 들리는지 나에게 말해줘. • 좌석이 올바른 높이로 맞춰졌는지 점검하시오. 첫 번째와 두 번 째 문장은 조건절을 이끄는 if가, 세 번째와 네 번째 문장은 명사 절을 이끄는 if가 들어갈 자리이다.

04 (1) 나는 그 집에 정원이 있는지 알고 싶다. if가 이끄는 목적어 부분을 직접의문문으로 바꿔 쓰는 것이 적절하다. (2) 그녀는 그 들이 이번 주말에 캠핑을 갈지 확실하지 않다. whether가 이끄 는 목적어 부분을 직접의문문으로 바꿔 쓰는 것이 적절하다.

05 'It's (high) time that+주어+과거동사 또는 should+동사원 형'. 제시된 우리말에는 '가르쳤어야 했다'는 화자의 안타까움이 나타내는 주관적인 감정이 들어가 있으므로 that 뒤에 따라오는 절의 동사를 teach의 과거형 taught를 쓰는 것이 적절하다.

06 It is (about[high]) time (that)+주어+과거형 동사

07 우리는 관광이 해롭다거나 이롭다고 말할 수 없다. whether A or B: A이든 B이든

08 It is (about[high]) time (that)+주어+과거형 동사'로 이미 일어났어야 하는 데 일어나지 못한 상황에 대한 주관적 감정을 나타낸다.

09 (1) 주관적 감정이 드러난 문장은 '과거 동사'를 써서 'we asked for a raise'로 쓰는 것이 적절하다. (2) 당위성을 나타 내는 문장은 'should+동사원형'을 써서 we should settle the matter.로 쓰는 것이 적절하다. (3) 'I wish 가정법 과거'는 'I wish+주어+과거 동사'로 쓴다.

교과서

Reading

확인문제   p.91

1 T 2 F

확인문제   p.92

1 T 2 F

01 Mysterious
02 *fails to buy, lying*
03 whether, or not, drunk, okay, Why
04 Put simply
05 outside
06 *greets, has brought nothing*
07 were supposed to, nothing
08 enough money to buy, fault, Don't you think
09 *with pity*
10 *for the first time*
11 *support himself*
12 It's time you started, to work
13 *blank*   14 *thanks to, order*
15 that have to last, I'm not sure whether
16 *for the second time*
17 Don't worry
18 *leaves*
19 leather boots
21 *instead of*
22 there should be
23 stop making, instead, died of
24 *in surprise*
26 *customer*
27 to buy
28 *seeing*, about, if
29 real, giving birth to, so much that
31 *shines from*
32 shining
33 about, left
34 why, just smile
35 was sent, was supposed to, Every time, am ready to
36 have you learned
37 *thinks back to*
38 dwells in, pitied, pitied, what, to figure out
40 what, were to last, know little about
41 last
42 brought them up, by having true love for, What people live by

1 Three Mysterious Smiles
2 It's winter. A poor shoe maker, Simon, fails to buy a warm coat. On his way back home, he finds a man, Michael, lying in the street without any

clothes.

3 Simon: I'm not sure whether he is dead or not. But I don't think I can save him because I'm drunk and have little money. (walking away from Michael at first, but coming back again) Poor man. Are you okay? Why are you lying here?

4 Michael: I can't tell you everything. Put simply, I am being punished.

5 Simon: But it's cold outside. Let's go home together.

6 Simon comes home and greets Matrena, his wife. She finds he has brought nothing.

7 Matrena: (surprised and angry) Simon, you were supposed to buy a coat for our family. But there's nothing. And who is this man?

8 Simon: I did not have enough money to buy the coat. I'm sorry. And I know nothing about this man. But it wasn't my fault. I had to bring him home. I mean just look at him. Don't you think he needs help?

9 Matrena: (looking at Michael with pity) Okay, Simon.

10 (Michael smiles for the first time.)

11 For a week, Michael does no work to support himself.

12 Simon: (looking at Michael) Michael, I'm afraid you've been doing nothing since you came here. It's time you started to earn a living for yourself. If you work for me, I will give you food. Would you like to work with me?

13 Michael: (with a blank face) Yes, I would.

14 A year later, Simon has become famous, thanks to Michael's great skills in making shoes. One day, a nobleman comes to order his boots.

15 Nobleman: I'd like to order fine leather boots that have to last for a year. I'm not sure whether you can make them. Can you do that?

16 (Michael watches the man carefully and smiles for the second time.)

17 Simon: Yes, sir. Don't worry.

18 (The nobleman leaves the shop.)

19 Simon: Michael, please make some thick leather boots.

20 Michael: Okay.

21 (However, Michael makes soft slippers instead of boots.)

22 Simon: (finding the slippers) Michael! I told you there should be no mistakes. What do you think you are doing?

23 Servant: (running into the shop) Please stop making boots and start making soft slippers for a dead body instead. My master has died of a heart attack.

24 Simon: (looking at Michael in surprise) How did you know?

25 Michael: Well …

26 A few years later, a woman customer visits the shoe shop with twin girls.

27 Customer: I'm here to buy some leather shoes for these twin girls.

28 Simon: (seeing that one of the girls has a disability) I'm sorry about your daughter's foot. May I ask you if she was born with a disability?

29 Customer: Oh, I'm not her real mother. Her mother hurt this girl's leg while she was giving birth to her. Their parents are both dead now. I felt sorry for them. I loved these twins so much that I decided to adopt them.

30 (Michael smiles for the third time.)

31 (Suddenly, a mysterious light shines from Michael.)

32 Simon: What's this light shining from you?

33 Michael: It's about time I left here.

34 Simon: What do you mean? And why did you just smile?

35 Michael: Let me explain. I am an angel. I was sent here as a punishment, and I was supposed to learn three truths. Every time I learned one of them, I smiled. Now that I have learned all three of them, I am ready to go back.

36 Simon: I see. What truths have you learned?

37 Michael thinks back to each time that he smiled. Simon and Matrena listen carefully to him.

38 Michael: First, I learned that love dwells in human beings when Matrena pitied me. This was the answer to the first lesson: Learn what dwells in human beings. I smiled because I learned the truth. But I still had two more to figure out.the answer to the first lesson: Learn what dwells in human beings. I smiled because I learned the truth. But I still had two more to figure out.

39 Simon: What were they?

40 Michael: The second was, "Learn what is not given to people." When the nobleman ordered that his boots were to last for a year, I knew he would die soon. Then I realized people know little

about their own future needs.

41 Simon: What was the last truth?

42 Michael: It was from the story of the woman and the twin girls. After the death of their mother, the woman brought them up with her love. Then, I learned people live by having true love for each other. That was the third lesson: What people live by.

시험대비 실력평가
p.99~103

01 that → whether 또는 if　　02 ②　　03 ④

04 ④　　05 ①　　06 earn a living

07 immediately　　08 ④　　09 if

10 ⑤　　11 ②　　12 so, as to　　13 ④

14 ③　　15 ⑤

16 the woman brought them up with her love

17 (1) Matrena가 그를 가여워했을 때 인간 내면에 사랑이 존재한다는 것을 깨달았기 때문이다.

(2) 귀족이 1년을 신어도 끄떡없는 부츠를 주문했을 때, 사람은 자신의 미래에 필요한 것을 알지 못한다는 사실을 깨달았기 때문이다.

(3) 쌍둥이 소녀와 여인의 이야기를 듣고 사람은 서로를 향한 참된 사랑으로 산다는 점을 알게 됐기 때문이다.

18 (A) that　(B) while　(C) adopt　　19 ②, ⑤

20 ④　　21 ③　　22 to make → making

23 (A) die　(B) for a year　　24 left　　25 ③

01 접속사 'that' 뒤에는 확실한 내용이 나와야 하므로, I am sure 뒤에는 that을 쓰지만, I'm not sure 뒤에는 'that' 대신 'whether' 또는 'if'로 쓰는 것이 적절하다.

02 위 글은 '희곡'이다. ① (신문·잡지의) 글, 기사, ③ 독후감, ④ 수필, ⑤ (책·연극·영화 등에 대한) 논평[비평], 감상문

03 Michael은 'Simon에게 말 못할 사정이 있다'고 했다.

04 ⓐ with pity: 불쌍하게, ⓑ with a blank face: 무표정한 얼굴로

05 ①번은 Simon을 가리키고, 나머지는 다 Michael을 가리킨다.

06 earn[make] a[one's] living = support oneself: 생계를 유지하다

07 It is time (that)+주어+가정법 과거: ~할 때이다. 현재 일어나지 않은 일에 관한 화자의 '불만족'이나 '당위성', '필요', '재촉' 등의 주관적인 감정을 나타내는 표현이므로, '즉시' 당신 자신을 위해 생계를 꾸려야 한다는 의미가 함축되어 있다.

08 앞에 나오는 내용과 상반되는 내용이 뒤에 이어지므로 However가 가장 적절하다. ① 게다가, 더욱이, ② 그러므로,

09 whether = if: ~인지 아닌지

10 이 글은 '한 귀족이 1년을 신어도 끄떡없는 튼튼한 가죽 부츠를 주문한 뒤에 심장마비로 죽게 되어 부츠 대신 죽은 사람에게 신길 부드러운 슬리퍼를 만들도록 상황이 바뀌었는데, 하인이 그런 내용을 말하기도 전에 Michael이 벌써 부츠 대신 부드러운 슬리퍼를 만들고 있어서, Simon이 놀라며 Michael에게 어떻게 알았는지 물어보는' 내용의 글이므로, 제목으로는 ⑤번 'Michael의 놀라운 선견지명'이 적절하다. foresight: 예지력, 선견지명

11 '손님'이 신발 가게에 방문한 것이므로 'customer'가 적절하다. ① 상인, ③ (변호사 등 전문가의 서비스를 받는) 의뢰인[고객], ④ 여주인, ⑤ 조수, 보조원

12 so ~ that 주어+동사 = so ~ as to부정사: 너무 ~해서 …하다

13 '쌍둥이 소녀들의 부모님이 왜 돌아가셨는지'는 대답할 수 없다. ① To buy some leather shoes for the twin girls. ② Because her mother hurt this girl's leg while she was giving birth to her. ③ No, she isn't. ⑤ Because she loved the twins so much.

14 ⓐ와 ①, ②, ④, ⑤: 현재분사, ③: 동명사

15 'What truths have you learned?'라고 Simon이 물었으므로, 뒤에 올 내용으로는 'Michael이 깨달은 진리'가 적절하다.

16 'bring up'은 목적어가 인칭대명사인 경우 'bring+목적어(대명사)+up'의 형식만 가능하다.

17 Michael이 세 가지 진리를 깨달은 순간을 쓰는 것이 적절하다.

18 (A) 목적어의 내용이 확실할 때는 접속사 'that'을 쓰는 것이 적절하다. whether: ~인지 아닌지, (B) 뒤에 '주어+동사'가 나오므로 while이 적절하다. during+기간을 나타내는 명사, (C) '입양'하기로 결정했다고 해야 하므로 adopt가 적절하다. adapt: (새로운 용도·상황에) 맞추다, 적응하다, adopt: 입양하다

19 ⓐ와 ②, ⑤: ~인지 아닌지, ①, ③, ④: (만약) ~이라면

20 그 여인은 아이의 생모가 아니고, 생모가 아이를 낳던 중에 아이가 다리를 다치게 되었다.

21 ⓐ와 ③: 주문하다(동사), ① 순서(명사), ② 명령하다, 지시하다(동사), ④ 정돈(된 상태)(명사), ⑤ 명령, 지시(명사)

22 '부츠는 그만 만들고'라고 해야 하므로, to make를 making으로 고치는 것이 적절하다. stop+to부정사: ~하기 위해 멈추다, stop ~ing: ~하기를 그만두다

23 귀족은 자신이 곧 '죽을' 것임을 몰라서, '1년'을 신어도 끄떡없는 튼튼한 가죽 부츠를 주문한다.

24 It's about time (that) 주어+가정법 과거: '~할 때다'라는 뜻으로, 현재 일어나지 않은 일에 관한 화자의 불만족이나 재촉 등의 주관적인 감정을 나타낸다.

25 주어진 문장의 내용이 ③번 앞 문장의 내용을 묻고 있는 것이므로 ③번이 적절하다.

01 (A) to buy   (B) clothes   (C) drunk
02 I'm not sure whether he is dead or not.
03 To put
04 have been doing
05 (1) should   (2) to start
06 pity
07 adopt
08 I'm here to buy some leather shoes for these twin girls.
09 (A) disability   (B) giving birth to
10 high
11 (A) a punishment   (B) three truths

01 (A) fail 뒤에는 to부정사를 써야 하므로 'to buy'가 적절하다. (B) '옷도 입지 않고'라고 해야 하므로 clothes가 적절하다. cloths: 옷감들, 천들, clothes: 옷, 의복, (C) 'drunken'은 '명사 앞'에만 쓰므로 drunk가 적절하다.

02 whether ~ or not: ~인지 아닌지, I'm not sure whether or not he is dead.처럼 or not을 whether 뒤에 붙여 쓰는 것도 가능하다.

03 put simply = to put it simply: 간단히 말해서

04 이곳에 온 이래로 지금까지 계속 빈둥거리고 있다고 말하는 것이므로, '현재완료진행형 시제(have/has been ~ing)'로 쓰는 것이 적절하다.

05 It's time (that) 주어+가정법 과거 = It's time (that) 주어+should 동사원형 = It's time+의미상의 주어(for 목적격)+to부정사: ~할 때이다, 현재 일어나지 않은 일에 관한 화자의 '불만족'이나 '당위성', '필요' '재촉' 등의 주관적인 감정을 나타내는 표현

06 Matrena는 Michael이 '불쌍히' 여겨져서 그를 자신의 집에 머물도록 허락한다. feel pity for ~: ~을 불쌍히 여기다, 딱하게 생각하다

07 adopt: 입양하다, 다른 사람의 아이를 자신의 가족으로 법률적으로 데리고 와서, 그 아이를 자신의 아이로 돌봐주다

08 buy는 4형식에서 3형식 문장으로 고칠 때 for를 사용한다. 주어진 어휘에 'for'가 있으므로, to buy these twin girls some leather shoes를 3형식으로 전환하여 배열하는 것이 적절하다.

09 쌍둥이 소녀들 중 한 명은 생모가 '아이를 낳던 중'에 그 아이의 다리를 다치게 했기 때문에 '장애'를 가지고 있다.

10 'It's time (that) 주어+동사의 과거형' 구문을 강조할 때 'about'이나 'high'를 사용하는 것이 적절하다.

11 Michael은 '벌'을 받아 여기로 보내어진 천사이다. 그가 깨달아야 했던 '세 가지 진리'를 하나씩 깨달을 때마다 그는 미소를 지었었다. 그는 세 가지 진리를 모두 깨달았기 때문에 돌아갈 준비를 마쳤다.

01 rush   02 ⑤   03 ②
04 In the distance we saw the ocean for the first time.
05 ①   06 ⑤   07 ③   08 ①
09 ④   10 ②
11 But you'll certainly regret missing it.
12 ④
13 (1) c (2) c (3) b (4) a (5) a (6) b   14 ④
15 (1) It's time that you cleaned it up.
    (2) It's time for her to study hard.
16 I'm not sure whether you can make a nice presentation.
17 ③   18 ②, ③   19 if → whether
20 I want to know whether she is angry or not.
21 ②
22 She has to decide whether she is going to accept the job or not.   23 ②, ③   24 ③
25 (A) Scene   (B) shoe   (C) lying
26 ②, ④, ⑤   27 ①
28 fine leather boots that have to last for a year
29 (A) some thick leather boots
    (B) soft slippers   30 ④

01 dwell(거주하다)과 reside(거주하다, 주재하다)는 동의어 관계에 있는 단어들이다. 따라서 hurry(서두르다)와 동의어 관계에 있는 단어는 rush(서두르다)이다.

02 ⑤ save는 '절약하다, 저장하다'라는 뜻으로 사용되었다.

03 주어진 문장에서 cross는 '건너다'라는 뜻으로 사용되었다. ① 화가 난, ③ 십자가, ④ 말소하다 ⑤ 혼합, 잡종

04 멀리서: in the distance

05 '비난 받을 만한 실수'라는 뜻의 영영풀이가 가리키는 것은 fault(잘못)이다.

06 B가 과거 시제를 이용해 '너의 잘못이었니'라고 물어볼 때 A의 대답은 No였다. 따라서 'it wasn't my fault.'가 빈칸에 들어갈 말로 가장 적절하다.

07 (A) 동사+부사로 구성된 문장에서 대명사 it은 동사와 부사 사이에 들어가야 한다. (B) 가정법 과거형 문장이므로 would tell이 적절하다. (C) 감탄사가 쓰이는 문장은 How와 What이는 쓰이는 경우로 나뉜다. How가 쓰이는 감탄사에서는 'How+형용사+주어+동사 ~!' 순으로 쓰는 반면 What은 'What (a/an)+형용사+명사+주어+동사 ~!' 순으로 쓴다.

08 주어진 (a)는 '도움'이라는 뜻으로 사용되었다. ② 손, ③ 나눠 주다, ④ 손, ⑤ 손

09 ④ 그(나)는 친구의 도움을 거절하지 않고, 친구의 도움이 필요하면 전화하겠다고("I'll call you if I need your help.") 말했다.

10 주어진 문장에서 First라는 단서를 미루어 볼 때, 'There are two interesting points about this play.'의 뒤에 위치하는 것이 가장 적절하다.

11 regret ~ing ~한 것을 후회하다 / certainly 분명히

12 위 글은 연극에 대해서 홍보하고 있는 글이므로 ④ to promote(홍보하기 위해)가 글의 목적으로 가장 적절하다.

13 (1) 새로 산 네 자전거를 타 볼 시간이야. (2) 이제 가야 할 시간이야. (3) 9시 버스가 올 때이다.(그러나 버스가 오지 않음) (4) 그녀는 지역 수영장에서 일주일에 다섯 번 훈련을 했다. (5) 오늘 두 번 연속으로 버스를 놓쳤어. (6) 네가 철이 들 때도 되었다.

14 ④ 진즉에 갔어야 할 시간인데. 즉, 현재 못가고 있는 상황을 나타낸다. you've gone을 you went로 고치는 것이 적절하다.
① 그녀가 생활을 정리해야 할 때였다. ② 잠잘 시간이다. ③ 슬슬 문제의 핵심으로 들어갈 때가 되었다. ⑤ 이제 사태를 수습하고 새롭게 다시 시작할 때이다.

15 (1)은 주어진 단어를 활용하여 조건과 우리말에 맞게 빈칸에 It's time that you cleaned it up.으로 쓰는 것이 적절하다. (2)는 주어진 단어를 활용하여 조건과 우리말에 맞게 It's time for her to study hard.로 쓰는 것이 적절하다. to부정사의 의미상의 주어는 'for+목적격'으로 쓴다.

16 '~인지 아닌지'라는 말은 whether를 활용하고 or not은 생략하여 쓴다. make nice presentation: 멋진 발표를 하다

17 나는 새 노트북을 사야 할지 확신할 수 없다. '~인지 아닌지'라는 뜻으로 명사절을 이끄는 접속사로 if와 whether 둘 다 사용 가능하지만 접속사 바로 뒤에 to부정사가 올 수 있는 것은 whether이다.

18 네가 지하철을 탈지 안 탈지 나에게 알려줘. 빈칸에 know의 목적어를 이끌 수 있는 접속사가 들어가야 한다. 문장 끝에 or not이 있으므로 if나 whether를 고르는 것이 적절하다.

19 '~인지 아닌지'라는 뜻으로 명사절을 이끄는 접속사로 if와

whether 둘 다 사용 가능하지만 접속사 바로 뒤에 to부정사가 올 수 있는 것은 whether이다. 따라서 if를 whether로 고쳐서 쓰는 것이 적절하다.

20 괄호 안의 단어를 활용하여 '~인지 아닌지'라는 의미를 나타내려면 'whether A or not'을 이용하는 것이 적절하다.

21 • 나는 벽을 초록으로 칠할지 파랑으로 칠할지 결정할 수 없다.
• 그녀는 웃어야 할지 울어야 할지 알 수 없었다. 'A로 할지 B로 할지'와 '~인지 아닌지'의 의미를 갖고 빈칸 뒤에 to부정사와 함께 쓰일 수 있는 접속사는 whether이다.

22 '~할지 안 할지'라는 의미를 갖고 괄호 안의 단어를 활용하여 영작하면 She has to decide whether she is going to accept the job or not.으로 쓰는 것이 적절하다.

23 • 나는 그저 네가 나하고 커피 한 잔 할 시간이 있는지 궁금했다.
• 그가 한국인인지 아닌지 모르겠다. 두 문장 모두 '~인지 아닌지'의 의미로 동사의 목적어를 이끄는 접속사 whether와 if가 적절하다.

24 ⓐ와 ③: 구하다, ① 저축하다, ② (나중에 쓰거나 먹으려고) 남겨 두다[아끼다], ④ 저장하다, ⑤ 절약하다, (낭비하지 않고) 아끼다

25 (A) '장면 1'이라고 해야 하므로 Scene이 적절하다. scene: 장면, scenery: 경치, (B) '명사+명사'로 이루어진 복합명사의 경우, 앞의 명사가 형용사적 성질을 지니므로 '단수형'으로 쓰는 것이 적절하다. shoe maker: 구두장이, (C) '길거리에 누워 있는'이라고 해야 하므로 'lie'의 현재분사형인 'lying'이 적절하다. lay: ~을 두다, 놓다

26 옷도 입지 않고 길거리에 누워 있는 Michael에게, 밖이 추우니까 같이 집으로 가자고 제안하는 것으로 보아 Simon의 성격은 '자선을 베푸는', '마음이 따뜻한', '인도적인, 인정 있는'이 적절하다. ① 무자비한, ② 자선을 베푸는, ③ 가혹한, 냉혹한, ④ 마음이 따뜻한, ⑤ 인도적인, 인정 있는

27 ⓐ die of: ~로 죽다, ⓑ in surprise: 놀라서

28 '1년을 신어도 끄떡없는 튼튼한 가죽 부츠'를 가리킨다.

29 '제가 실수하지 말라고 했잖아요.'라는 말은 '부드러운 슬리퍼 대신 두꺼운 가죽 부츠를 만들어야 했잖아요.'라는 의미이다. should have p.p.: ~했어야 했는데

30 (C)의 This가 주어진 글의 내용을 가리키므로 제일 먼저 오고 (C)의 결과로 (A)에서 웃은 것이므로 (C) 다음에 (A)가 이어지고 (B)의 But 뒤에서 앞에 나오는 내용과 상반되는 내용을 말하고 있으므로 (A) 다음에 (B)가 와야 한다. 그러므로 (C)-(A)-(B)의 순서가 적절하다.

01 ③

02 (1) give birth to   (2) die of   (3) in advance

03 ⑤

04 I was not sure whether or not it is safe for him to drink milk.

05 ⑤   06 ①

07 You're supposed to make your bed in the morning.

08 ④   09 ⑤

10 took 또는 should take

11 I don't know whether to buy the blue one or the red one.

12 I don't know if I can drive.

13 ①, ②   14 ①   15 blank

16 ②, ③, ⑤   17 ④   18 ②

19 (A) love   (B) their own future needs
    (C) having true love   20 ③   21 ⑤

01 '한 사람이나 몇몇 사람에게만 알려지고 다른 사람들에게 말해서는 안 되는 정보의 조각'이라는 영영풀이가 가리키는 것은 ③ secret(비밀)이다.

02 (1) give birth to ~을 출산하다 (2) die of ~로 죽다 (3) in advance 먼저, 앞서

03 '난 그가 곧 나아지길 바라.'라는 문장은 글의 문맥상 '네 보살핌과 사랑으로 분명히 나아질 거야'라고 말하는 B의 말 앞인 ⑤에 위치하는 것이 가장 적절하다.

04 whether or not ~인지 아닌지 / it ~ for 진주어 to ... (진주어)가 …하는 것이 ~하다

05 'Do you think ~'와 'what is important for staying healthy' 두 문장이 결합된 문장으로, 이때 의문사 what은 문장의 맨 앞에 위치하게 된다. 따라서 ⑤ What do you think is important for staying healthy?가 가장 적절하다.

06 위 대화에서 B의 마지막 말은 '건강을 유지하기 위해서는 과일과 채소를 많이 먹어야 한다'라는 문장이 되어야 한다. 따라서 빈칸에는 의무를 나타내는 표현들이 들어가야 한다.

07 'be supposed to ~'는 '~하기로 되어 있다', '~해야 한다'라는 의미로, 의무를 나타내는 표현이다.

08 앞서 A가 왜 침대를 정리하는 것이 부모님을 기쁘게 만드냐고 물어봤으므로 B의 대답은 ④because가 들어간 문장이어야 한다.

09 ⑤에서 A가 '넌 경주에 이기기를 원하니?'라고 묻자 B가 '경주에 이기기 위해 포기해서는 안 돼'라고 말하는 것은 문맥상 적절하지 않다.

10 이제는 우리가 지구 온난화를 막기 위해 모든 조치를 취해야 할 때다.

11 파란 것과 빨간 것 중 어느 것을 사야 할지 모르겠다. don't know에 대한 목적어를 이끌고 to부정사와 함께 쓰일 수 있는 것은 whether이므로 if를 whether로 고쳐 쓰는 것이 적절하다.

12 '~인지 아닌지'의 의미를 갖고 접속사 if를 사용하여 우리말에 맞게 I don't know if I can drive.로 쓰는 것이 적절하다.

13 A: 엄마, 청바지가 닳았어요. B: 새 바지를 살 때가 됐구나. 'It's hight time (that)+주어+과거동사 또는 should+동사원형'으로 ①, ②를 고르는 것이 적절하다.

14 빈칸 뒤의 문장은 '그들은 몇 달 동안 이 일을 해 왔다.'이므로 빈칸에는 몇 달에 걸쳐 무언가를 끝내지 못한 불만 등 주관적 감정이 들어가는 내용이 자연스러우므로 ①을 고르는 것이 적절하다.

15 with a blank face: 무표정한 얼굴로, void of: ~이 결여된. expression: 표정

16 '이 남자를 보세요. 도움이 필요해 보이지 않나요?'라는 Simon의 말에 Michael을 불쌍하게 바라보며 '그래요, Simon.'이라고 대답하는 것으로 보아, Matrena의 성격은 '동정적인', '연민 어린'이 적절하다. ① 동정적인, ② 냉혹한, ③ 잔인한, ④ 연민 어린, 동정하는, ⑤ 교만한

17 Michael이 Simon 집에 와서 계속 빈둥거리고 있었다.

18 ⓐ와 ②, ⑤: 형용사적 용법, ①, ③ 명사적 용법, ④ 부사적 용법

19 (A) Michael이 배운 첫 번째 교훈은 인간 내면에 '사랑'이 존재한다는 것이다. (B) Michael이 배운 두 번째 교훈은 사람은 '자신의 미래에 필요한 것'을 알지 못한다는 것이다. (C) Michael이 마지막으로 배운 교훈은 사람은 서로를 향한 '참된 사랑으로' 산다는 것이다.

20 위 글은 '독후감'이다. ① 전기, ② 일기, ④ (신문·잡지의) 글, 기사, ⑤ 수필

21 'Michael이 돌아갈 곳'은 알 수 없다. ① What People Live By, ② Leo Tolstoy, ③ Simon and Michael, ④ 이 글은 Michael이 Simon과 같이 사는 동안 사람에 대한 진리를 깨닫는 내용이다.

01 How

02 But it is not my fault.

03 The tortoise won the race.

04 It's because the tortoise didn't give up.

05 (1) I don't like traffic jam! It's high time we

arrived[또는 should arrive] at home.

(2) 〈없음〉

(3) It's time for us to be on our way.

06 (1) Do you know whether[if] this is

(2) if you got the right answer

(3) whether it'll be warmer tomorrow

07 make fine leather boots that have to last for a year

08 I told you there should be no mistakes.

09 what

10 two more to figure out

11 (1) 인간 내면에 무엇이 존재하는가?

(2) 인간에게 주어지지 않은 것은 무엇인가?

(3) 사람은 무엇으로 사는가?

---

01 How may I help you?: 어떻게 도와드릴까요?

02 '~의 잘못이 아니다'라는 의미로 책임이나 비난에 대해 부인하는 표현으로는 'It's not one's fault.'를 사용할 수 있다.

03 M의 말에서 알 수 있듯이, 거북이 경주에서 승리했다.

04 거북이 경주에서 이긴 이유는 포기하지 않았기 때문("In order to win the race, you must not give up.")이다.

05 (1) 교통체증은 싫어. 우리는 집에 도착했을 시간이야. 'It's high time+주어+과거형 동사 또는 should 동사원형' 구문이므로 arriving을 arrived 또는 'should arrive'로 고쳐서 쓰는 것이 적절하다. (2) 아침 먹을 시간이다. (3) 우리 그만 가야 할 시간이에요. 'It's time to 동사원형'은 '~할 시간이다'라는 의미이고 to부정사의 의미상의 주어는 'for+목적격'이므로 'of us'를 'for us'로 쓰는 것이 적절하다.

06 괄호 안의 단어와 단어 개수, 우리말에 맞게 영작하면 (1) Do you know whether[if] this is (2) if you got the right answer (3) I'm not certain whether it'll be warmer tomorrow or not.이다.

07 '1년을 신어도 끄떡없는 튼튼한 가죽 부츠를 만드는 것'을 가리킨다.

08 유도부사 'there'를 사용하여 쓰는 것이 적절하다.

09 ⓐ와 ⓑ 공통으로, 동사 'Learn'의 목적어에서 주어 역할을 하는 선행사를 포함한 '주격 관계대명사 what'을 쓰는 것이 적절하다.

10 '두 가지 더 알아내야만 하는 것'을 가리킨다.

11 (1) What dwells in human beings? (2) What is not given to people? (3) What do people live by?

|모범답안|

01 (1) You should clean your room.

(2) You had better try not to make a mess.

(3) You have to clear it up regularly.

02 (A) *What People Live By*   (B) Leo Tolstoy

(C) Simon's wife   (D) Love

(E) some leather boots

(F) their own future   (G) had adopted twin girls

(H) love

---

01 의무를 나타내는 표현으로는 조동사 had better/should/ought to/have to/must 등이 있다. 이 표현들은 모두 '~해야 한다'라는 뜻을 지닌다.

단원별 모의고사   p.119~124

| 01 ① | 02 ⑤ | 03 Now that |

04 ②

05 Ryan got so angry that he wouldn't talk with me.

06 ③

07 (A) First   (B) Second   (C) certainly

| 08 ①, ④ | 09 ⑤ | 10 ③ | 11 ⑤ |

12 I would tell the teacher why you couldn't hand it in.

| 13 ③ | 14 ① |

15 it's about time that our laws should reflect this reality

16 ②

17 (1) I don't know whether you remember me (or not).

(2) I didn't know whether to wake you up or not.

18 (1) It's about time that Korea helped other countries

(2) It's time that we had

(3) it's time that Korea joined it   19 ④

20 working → to work

| 21 ⑤ | 22 ③ |

23 I loved these twins so much that I decided to adopt them.   24 ②

| 25 ③ | 26 ①, ②, ⑤ | 27 ②, ④ | 28 ② |

| 29 ③, ④, ⑤ | 30 ② |

---

01 '만족스러운 삶을 위해 반드시 가져야 할 것들'이라는 뜻의 영영 풀이가 가리키는 것은 ①needs(요구, 욕구)이다.

02 나는 종이컵보다는 텀블러를 사용함으로써 환경을 보호하려고 노력한다. / instead of ~ 대신에

03 now that 이제 ~이므로, ~이기 때문에

04 위 대화에서 Inho가 Lina에게 과거 시제로 'Was it your fault?'라고 물어봤으므로 ⓑisn't는 wasn't로 고치는 것이 적절하다.

05 '너무 ~해서 …하다'라는 뜻을 가진 'so ~ that ...' 구문을 이용해 문장을 완성할 수 있다.

06 위 대화에서 Lina는 Ryan과의 싸움으로 인해 걱정하고 있었지만 Inho의 조언으로 화해하기로 결정했다. 따라서 Lina의 심경 변화는 ③ worried(걱정하는) → hopeful(희망적인)이 가장 적절하다.

07 first 첫째로, 첫번째로 / second 둘째로 / certainly 분명히, 확실히

08 need to ~는 '~할 필요가 있다'라는 뜻으로 의무를 나타내는 표현이다. 이때 (a)에서는 미래 시제가 사용되었으므로 조동사 will과 함께 사용한다.

09 ⑤ 티켓은 온라인과 오프라인으로 예매할 수 있다는 말은 언급되지 않았다.

10 의무를 나타내는 표현으로는 had better/should/ought to/have to/be supposed to 등과 같은 표현들이 있다. could는 can의 과거형으로 무엇을 할 수 있었다는 뜻으로 사용된다.

11 'It was all my fault.'는 '모두 내 잘못이었다.'라는 의미로 책임이나 비난에 대해 인정하는 표현이다.

12 why 이하는 간접의문문으로 tell의 직접목적어이다.

13 우리말에 맞게 영어로 바꿔 쓰면 빈칸에 ③이 들어가는 것이 적절하다.

14 주어진 우리말은 네가 좋은 사람인지 나쁜 사람인지 모르겠다는 뜻이므로 알맞게 영작하면 ①을 고르는 것이 적절하다. ② 나는 네가 좋은 사람이란 것을 확신한다. ③ 네가 좋은 관계를 갖고 있는지 알 수 없다. ④ 네가 좋은 위치에 있는지 아닌지 나는 모르겠다. ⑤ 네가 옳은지 아닌지 나는 확신할 수 없다.

15 빈칸에는 '우리의 법이 이런 현실을 반영해야 할 때입니다.'라는 말이 들어가야 하므로 보기의 단어를 활용하여 it's about time that our laws should reflect this reality로 영작하는 것이 적절하다.

16 '~할 때이다'의 의미를 갖는 ②를 고르는 것이 적절하다.

17 괄호 안의 어휘를 활용하여 우리말에 맞게 영작하면, (1) I don't know whether you remember me (or not). (2) I didn't know whether to wake you up or not.이다.

18 (1), (2), (3) 'It's about time+주어+과거동사'로 쓰는 것이 적절하다.

19 ⓐ, ⓒ, ⓓ: Michael, ⓑ, ⓔ: Simon

20 would like 뒤에는 to부정사를 쓰는 것이 적절하다.

21 ⓐ와 ⑤: (기능이) 지속되다, 오래가다(자동사), ① 가장 ~할 것 같지 않은(형용사), ② (특정 기간 동안 사용할 수 있도록) 충분하다(타동사), ③ 바로[이] 앞의, 지난 ~(형용사), ④ 마지막 (남은)(형용사)

22 Michael은 '부츠' 대신 '부드러운 슬리퍼'를 만든다.

23 so+형용사/부사+that+주어+동사: 너무 ~(형용사/부사)해서 …하다

24 이 글은 '부모님이 이미 돌아가신 쌍둥이를 너무 불쌍하게 여기는 한편 그 아이들을 너무 사랑해서 입양하기로 결정한 여인'에 관한 글이므로, 주제로는 ②번 '쌍둥이 소녀들에 대한 여인의 사랑'이 적절하다.

25 ③번 다음 문장의 they에 주목한다. 주어진 문장의 two more to figure out을 받고 있으므로 ③번이 적절하다.

26 bring up = rear = raise = nurture: 양육하다, ③ turn up: 나타나다, ④ lift: (위로) 들어올리다

27 ⓐ와 ②, ④: 부사적 용법, ①: 형용사적 용법, ③, ⑤: 명사적 용법

28 Michael은 이제 제가 '떠날' 때가 왔다고 말한다.

29 figure out = find out = discover: 알아내다, ③ 분석하다 ④ 후회하다 ⑤ 설명하다

30 이 글은 'Michael이 인간에 대한 진리를 깨달을 때마다 미소를 지은 세 가지 경우'에 관해 설명하는 글이므로, 제목으로는 ②번 '인간에 대한 세 가지 진리'가 적절하다.

교과서 파헤치기

Lesson 7

1 side effect, 부작용   2 increase, 증가하다
3 alternative, 대체 가능한, 대체의   4 prefer, 선호하다
5 climate, 기후   6 exercise, 운동하다   7 control, 통제하다
8 experience, 경험하다   9 source, 원천, 근원
10 environment, 환경   11 personality, 성격, 인격
12 invest, 투자하다   13 disaster, 재난, 재해
14 retirement, 은퇴, 퇴직   15 will, 유언장
16 career, 경력, 직업

단어 TEST Step 1   p.02

01 피하다, 방지하다 02 폭풍
03 정기적으로, 규칙적으로   04 침착한
05 동료의   06 대체 가능한, 대체의
07 줄이다, 낮추다 08 건축가   09 은퇴, 퇴직
10 재난, 재해   11 졸업생; 졸업하다 12 부작용
13 씨 뿌리기   14 재능을 발휘하는 사람
15 건축학, 건축 양식 16 원천, 근원   17 성격, 인격
18 도움이 되는, 유용한   19 인생 말기의
20 완벽하게   21 (주변의) 환경 22 유언장
23 다루다, 처리하다 24 에너지를 절약하는
25 투자하다   26 현대의, 근대의 27 목적
28 증가하다, 증가시키다   29 경력, 직업
30 작동하다, 가동시키다   31 방지하다, 막다
32 문학   33 부유한, 재산이 많은
34 통제하다   35 ~ 덕분에
36 (힘쓴 끝에) ~를 얻다   7 ~ 대신에
38 크게 박수 치다 39 또한   40 긍지를 느끼다
41 계속해서 ~하다 42 ~와 잘 지내다 43 ~에 성공하다

단어 TEST Step 2   p.03

01 architecture 02 regularly 03 alternative
04 avoid 05 retirement 06 personality
07 handle 08 architect 09 helpful
10 end-of-life 11 reduce 12 fellow
13 graduate 14 energy-saving 15 purpose
16 wealthy 17 feed 18 perfectly
19 environment 20 prevent 21 literature
22 bloomer 23 source 24 control
25 operate 26 will 27 increase
28 invest 29 disaster 30 seeding
31 side effect 32 modern 33 storm
34 career 35 instead of ~ 36 believe in
37 thanks to ~ 38 succeed in 39 keep on -ing
40 give a big hand   41 feel proud
42 get along well with
43 not only A but also B

대화문 TEST Step 1   p.05~07

Think Back A
Let's, together / make shoes / don't, doing better
than / playing, better, making, musician / What, think
about / because

Everyday English 1 Listen and Check
(1) basketball / prefer, to / teach, play
(2) forward / Which, prefer / prefer, to / would, if /
together

Everyday English 1 B Listening Activity
looking, here, someone, care, while, vacation,
regularly, By the way, prefer, long time to, from, to,
taking

Everyday English 2 A Listen and Check
(1) feel, weekend / don't, going / Then, how about /
Sounds
(2) How / like / about, popular / looks, take
(3) doing / taste / like / feel / put, salt / right

Everyday English 2 B Listening Activity
This / up / received, present / like, feel / help, well /
hear / rains, use / hope

In Real Life
busy / minute / wrong, worried / worried, future,
want / becoming, literature / science, literature / Why
don't, student hall, graduates / helpful / problem

Check Your Progress 1
come / getting ready, birthday / trying, on several /
how, look / looks good on, wear / prefer, other /
How, about wearing / match, Thanks

Check Your Progress 2
ticket / lucky / thinking, with / how, feel / exciting,
aren't / album / different

Think Back A

W: Miguel! Let's make some shoes together.

B: Grandma, I don't want to make shoes.

W: You don't like it? Then, what do you like doing better than making shoes?

B: I like playing music better than making shoes! I want to be a musician.

B: What do you think about music?

W: Music is bad! My grandfather left the family because of music.

Everyday English 1 A Listen and Check

(1) G: Do you like basketball?

B: Yes, I do. But I prefer soccer to basketball.

G: Oh, really? Can you teach me how to play soccer?

B: Sure.

(2) B: I'm looking forward to the music festival.

G: Me too. Which do you prefer, singing or dancing?

B: I prefer dancing to singing.

G: I like singing. It would be very fun if we can sing and dance together.

Everyday English 1 B Listening Activity

W: Are you looking for a job? And are you an animal lover? If you are, here is the best job for you. We need someone to take care of some pets while their family is on vacation. You will need to wash the pets, feed them regularly, and play with them. By the way , we prefer people who can work with us for a long time to those who can only work for a short time. You will work from 9 to 5, Monday to Friday. If you are interested in taking care of pets, please call 567-1234.

Everyday English 2 A Listen and Check

(1) B: How do you feel about going on a picnic this weekend?

G: I don't think it's a good idea. It's going to rain this weekend.

B: Then, how about going to a concert?

G: Sounds great.

(2) M: How can I help you?

G: I'd like to buy a hat for my mother.

M: How do you feel about this red one? It's very popular.

G: looks good. I'll take it.

(3) G: What are you doing?

B: I'm making a new soup. Would you like to taste it?

G: Sure. Um... (*Tasting the soup*)

B: Do you like it? How do you feel about this new recipe?

G: Well, I think you need to put some salt in it.

B: You're right. Thank you.

Everyday English 2 B Listening Activity

B: Hello?

G: Hello, Minwoo. This is Yena.

B: Hi, Yena. What's up?

G: I received your present for my birthday today. Thank you so much.

B: Do you like it? How do you feel about its bright color?

G: I really like it. It can help drivers see me well in the rain.

B: I'm glad to hear that.

G: Thank you again. I hope it rains soon so that I can use it.

B: Haha. I hope so. See you soon!

In Real Life

Jisu: Hello, Mr. Brown. Are you busy now?

Mr. Brown: Not really.

Jisu: Then, can I talk to you for a minute?

Mr. Brown: Of course. Jisu, what's wrong? You look worried.

Jisu: I'm worried about my future. I don't know what I want to be in the future.

Mr. Brown: How do you feel about becoming a writer? You like literature, don't you?

Jisu: Well, no. I prefer science to literature. But I don't know what kinds of jobs I could do.

Mr. Brown: Why don't you come to the student hall tomorrow? Our graduates will talk about their jobs.

Jisu: That will be very helpful. Thank you.

Mr. Brown: No problem.

Check Your Progress 1

B: Mom, can you come to my room?

W: Yes. What are you doing?

B: I'm getting ready for a date. It's Jina's birthday.

W: Aha! So, you're trying your clothes on several times.

B: Yes. Mom, how do I look in this blue shirt?

W: It looks good on you, but are you going to wear those blue jeans, too?

B: I think so. I prefer jeans to my other pants.

W: How do you feel about wearing a white shirt

instead?

B: I think the white one and the jeans match better. Thanks for your advice.

W: No problem.

Check Your Progress 2

B: I got a ticket for the Coolboys concert.

G: You're so lucky! When is it?

B: It's next Saturday. I'm thinking of going there with my friends.

G: By the way, how do you feel about their new album?

B: I like it. All the songs are so exciting, aren't they?

G: Yes, but I prefer their last album to the new one.

B: Why?

G: It has more songs of different genres.

본문 TEST Step 1   p.11~13

01 Welcome, Careers Day

02 Welcome to, Careers Day

03 days, hard, come by

04 keep on, succeed in

05 welcome, some, graduates, jobs

06 excited about meeting

07 So am

08 think, what, would like

09 welcome, speaker, weather controller

10 everyone, I'm Ilkem

11 scientist studying, weather

12 few, weather, impossible, control

13 So did   14 Thanks, technology, fellow, as

15 example, control, using, seeding

16 spray, into, make, rain

17 another, instead, closing, well

18 reduce, effects, controlling, climate

19 control, perfectly yet, able

20 prevent, natural disasters, floods

21 able, better, safer environment

22 Why don't, join, controlling

23 architect, net-zero energy houses

24 worried, using, much energy

25 So were, parents

26 When, How, have to

27 Turn off, when, watching

28 Since, design energy-saving houses

29 environmental engineering, come true

30 other alternative energy sources

---

31 make more energy than

32 need, wasting energy anymore

33 interested in designing, talk

34 an end-of-life planner

35 As, increasing, interested, wealthy

36 not only, but also

37 example, help, exercise regularly

38 invest, retirement, get along

39 even, how to, will

40 avoid, lot, after, dies

41 feel proud of what

42 Let's give, big hand

43 talks have been helpful

44 having, hard, learning, while

45 worried that, slow learners

46 So was

47 a late bloomer

48 what, good at, finally

49 So, Believe in yourself

본문 TEST Step 2   p.14~16

01 Careers Day

02 Welcome to

03 hard to come by

04 keep on trying, succeed in

05 the graduates, listen to them talk

06 excited about meeting

07 So am I

08 would like to, in the future

09 welcome, the weather controller

10 I'm Ilkem

11 studying the weather

12 a few years, impossible to control

13 did

14 Thanks to, however, fellow scientists

15 control, using, seeding, system

16 make them rain

17 instead of, during, as well

18 the side effects, bu controlling

19 control the weather, able to

20 natural disasters like floods, storms

21 in a better and safer environment

22 Why don't you join, controlling

23 architect, net-zero energy houses

24 using too much energy

25 were   26 do I have to tell

---

27 Turn off

28 Since, energy-saving houses

29 environmental engineering, come true

30 alternative energy sources

31 make more energy than

32 wasting energy

33 are interested in

34 end-of-life planner

35 As, is increasing, interested in

36 not only, but also, death

37 example, exercise regularly

38 invest for retirement, get along well with

39 make a will

40 avoid a lot of problems after, dies

41 feel proud of what

42 give a big hand to

43 helpful for

44 having a hard time learning, while worrying

45 slow learners 46 was

47 a late bloomer

48 what I was good at

49 Believe in yourself

본문 TEST Step 3   p.17~19

1 직업의 날에 온 것을 환영합니다!

2 우리 직업의 날에 온 것을 환영합니다!

3 요즘은 직업을 얻기가 어렵습니다.

4 하지만 여러분이 계속해서 노력한다면, 여러분의 진로에서 성공할 수 있을 것입니다.

5 오늘, 우리는 우리 학교 졸업생 몇몇을 맞이하고, 그들의 직업에 관해 이야기를 들을 거예요.

6 그들을 만나는 게 신나나요?

7 저도 그렇습니다.

8 그들의 이야기를 들으면서 여러분이 미래에 무엇을 하고 싶은지 생각해 보세요.

9 첫 번째 연설자인 날씨 조절자 Ilkem을 환영합시다.

10 안녕하세요, 여러분. 저는 Ilkem입니다.

11 저는 날씨를 연구하는 과학자입니다.

12 몇 년 전까지만 해도, 사람들은 날씨를 조절하는 것이 불가능하다고 생각했어요.

13 저도 그랬습니다.

14 그러나 현대 기술 덕분에 저의 동료 과학자들과 저는 원하는 대로 날씨를 바꿀 수 있습니다.

15 예를 들어, 우리는 구름 씨 뿌리기 기술을 이용해 강우를 조절할 수 있습니다.

16 우리는 구름 속에 드라이아이스를 뿌려 구름을 비로 만듭니다.

17 중국에서는 올림픽의 개막식과 폐막식에 북경 대신 다른 도시에 비가 오게끔 했습니다.

18 또한 우리는 기후를 조절함으로써 지구 온난화의 부작용들을 줄일 수 있습니다.

19 아직은 날씨를 완벽하게 조절할 수 없지만, 곧 그렇게 할 수 있을 것입니다.

20 그러면 홍수나 폭풍 같은 다양한 자연재해를 예방할 수 있을 것입니다.

21 그래서 여러분이 좀 더 안전하고 좋은 환경에서 살 수 있을 거예요.

22 여러분도 날씨를 조절하여 더 나은 환경을 만드는 데에 함께하는 게 어때요?

23 안녕하세요, 저는 Eva입니다. 저는 건축가로, net-zero 에너지 집을 설계합니다.

24 많은 사람들이 집에서 너무 많은 에너지를 사용하는 것에 대해 걱정합니다.

25 저희 부모님도 그랬습니다.

26 제가 어릴 때 부모님께서는 "Eva! 내가 몇 번을 말해야 하니?

27 TV를 보지 않을 때는 꺼!"라고 자주 말씀하셨습니다.

28 그때부터 저는 에너지를 절약하는 집을 설계하고 싶었습니다.

29 저의 꿈을 실현하기 위해 저는 건축과 환경 공학을 공부했습니다.

30 이제 저는 풍력이나 다른 대체 에너지 자원을 사용하는 집들을 설계합니다.

31 그 집들은 사용하는 것보다 더 많은 에너지를 만들어 냅니다.

32 더 이상 에너지를 낭비하는 것을 걱정할 필요가 없습니다.

33 여러분이 net-zero 에너지 집을 설계하는 것에 관심이 있다면, 저에게 와서 얘기하세요.

34 안녕하세요. 제 이름은 지원이고, 저는 임종 설계사입니다.

35 고령 인구가 증가함에 따라 사람들은 어떻게 하면 노년에 행복하고 부유하게 살 수 있는지에 대해 관심을 가집니다.

36 저는 사람들이 건강한 삶을 사는 것을 도울 뿐만 아니라 그들의 죽음을 계획할 수 있게 돕습니다.

37 예를 들어, 저는 그들이 규칙적으로 운동하도록 돕습니다.

38 또한 은퇴 후에 투자를 하는 방법이나 그들의 가족과 잘 어울려 지내는 것에 대한 조언을 합니다.

39 그리고 저는 심지어 그들에게 유언장 쓰는 법을 가르칩니다!

40 이것은 그가 죽고 난 후 가족들이 많은 문제들을 피하는 데에 도움을 줍니다.

41 저는 제가 하는 일이 자랑스럽습니다.

42 선생님: 연설자들에게 큰 박수를 보냅시다.

43 오늘 이야기들이 여러분에게 도움이 되었기를 바랍니다.

44 저는 많은 학생들이 새로운 것을 배우는 데에 어려움을 겪고 그들의 미래에 대해 걱정하는 것을 봅니다.

45 그들은 배우는 속도가 느리다고 걱정합니다.

46 저 또한 그랬습니다.

47 저는 늦게 꽃피우는 사람이었죠.

48 내가 무엇을 잘하는지 찾기 위해 노력했고, 결국은 선생님이

49 그래서 여러분에게 이렇게 말하고 싶습니다. "여러분 자신을 믿으세요, 그러면 할 수 있습니다."

본문 TEST Step 4-Step 5   p.20~25

1 Welcome to Careers Day!

2 Welcome to our Careers Day!

3 These days, jobs are hard to come by.

4 But if you keep on trying your best, you will succeed in your career.

5 Today, we will welcome back some of the graduates of our school, and listen to them talk about their jobs.

6 Are you excited about meeting them?

7 So am I.

8 As you listen to their talks, think about what you would like to do in the future.

9 Please welcome our first speaker, Ilkem, the weather controller.

10 Hello, everyone. I'm Ilkem.

11 I'm a scientist studying the weather.

12 Just a few years ago, people thought the weather was impossible to control.

13 So did I.

14 Thanks to modern technology, however, my fellow scientists and I can change the weather as we want.

15 For example, we can control the rain, using a cloud seeding system.

16 We spray dry ice into clouds to make them rain.

17 In China, they made rain in another city instead of Beijing during the opening event of the Olympics and its closing event as well.

18 We can also reduce the side effects of global warming by controlling the climate.

19 We can't control the weather perfectly yet, but may be able to do so soon.

20 Then, we could prevent many kinds of natural disasters like floods and storms.

21 So you will be able to live in a better and safer environment.

22 Why don't you join us in making a better environment by controlling the weather?

23 Hi, I'm Eva. I'm an architect, and I design net-zero energy houses.

24 Many people are worried about using too much

energy at home.

25 So were my parents.

26 When I was young, my parents often said, "Eva! How many times do I have to tell you?

27 Turn off the TV when you're not watching it!"

28 Since then, I have wanted to design energy-saving houses.

29 I studied architecture and environmental engineering to make my dream come true.

30 Now, I design houses that use wind power or other alternative energy sources.

31 The houses make more energy than they use.

32 You don't need to worry about wasting energy anymore.

33 If you are interested in designing net-zero energy houses, please come and talk to me.

34 Hello. My name is Jiwon, and I'm an end-of-life planner.

35 As the number of old people is increasing, people are interested in how to be happy and wealthy in their old age.

36 I help people not only to live a healthy life but also to plan for their death.

37 For example, I help them exercise regularly.

38 I also give them some tips on how to invest for retirement and get along well with their family.

39 And I even teach them how to make a will!

40 This helps their family members avoid a lot of problems after the person dies.

41 I feel proud of what I'm doing.

42 Teacher: Let's give a big hand to the speakers.

43 I hope today's talks have been helpful for you.

44 I see many students having a hard time learning something new, while worrying about their future.

45 They are worried that they are slow learners.

46 So was I.

47 I was a late bloomer.

48 I tried to find what I was good at, and finally became a teacher.

49 So, I want to say, "Believe in yourself, and you can do it."

구석구석지문 TEST Step 1   p.26

Everyday English 2 C. Communication Activity

1. How do you feel about

2. because, boring, How about you

3. I think, feel calm when

4. why don't you become, in the future

5. good idea

1. using a cloud seeding system

2. By controlling, can reduce the side effects

3. net-zero energy houses

4. wind power, other alternative energy sources

5. not only to live, but also to plan

6. helps their family avoid, after the person dies

Culture & Project Step 1

1. to look for space tour guides

2. In the future, be able to travel

3. to guide us around space

4. a lot, so that, about space to tourists

5. Also, help people travel safely, comfortably

---

things about space to tourists.

5. Also, they should be healthy and help people travel safely and comfortably.

구석구석지문 TEST Step 2   p.27

Everyday English 2 C. Communication Activity

1. A: How do you feel about classical music?

2. B: I don't like it, because it's too boring. How about you?

3. A: I think it's very good. I feel calm when I listen to classical music.

4. B: Then why don't you become a musician in the future?

5. A: That's a good idea.

After You Read A

1. I can control the rain, using a cloud seeding system.

2. By controlling the climate, I can reduce the side effects of global warming.

3. I design net-zero energy houses.

4. I make houses that use wind power or other alternative energy sources.

5. I help people not only to live a healthy life but also to plan for their death.

6. This job helps their family avoid a lot of problems after the person dies.

Culture & Project Step 1

1. Our group has made a poster to look for space tour guides.

2. In the future, we will be able to travel to space.

3. So, we need someone to guide us around space.

4. The space tour guides should know a lot about planets and space so that they can explain many

단어 TEST Step 1 　　　　　　　p.28

01 설명하다	02 잘못	03 싸움, 다툼
04 빛나다	05 주인	06 입양하다
07 요구, 욕구	08 논쟁	09 탓하다
10 갑작스러운	11 부양하다	12 가죽
13 술에 취한	14 처벌	15 쓰레기
16 하인	17 후회하다	18 장애
19 거주하다	20 진실, 진리	21 전달하다, 나르다
22 죽음	23 갑자기	24 장애를 가진
25 발생하다, 일어나다		26 인사하다
27 자랑스러워하는	28 분명히	29 판단하다
30 지속하다, 계속되다		31 귀족
32 처벌하다	33 동정, 연민, 유감	34 ~에 따라 살다
35 이제 ~이므로, ~이기 때문에		36 ~ 대신에
37 양육하다	38 ~로 죽다	39 무표정으로
40 먼저, 앞서	41 돌이켜 생각하다	42 간단히 말해
43 ~에게서 멀어지다		

단어 TEST Step 2 　　　　　　　p.29

01 proud	02 adopt	03 while
04 dwell	05 fault	06 punish
07 nobleman	08 fine	09 argument
10 greet	11 certainly	12 punish
13 human beings	14 blame	15 conflict
16 disability	17 heart attack	18 convey
19 judge	20 last	21 disabled
22 leather	23 punishment	24 regret
25 servant	26 needs	27 master
28 sudden	29 pity	30 twin
31 truth	32 serve	33 death
34 support	35 thanks to	36 die of
37 bring up	38 fail to	39 think back
40 walk away from		31 instead of
42 in advance	43 figure out	

단어 TEST Step 3 　　　　　　　p.30

1 discount, 할인　2 dwell, 거주하다

3 last, 지속하다, 계속되다　4 neighbor, 이웃

5 needs, 요구, 욕구　6 argument, 논쟁　7 fault, 잘못

8 servant, 하인　9 regret, 후회하다　10 save, 구하다

11 explain, 설명하다　12 secret, 비밀

13 judge, 판단하다　14 disability, 장애
15 adopt, 입양하다　16 punish, 처벌하다

대화문 TEST Step 1 　　　　　　　p.31~33

Everyday English 1 A Listen and Check

1 made, clean / fault, did / goodness, take, clear, up / together

2 why, late for / all / happened / late, missed

3 this, How / problem with, bought / problem with / dirty, fault, never / about, visit

Everyday English 1 B Listening Activity

sick, worried / feed / gave / should not feed / whether, safe, to drink, all, fault / worry, take, to, doctor / get better / certainly, with, care

Everyday English 2 A Listen and Check

1 hospital / Aren't, supposed / anyone, worried, missing classes / copy of / idea

2 confused, matter / cannot, anything, how to communicate / tried, with / always / supposed, sign

Everyday English 2 B Listening Activity

planning / thinking of doing, volunteer, disabilities, join / worried / makes / whether, ready to, advice / supposed to respect / mean, needs / only, ask

In Real Life

depressed, matter / argument / fault / misunderstanding / case, supposed to make, possible / angry / knows, regret / so / maintain, friendships / advice, make up, with

Check Your Progress 2

watching, looking forward, interesting, century, changed, costumes, audiences, Second, appears, performance, deep understanding, bear, book, fault, miss, regret missing

Check Your Progress 3

How / seats / check, performances, prefer / left / Never / enough, total / discount / off / should, get, discount / supposed to bring

대화문 TEST Step 2 　　　　　　　p.34~36

Everyday English 1 A Listen and Check

1 B: Who made this mess? It was clean this morning.

G: It's not my fault. Your dog did it.

B: Oh, my goodness! It will take a lot of time to clear it up.

G: Let's do it together. I'll help you.

2 G: Minsu, why were you late for school today?

B: It was all my fault.

G: What happened?

B: I got up late this morning, so I missed the bus.

3 W: Hello, this is the shoe shop. How may I help you?

M: I have a problem with the boots that I bought there yesterday.

W: What's the problem with them?

M: They're a bit dirty. But it is not my fault. I've never worn them.

W: Sorry about that. Please visit our shop this week.

Everyday English 1 B Listening Activity

G: My dog got sick this morning. I'm so worried about him.

B: What did you feed him yesterday?

G: I gave him some milk last night.

B: Oh, you should not feed a dog milk.

G: I was not sure whether or not it is safe for him to drink milk. It was all my fault.

B: Don't worry too much. Did you take him to the animal doctor?

G: Yes, I did. I hope he'll get better soon.

B: He'll certainly get better with your care and love.

Everyday English 2 A Listen and Check

1 B: Did you hear that Minsu is in the hospital?

G: Oh, I didn't know that. Aren't we supposed to visit him?

B: No, he doesn't want anyone to visit him. He is just worried about missing classes.

G: Then should I make a copy of my notes for him?

B: That's a good idea.

2 B: Jina, you look confused. What's the matter?

G: My partner cannot hear anything. I don't know how to communicate with her.

B: Have you tried communicating with her by writing?

G: Yes, I have. But the problem is that we do not always have a pencil.

B: Then, you are supposed to learn how to use sign language.

Everyday English 2 B Listening Activity

B: Jina, what are you planning to do this winter vacation?

G: I'm thinking of doing some volunteer work for people with disabilities. Would you like to join me?

B: Oh, that's a good idea. But I'm a bit worried about it.

G: What makes you feel like that?

B: I'm not sure whether I am ready to help them. Could you give me some advice?

G: You're supposed to respect their needs.

B: What do you mean by their needs?

G: You should help them only when they ask you to do so.

In Real Life

Inho: Lina, you look so depressed. What's the matter?

Lina: Oh, Inho. I had an argument with Ryan.

Inho: Was it your fault?

Lina: No, it wasn't my fault! There was just a misunderstanding between us.

Inho: In that case, you're supposed to make up with him as soon as possible.

Lina: Well, Ryan got so angry that he wouldn't talk with me.

Inho: But who knows? He might regret it now, just like you.

Lina: Do you think so?

Inho: Yes, everyone wants to maintain good friendships.

Lina: Thanks for your advice. I hope I can make up with him soon.

Check Your Progress 2

W: Thank you for watching "Play World." Are you looking forward to this month's play? This month's play is *Hamlet* There are two interesting points about this play. First, it is a 21st century version of Shakespeare's *Hamlet*. It has changed the costumes and the dead language of the 16th century that most of today's audiences might feel uncomfortable with. Second, the famous actor, Park Mujin, appears in this play. His performance shows a deep understanding of the main character, Hamlet. Please bear in mind that you will need to book your ticket online. It won't be your fault if you miss this play. But you'll certainly regret missing it.

Check Your Progress 3

W: Hello. This is the Culture Theater. How may I help you?

B: I'd like to book four seats for Sleeping Beauty this Friday.

W: Okay, let me check. The performances are at 6 p.m., and 8 p.m. Which one do you prefer?

B: 6 p.m. please.

W: Oh, I'm sorry but we only have two seats left for that time.

B: Never mind. It's all my fault for calling so late. What about 8 p.m.?

W: There are enough seats at 8 p.m. That will be 60 dollars in total.

B: Can I get a student discount? We are all students.

W: Sure, it's 30% off.

B: What should I do to get the discount?

W: You're supposed to bring your student ID card.

본문 TEST Step 1 p.37~39

01 Mysterious Smiles

02 *fails, On, back, lying*

03 whether, or, drunk, lying

04 Put simply, being punished

05 cold outside, Let's, together

06 *greets, has brought nothing*

07 *surprised*, supposed to, nothing

08 enough, nothing, fault, bring

09 *looking at, with pity*

10 *smiles for, first time*

11 *For, work, support himself*

12 been, since, earn, living

13 *with, blank face*, would

14 *famous, thanks, skills, order*

15 leather, last, sure whether

16 *carefully, smiles, second time*   17 Don't worry

18 *nobleman leaves, shop*

19 make, thick leather   20 Michael, Okay

21 *However, soft, instead of*

22 should, mistakes, What, think

23 stop making, instead, attack

24 *looking at, in surprise*   25 Michael, Well

26 *few, later, customer, with*

27 to buy, leather, twin

28 *seeing, disability*, born with

29 real, giving birth, adopt

30 *smiles for, third time*

31 *Suddenly, mysterious light shines*

32 light shining from

33 about time, left

34 mean, why, just smile

35 punishment, supposed, truths, ready

36 truths have, learned

본문 TEST Step 2 p.40~42

01 Mysterious

02 *fails to buy, On, way back, lying*

03 whether, or not, drunk, okay, Why, lying

04 Put simply, being punished

05 outside

06 *greets, has brought nothing*

07 were supposed to, nothing

08 enough money to buy, fault, Don't you think, help

09 *with pity*   10 *for the first time*

11 *support himself*

12 It's time you started, to work

13 *blank*   14 *thanks to, skills, order*

15 fine leather, that have to last, I'm not sure whether

16 *carefully, for the second time*

17 Don't worry   18 *leaves*   19 leather boots

21 *instead of*

22 there should be, mistakes, What

23 stop making, instead, died of, heart attack

24 *in surprise*   26 *later, customer*

27 to buy

28 *seeing*, about, if, with a disability

29 real, giving birth to, so much that

31 *shines from*   32 shining   33 about, left

34 why, just smile

35 was sent, as, punishment, was supposed to, Every time, Now that, am ready to

36 have you learned   37 *thinks back to*

38 dwells in, pitied, what, to figure out

40 what, were to last, realized, know little about, future needs

41 last truth

42 brought them up, by having true love for, What people live by

37 *thinks back to, carefully*

38 dwells, pitied, lesson, figure

39 What were they

40 what, last, realized, future

41 What, last truth

42 death, brought, up, by

1 세 가지의 신비로운 미소

2 겨울이다. 가난한 구두장이 Simon은 따뜻한 코트를 사는 데 실패한다. 그는 집에 돌아오는 길에 옷도 입지 않고 길거리에 누워 있는 Michael이라는 한 남자를 발견한다.

3 Simon: 저 남자가 죽은 건지 아닌 건지 모르겠군. 하지만 나는 취해 있고, 돈도 거의 없어서 저 남자를 구할 수 없을 것 같아. (처음엔 Michael에게서 발걸음을 돌리지만, 다시 돌아오며) 불쌍한 사람이군. 괜찮으세요? 왜 여기 누워 있는 거예요?

4 Michael: 당신에게 말 못할 사정이 있어요. 간단히 말하자면, 저는 벌을 받고 있어요.

5 Simon: 하지만 밖은 추워요. 같이 집으로 갑시다.

6 Simon은 집으로 와서 그의 아내인 Matrena와 인사한다. 그녀는 그가 아무것도 가져오지 않은 것을 알게 된다.

7 Matrena: (놀라서 화내며) Simon, 당신은 우리 가족을 위해 코트를 사 오기로 했잖아요. 하지만 아무것도 없네요. 그리고 이 남자는 누구예요?

8 Simon: 코트를 살 정도로 충분한 돈이 없었어요. 미안해요. 그리고 이 남자에 관해서는 아무것도 모르지만, 내 잘못이 아니에요. 나는 이 남자를 집에 데려와야만 했어요. 이 남자를 보세요. 도움이 필요해 보이지 않나요?

9 Matrena: (Michael을 불쌍하게 바라보며) 그래요, Simon.

10 (Michael은 처음으로 미소를 짓는다.)

11 1주일간, Michael은 스스로 자신의 생계를 유지하기 위해 아무 일도 하지 않는다.

12 Simon: (Michael을 바라보며) Michael, 당신이 이곳에 와서 계속 빈둥거리고 있어 걱정되네요. 당신 자신을 위해 생계를 꾸려야 할 때예요. 저를 위해서 일해 준다면, 제가 당신에게 음식을 제공할게요. 저랑 같이 일하시겠어요?

13 Michael: (무표정한 얼굴로) 네, 그렇게 할게요.

14 1년 후, Simon은 Michael의 훌륭한 구두 제작 솜씨 덕분에 유명해졌다. 어느 날, 한 귀족이 부츠를 주문하러 가게에 온다.

15 귀족: 나는 1년을 신어도 끄떡없는 튼튼한 가죽 부츠를 주문하고 싶습니다. 당신이 그 부츠를 만들 수 있을지 모르겠네요. 할 수 있겠습니까?

16 (Michael은 귀족을 유심히 살펴보고는 두 번째로 미소 짓는다.)

17 Simon: 네, 나리. 걱정하지 마세요.

18 (귀족은 가게를 떠난다.)

19 Simon: Michael, 두꺼운 가죽 부츠를 만들어 주세요.

20 Michael: 네.

21 (하지만, Michael은 부츠 대신 부드러운 슬리퍼를 만든다.)

22 Simon: (슬리퍼를 발견하며) Michael! 제가 실수하지 말라고 했잖아요. 지금 뭐 하고 있는 겁니까?

23 하인: (가게로 뛰어들며) 부츠는 그만 만들고 대신 죽은 사람에게 신길 부드러운 슬리퍼를 만들어 주세요. 나리가 심장마비로 돌아가셨습니다.

24 Simon: (놀라서 Michael을 바라보며) 당신은 어떻게 알았습니까?

25 Michael: 글쎄요…

26 몇 년 후, 한 여인이 쌍둥이 소녀들과 함께 신발 가게에 방문한다.

27 손님: 이 쌍둥이 소녀들에게 신길 가죽 신발을 사러 왔습니다.

28 Simon: (장애를 가진 한 소녀를 보며) 따님 한쪽 발이 안타깝네요. 실례지만, 태어날 때부터 장애가 있었는지 여쭤봐도 될까요?

29 손님: 오, 저는 이 아이의 생모가 아니에요. 생모가 아이를 낳던 중에 아이가 다리를 다치게 됐어요. 그들의 부모님은 이미 돌아가셨습니다. 나는 이 쌍둥이가 너무 불쌍했어요. 이 아이들을 너무 사랑해서 입양하기로 결정했습니다.

30 (Michael은 세 번째로 미소를 짓는다.)

31 (갑자기 Michael에게서 신비한 빛이 빛난다.)

32 Simon: 당신에게서 나오는 이 빛은 도대체 뭔가요?

33 Michael: 이제 제가 떠날 때가 왔군요.

34 Simon: 무슨 말씀이시죠? 그리고 당신은 왜 미소를 지었던 건가요?

35 Michael: 설명해 드릴게요. 저는 천사입니다. 저는 벌을 받아 여기로 보내졌고, 세 가지 진리를 깨달아야 했습니다. 제가 진리를 하나씩 깨달을 때마다 미소를 지었던 것입니다. 저는 세 가지 진리를 모두 깨달았기 때문에 돌아갈 준비를 마쳤습니다.

36 Simon: 그렇군요. 당신이 깨달은 진리는 무엇이었나요?

37 Michael은 그가 미소 지었을 때를 회상한다. Simon과 Matrena는 그의 말을 주의 깊게 듣는다.

38 Michael: 첫째, Matrena가 저를 가여워했을 때 인간 내면에 사랑이 존재한다는 것을 저는 깨달았습니다. 이는 '인간 내면에 무엇이 존재하는가'라는 첫 번째 교훈에 관한 답이었던 것입니다. 저는 그 진실을 깨달았기 때문에 미소를 지었습니다. 하지만 저는 아직도 두 가지를 더 알아내야만 했어요.

39 Simon: 그것들은 뭐였나요?

40 Michael: 두 번째는 "인간에게 주어지지 않은 것은 무엇인가"였습니다. 그 귀족이 1년을 신어도 끄떡없는 부츠를 주문했을 때, 저는 그가 곧 죽을 것을 알고 있었습니다. 사람은 자신의 미래에 필요한 것을 알지 못한다는 사실을 그때 저는 깨달았습니다.

41 Simon: 마지막 진리는 무엇이었나요?

42 Michael: 쌍둥이 소녀와 여인의 이야기를 듣고 깨달았습니다. 쌍둥이의 생모가 사망한 후, 그 여인은 그들을 사랑으로 키웠습니다. 그때, 저는 사람은 서로를 향한 참된 사랑으로 산다는 점을 알게 됐습니다. 그것이 '사람은 무엇으로 사는가'에 관한 세 번째 교훈이었습니다.

35

1 Three Mysterious Smiles

2 It's winter. A poor shoe maker, Simon, fails to buy a warm coat. On his way back home, he finds a man, Michael, lying in the street without any clothes.

3 Simon: I'm not sure whether he is dead or not. But I don't think I can save him because I'm drunk and have little money. (walking away from Michael at first, but coming back again) Poor man. Are you okay? Why are you lying here?

4 Michael: I can't tell you everything. Put simply, I am being punished.

5 Simon: But it's cold outside. Let's go home together.

6 Simon comes home and greets Matrena, his wife. She finds he has brought nothing.

7 Matrena: (surprised and angry) Simon, you were supposed to buy a coat for our family. But there's nothing. And who is this man?

8 Simon: I did not have enough money to buy the coat. I'm sorry. And I know nothing about this man. But it wasn't my fault. I had to bring him home. I mean just look at him. Don't you think he needs help?

9 Matrena: (looking at Michael with pity) Okay, Simon.

10 (Michael smiles for the first time.)

11 For a week, Michael does no work to support himself.

12 Simon: (looking at Michael) Michael, I'm afraid you've been doing nothing since you came here. It's time you started to earn a living for yourself. If you work for me, I will give you food. Would you like to work with me?

13 Michael: (with a blank face) Yes, I would.

14 A year later, Simon has become famous, thanks to Michael's great skills in making shoes. One day, a nobleman comes to order his boots.

15 Nobleman: I'd like to order fine leather boots that have to last for a year. I'm not sure whether you can make them. Can you do that?

16 (Michael watches the man carefully and smiles for the second time.)

17 Simon: Yes, sir. Don't worry.

18 (The nobleman leaves the shop.)

19 Simon: Michael, please make some thick leather boots.

20 Michael: Okay.

21 (However, Michael makes soft slippers instead of boots.)

22 Simon: (finding the slippers) Michael! I told you there should be no mistakes. What do you think you are doing?

23 Servant: (running into the shop) Please stop making boots and start making soft slippers for a dead body instead. My master has died of a heart attack.

24 Simon: (looking at Michael in surprise) How did you know?

25 Michael: Well …

26 A few years later, a woman customer visits the shoe shop with twin girls.

27 Customer: I'm here to buy some leather shoes for these twin girls.

28 Simon: (seeing that one of the girls has a disability) I'm sorry about your daughter's foot. May I ask you if she was born with a disability?

29 Customer: Oh, I'm not her real mother. Her mother hurt this girl's leg while she was giving birth to her. Their parents are both dead now. I felt sorry for them. I loved these twins so much that I decided to adopt them.

30 (Michael smiles for the third time.)

31 (Suddenly, a mysterious light shines from Michael.)

32 Simon: What's this light shining from you?

33 Michael: It's about time I left here.

34 Simon: What do you mean? And why did you just smile?

35 Michael: Let me explain. I am an angel. I was sent here as a punishment, and I was supposed to learn three truths. Every time I learned one of them, I smiled. Now that I have learned all three of them, I am ready to go back.

36 Simon: I see. What truths have you learned?

37 Michael thinks back to each time that he smiled. Simon and Matrena listen carefully to him.

38 Michael: First, I learned that love dwells in human beings when Matrena pitied me. This was the answer to the first lesson: Learn what dwells in human beings. I smiled because I learned the truth. But I still had two more to figure out.the answer to the first lesson: Learn what dwells in human beings. I smiled because I learned the truth. But I still had two more to figure out.

39 Simon: What were they?

40 Michael: The second was, "Learn what is not given to people." When the nobleman ordered that his boots were to last for a year, I knew he would die soon. Then I realized people know little about their own future needs.

41 Simon: What was the last truth?

42 Michael: It was from the story of the woman and the twin girls. After the death of their mother, the woman brought them up with her love. Then, I learned people live by having true love for each other. That was the third lesson: What people live by.

구석구석지문 TEST Step 1 p.53

After You Read A

1. enough money to buy

2. know nothing about

3. fault, had to bring

4. look at, Don't, needs help

5. so pitiful that, couldn't help giving

After You Read B

1. was supposed to, truths as a punishment

2. lets, stay in, dwells in human beings

3. orders fine leather, have to last

4. The servant, stop making, start making soft slippers, instead, died of a heart attack

5. adopted, one of whom was disabled

Check Your Progress 1

1. did, hand in

2. didn't

3. supposed to hand it in

4. all my fault, completed, was going to save, broke down

5. What a pity, were, would tell, why you couldn't hand it in

6. agree, better do, as soon as possible

7. give you a hand

8. How kind of, call, if, need your help

구석구석지문 TEST Step 2 p.54

After You Read A

1. I did not have enough money to buy the coat. I'm sorry.

2. And I know nothing about this man.

3. But it wasn't my fault. I had to bring him home.

4. I mean just look at him! Don't you think he needs help?

5. He looked so pitiful that I couldn't help giving him some help.

After You Read B

1. Michael was supposed to learn three truths as a punishment.

2. When Matrena lets Michael stay in her home, he learns that love dwells in human beings.

3. The nobleman orders fine leather boots that have to last for a year.

4. The servant of the nobleman said, "Please stop making boots and start making soft slippers for a dead body instead. My master has died of a heart attack."

5. The woman adopted the twin girls, one of whom was disabled.

Check Your Progress 1

1. B: Jina, did you hand in your English homework?

2. G: No, I didn't.

3. B: Why? You're supposed to hand it in today.

4. G: It was all my fault. I completed my homework. But just before I was going to save it, the computer broke down.

5. B: What a pity! If I were you, I would tell the teacher why you couldn't hand it in.

6. G: Yeah, I agree. But I think I'd better do it again as soon as possible.

7. B: Can I give you a hand with that?

8. G: How kind of you! I'll call you if I need your help.

MEMO

MEMO

MEMO

적중100

영어 기출 문제집

정답 및 해설

금성 | 최인철